MODERN READERS' SERIES
ASHLEY H. THORNDIKE, *General Editor*

SHORT PLAYS
BY
REPRESENTATIVE AUTHORS

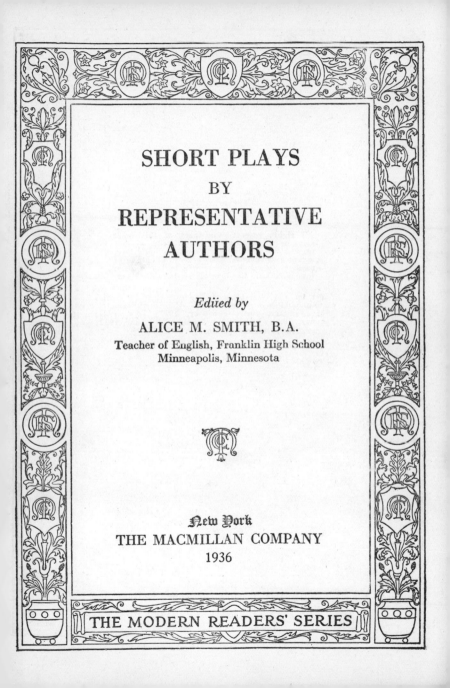

SHORT PLAYS
BY
REPRESENTATIVE AUTHORS

Edited by

ALICE M. SMITH, B.A.
**Teacher of English, Franklin High School
Minneapolis, Minnesota**

New York
THE MACMILLAN COMPANY
1936

THE MODERN READERS' SERIES

Printed in the United States of America

PREFATORY NOTE

In these latter days when all places on the earth have grown of interest and a feeling of world kinship is to be desired, it is well that not only the student and the general reader, but young persons as well, should feel the thought of nations through their literatures. What more efficacious than a record of life through the medium of drama? Morsels in the form of the short play may lead to further acquaintance with not only these dramatists, but with others of equal or greater rank.

For a visit with strong personalities, here is offered the acquaintance of the agrarian hero, the Scandinavian pioneer of Iceland in "The Hraun Farm," the homely sweet Welsh soul in "The Merry Merry Cuckoo," and the Amazonian determination of the woman of the Sagas in "The Locked Chest."

To move in a mystical atmosphere, the reader may live with the very heart of India in the spiritually beautiful "Post Office."

For humor, there is enjoyment of the fanciful in "Six Who Pass," and the sharing of a laugh both last and best in a return to the past with an innovation in England's literature in "The Silver Lining." A surreptitious peep into domestic foibles in "By Ourselves" is allowed by a modern German who is not a materialist; an open invitation is extended by an

v

American to view the negro mind laid bare in "The Rider of Dreams," and the spirit of Irish humor and naïveté is realistic, indeed, in "Spreading the News."

Lastly, pathos has its mission for us in the sad solo of the Russian in "The Swan Song," and poverty and injustice claim attention from the Anglo-Saxon to the victim in his native home as seen in "The Man on the Kerb," and to the victim of adoption in "The Shadowed Star."

A. M. S.

Minneapolis, Minnesota.

CONTENTS

		PAGE
THE HRAUN FARM	*Jóhann Sigurjónsson* . .	1
THE MERRY MERRY CUCKOO .	*Jeannette Marks*	55
THE LOCKED CHEST	*John Masefield*	73
THE POST OFFICE	*Rabindranath Tagore* . .	107
SIX WHO PASS WHILE THE LENTILS BOIL	*Stuart Walker*	139
THE SILVER LINING	*Constance d'Arcy Mackay*	171
BY OURSELVES	*Ludwig Fulda*	183
THE RIDER OF DREAMS . . .	*Ridgely Torrence*	221
SPREADING THE NEWS	*Lady Augusta Gregory* .	247
THE SWAN SONG	*Anton Tchekhoff* . . .	271
THE MAN ON THE KERB . . .	*Alfred Sutro*	283
THE SHADOWED STAR	*Mary MacMillan* . . .	299

THE HRAUN FARM[1]
(Gaarden Hraun)

BY

JÓHANN SIGURJÓNSSON

TRANSLATED BY

HENNINGE KROHN SCHANCHE

[1] Reprinted by permission of the translator, representing the author, and by permission of the American-Scandinavian Foundation.

For permission to perform this play application must be made to the translator.

Jóhann Sigurjónsson, the Icelandic dramatist, may not be well known to many, but three great dramas, "Mr. Rand," "Bjoerg-Ejvind," and "The Hraun Farm," will account for the acclamation of some critics that he is the equal of Ibsen, Bjornson, and Strindberg. Human feelings are powerfully portrayed, and pictures of his passionately loved Iceland are vigorously drawn. Yet with this intensity of devotion and poetic vision, there is the diction of fine self-possession and exactness of analysis.

In "The Hraun Farm" ("hraun" meaning a field covered with volcanic stone) the reader is reminded of the ancient tribal people in the terrible struggle of the father between love for his land and love for his child. The very height of poetic feeling is reached in Sveinungi's reminiscent speech in the second act. The loving tactfulness of Jorunn brings the play to a happy ending.

THE HRAUN FARM

Dramatis Personæ

SVEINUNGI, *owner of the Hraun Farm*
JORUNN, *his wife*
LJOT, *their daughter*
EINAR, *a relative of Jorunn*
JAKOBINA, *an old woman*
FRIDA, *a child, eleven years old*
SØLVI, *a geologist*
JON
INDRIDI
HELGI
RANNVEIG } *Servants*
BJØRG
THORA
A Shepherd Boy

The action takes place in Iceland. TIME: the present. "Hraun" is the Icelandic word for lava-field.

ACT I

[*The farm. Five white gables, all adjoining and separated by heavy partitions. The roof is covered with turf, the walls are of earth and stone. The gable farthest to the left is without a door, but has two windows on the ground floor and a smaller window above. The next has a door leading into the "badstofa" or servants' quarters. The third is a dairy and storehouse; the*

3

fourth, a smithy; the fifth, a drying-shed. In the yard is a horse-block; to the left, a picket fence. Before the doors lie the packs unloaded from nine horses: two green chests, sacks of grain and household stuff, lumber, and a number of other articles. JAKOBINA *stands feeling one of the sacks.* HELGI *is undoing the strappings. The door to the smithy is open.* EINAR *is seen within, forging horseshoe nails.*]

[*It is morning, before breakfast.*]

JAKOBINA [*talking half to herself*]. This must be coffee. [*Lays her hand on one of the chests.*] And what has Jorunn got in these, I wonder! I fancy there are many pretty things there.

HELGI. You may be sure of that.

JAKOBINA. Nineteen years I've been here now, and it's never happened yet that the mistress has forgotten to bring something or other to please me when she came back from town, — and it wasn't always little things either, God bless her! Oh, but there they have knocked off the paint. What a shame! [*Sits down on the chest and runs her hand over the paint.*]

[*Enter* BJØRG *and* RANNVEIG *from the left, carrying pails full of milk, which they set down.*]

RANNVEIG. They brought home quite a bit. We shall not go hungry for a while yet. Where are they?

HELGI. They are inside, drinking coffee.

BJØRG. Is Jon drunk?

HELGI. Not so very; he's just a little gay.

THE SHEPHERD BOY. Are you through milking already?

BJØRG. Can't you see for yourself?

THE SHEPHERD BOY. Oh, pshaw! [*His eyes light on the lumber piles. He bends down and begins to count the knots in the wood.*] One, two, three —

[*Enter* SVEINUNGI *from the "badstofa."*]

SVEINUNGI. What do you say, girls? Quite a pack, isn't it?

BJØRG. I should say so!

SVEINUNGI [*to* HELGI]. You've begun to undo the strappings? That's fine. And here come the others.

[*Enter* JON *and* INDRIDI *from the house.* JON *is somewhat intoxicated.*]

JON. Here stands our dear master. Good day to you, Rannveig! Good day!

BJØRG *and* RANNVEIG. Good day, and welcome home!

SVEINUNGI [*laughing*]. Why don't you put your arms around the girls and give them a kiss? Are you afraid?

JON. No, Jon isn't afraid.

SVEINUNGI. You didn't get anything with your coffee. [*Runs into the house.*]

JON. He is the same as ever.

[BJØRG *and* RANNVEIG *carry the milk into the storehouse.*]

JAKOBINA [*rising*]. You didn't take notice of anything in particular on your way back?

INDRIDI. Not that I remember.

JAKOBINA. Did you see many birds?

INDRIDI. Come to think of it, I don't believe I saw any.

JAKOBINA. That's what I thought. [*Goes into the house. Enter* SVEINUNGI *from the house with a flask and a glass, which he fills.*]

SVEINUNGI. Here, this is for you.

JON [*drinks*]. Thanks.

SVEINUNGI [*fills the glass again for* INDRIDI *and* HELGI]. Won't you take a drop too, Einar?

[EINAR *appears in the doorway of the smithy.*]

EINAR. Thank you. [*Drinks.*]

SVEINUNGI [*sees* THE SHEPHERD BOY]. Are you here? Why, the girls are all through milking. Do you suppose you can keep the sheep standing in the fold all day? [THE SHEPHERD BOY *is about to go.*] Wait a minute! I have a little thing here that I bought for you yesterday. [*Takes a knife from his vest pocket.*] I think the blade is good iron, and that is the main thing. [*Gives him the knife.* THE SHEPHERD BOY *kisses him.*] It is not much. You are welcome to it.

THE SHEPHERD BOY [*opens his knife*]. Look, Einar, it's a regular hunting knife. [*Closes it, runs to the left, calling.*] Snati! Pila! Snati!

RANNVEIG. You needn't call the dogs. They are up at the fold. [*Exit* THE SHEPHERD BOY.]

SVEINUNGI. That boy will amount to something in time. It's well done for one so young to tend more than fourscore sheep, and he hasn't lost one yet. [*Takes the flask back to the house.*]

JON. He's in mighty good humor to-day, the old man.

BJØRG. I should say so.

INDRIDI. Why, he got the highest price for his wool.

JON. And a sorry day it would be when we didn't get that!

INDRIDI. What do you think Jakobina had in mind when she asked about the birds?

Jon. It's hard to tell! She has her mind on so many things. [*Enter* Sveinungi *and* Jorunn *from the house.*]

Sveinungi [*in the door, laughing and talking*]. I believe the girls have their eye on the green chests. Indridi, will you carry them in? [Indridi *goes with one of the chests.*]

Jorunn. You can put them in the little room.

Sveinungi. Rannveig, will you bring me the key to the drying shed? You know where it hangs. [Rannveig *runs in.*] You boys will have to carry the breadstuffs up into the loft of the storehouse, and the coffee and sugar too, and while I think of it, you had better take one sack out to the mill, Helgi.

Helgi. I will.

Sveinungi [*opening a bag*]. Here, Einar, you'll find iron and nails and brazil-wood, and here's something for yourself. [*Hands him a plug of tobacco.*] See if you can be a bit saving of it.

Einar [*pats him on the shoulder*]. God bless you! [*Goes into the smithy.*]

Rannveig [*comes out*]. Here is the key.

Sveinungi [*unlocks the door to the drying-shed*]. You can stack the timber on top of the old pile. After you have had your breakfast, you, Jon, and Indridi had better go and lie down. You must be tired.

Jon. I am sure I could keep on working all day if need be, and just as hard as those who have had their sleep. [Indridi *comes for the other chest.*]

Sveinungi [*laughs*]. There are not many like you.

Jorunn. Where is Ljot? I thought she was here.

Helgi. I saw her walking in the yard. I have not seen her come back.

SVEINUNGI [*goes to the picket fence; calls*].   Ljot!
LJOT [*is heard answering*].   Yes!
SVEINUNGI.   Are you there? Aren't you coming
home?
LJOT [*is heard answering*].   I am coming.
JORUNN.   Have you set the milk?
RANNVEIG.   Yes.
JORUNN.   Then come in, if you want to see what I
have brought.

EINAR [*steps to the door of the smithy. He holds a
snuff-box in his hand, and is rolling up a long plug of
tobacco, which he puts into the box*].   This tastes better;
the old stuff was getting as dry as hay. [*Spits.*] Oh,
well, there was a time, but that's so long ago.

HELGI.   What are you talking about?

EINAR.   It was a winter night, and I was lying in
wait for the fox.   Well, what happened was neither
more nor less than this, that when I wanted to take a
chew of tobacco, I found I'd left the box at home.   I
can stand it for one night, I thought, but it was cold
where I was lying, and the fox made himself scarce.
Let me tell you, when I had been waiting till nearly
dawn, I'd gladly have given my soul for a good honest
chew.

[LJOT *passes through from the right, carrying some
freshly gathered flowers in her hand. Goes into the
house.*]

HELGI.   And did you get the fox?

EINAR.   I did.   It came just as I was about to go
home.

[*Enter* INDRIDI *from the house.*]

JON.   When you got home, I'm sure you went
straight for a good big plug of tobacco.

EINAR. Maybe I did! It was the finest blue fox I've ever shot.

[*Enter* FRIDA *from the left. She is warm from running.*]

FRIDA. Now I've turned the horses out on the grass. [*Wipes her forehead.*] Do you want me to pull the bellows for you?

EINAR. You'd better go in and see if Jorunn should happen to have something for you. Then you can come back here. [FRIDA *runs in.*]

[*Enter* BJØRG *and* RANNVEIG *from the house.*]

BJØRG. See what the mistress has brought for me! [*Holding up a piece of cloth.*] It will be fun to make that into an apron.

RANNVEIG. I got a head-kerchief with red flowers [*holds it up*] and a piece of soap. [*Smells it.*]

JON. May I? [*Smells it.*] You'll be good to kiss, when you have washed with that soap.

RANNVEIG. Only I won't let you.

THORA [*in the doorway*]. I must show you what I got, too.

[*Enter* SØLVI *from the left, carrying a gun over his shoulder and a small knapsack on his back.*]

SØLVI. Good day to you!

THE SERVANTS. Good day!

INDRIDI. We did not see you coming.

SØLVI. I took the short cut. May I have something to drink? I am thirsty.

RANNVEIG. I'll get it for you.

SØLVI [*lowering his voice*]. And may I see Ljot for a moment? I have something for her.

RANNVEIG. I'll tell her. [*Exeunt Girls.*]

INDRIDI. Have you any news?

SØLVI. No.

INDRIDI. You are still at Hol?

SØLVI. Yes.

INDRIDI. Have they begun to cut the hay?

SØLVI. Not yet.

INDRIDI. They generally start before any of the other farms.

SØLVI. They need to. They don't keep much help. [*Enter* RANNVEIG *with the milk.*]

RANNVEIG. Here it is, and you are welcome to it.

SØLVI [*drinks*]. Thanks.

RANNVEIG. I have told Ljot. [*Goes in.*]

HELGI. Here, give me a hand! [INDRIDI *lifts the sack to* HELGI's *back;* HELGI *carries it out to the left.*]

JON [*coiling the last ropes*]. We can start carrying the lumber into the shed.

[*Enter* LJOT *from the house.*]

SØLVI. Good day to you, Ljot!

LJOT. Good day! You wished to see me?

SØLVI. You won't be angry with me? — I thought perhaps you would like this. [*Takes the skin of a duck from his knapsack.*] I shot it on the creek the other day, and I thought it was so pretty that I took off the skin and dried it. Do you think you could make use of it — say for a riding-cap?

LJOT. It is beautiful.

SØLVI. When you hold the wing this way the spot is blue, and when you hold it so it is green; it's the way the light falls.

LJOT. I doubt if I dare take it. I scarcely know you.

SØLVI. You would make me very happy if you would take it.

Ljot. Then I will, and thank you. [*Gives him her hand.*] How lovely it is!

Sølvi [*lowering his voice*]. Do you never go for a walk by yourself in the *hraun?*

Ljot. Why do you ask?

Sølvi. You know the pretty spot by the old roan tree; it is not more than a good ten minutes' walk from here. I thought perhaps you might go there sometimes on Sundays.

Ljot [*blushes*]. I don't know —

Sølvi. I shall be there all day Sunday. Good-bye, Ljot.

Ljot [*confused*]. Good-bye.

Sølvi. I shall be there at sunrise, and I shall be there when the sun goes down. [*Exit to the left.*]

[*Enter* Sveinungi, *hurriedly.*]

Sveinungi. Who was it that went just now?

Indridi. Is he gone? It was Sølvi.

Sveinungi. What did he want here?

Indridi. He got a cup of milk.

Sveinungi [*to* Ljot]. It seemed to me he was talking to you. What have you there?

Ljot. He gave me a bird's skin.

Sveinungi. Pshaw! You should have made him keep it himself.

Ljot. There was no harm meant.

Sveinungi. Einar could have brought you down one just like it, if you had cared for it. Why are you blushing so?

Ljot. I did not think you would be so angry because I took the bird's skin.

Sveinungi. I can't bear him, that stone-picker! He roves from place to place like a tramp. Let him dare to set his nets for you! Give me the creature, and I'll hand it back to him the next time he comes; for he's sure to come.

LJOT. I can burn it myself, if you grudge me the keeping it. [*Goes in.*]

SVEINUNGI [*talking in the doorway*]. And then you get angry to boot. [*To* INDRIDI.] I see you have undone all the strappings.

INDRIDI. Yes.

SVEINUNGI. Where is Helgi?

INDRIDI. He went to the mill.

[*Enter* HELGI *from the left.*]

SVEINUNGI. There he comes. Then you can do what I told you. [*Goes in.*]

HELGI. Anything amiss? The master seemed cross.

INDRIDI. That's nothing.

HELGI. Is Sølvi gone?

INDRIDI. Yes. Let's get through with this. You go into the storehouse and take the things as I hand them to you.

[*They carry the breadstuffs into the storehouse.* EINAR *appears in the door of the smithy.*]

EINAR. H'm, I feel I'm getting old. There was a time when I could forge three nails in one heating, and now it's a hard rub getting through with one.

INDRIDI. We can't be young more than once.

EINAR. And we can't cast the slough of old age, as they could once upon a time.

INDRIDI. Would you care to?

EINAR. I don't know. I almost think these new times are not for me. [*Enter* FRIDA.]

FRIDA. Einar, I was to call you to breakfast. [*Runs against* SVEINUNGI, *who is coming out.*]

SVEINUNGI. There, there! Why, you have brought it all under cover and the ropes in the shed. That's fine. Now, Helgi, when you have eaten, you can go and begin to cut turf. The others will join you when they have had their sleep. [*Lowering his voice.*] Einar, will you ask Ljot to come out? I want to have a little talk with her.

EINAR. I will. [EINAR *and* FRIDA *go in.* SVEINUNGI *locks the drying-shed and looks into the storehouse, pretending to be very busy.*]

[*Enter* LJOT *from the house.*]

LJOT. Here I am, father.

SVEINUNGI. I did not hear you. [*Smiles.*] You step as lightly as a young foal. You are not hurt at what I said a moment ago? It was only for your own good. I won't have any shiftless straggler around here making eyes at you. The parish can gossip about something else. [LJOT *goes to the fence, resting her hands on it.*] But that was not what I wanted to talk to you about. [*Goes to her.*] You know Arne, the farmer at Skrida. You have seen his son Halfdan. What do you think of him?

LJOT. I have seen him only a few times.

SVEINUNGI. There are two brothers. The older one is married and is going to take the farm, but Halfdan is most like his father. You should see the way their place is kept. Their yard is nearly as big as this, and there are long stretches where the grass stands so high that it falls over. It's as fine a sight as I have ever seen. We stopped there, Jorunn and I, for a full hour, on our way back from town, and there was no lack of welcome. Can you guess what we talked about?

LJOT. No.

SVEINUNGI [*laughs*]. You can't? Arne asked me whether I would have his son Halfdan for a son-in-law.

LJOT. And what did you say?

SVEINUNGI. I said I had nothing against it — quite the contrary. I should be content if you had a husband like him, and we are getting old, your mother and I. We don't know when death may strike us. It may come at any time, and I should like to see the man who is to take my place when I am gone.

LJOT. I don't think you are getting old.

SVEINUNGI. Oh, yes, I feel it. Sometimes when I want to use this or that for my work I find that I have clean forgotten where I put it. That could never have happened when I was young; there was not a thing that slipped my mind. But what do you say, Ljot? Your mother thinks as I do, so it lies solely with you whether you will accept this happiness or not.

LJOT. I don't think I care for that happiness.

SVEINUNGI. You should weigh your words well before you speak. Perhaps you fancy there will be a wooer like Halfdan coming every day. But you don't mean that; you only mean that he must come and speak for himself.

LJOT. I am so young, father.

SVEINUNGI. You are past nineteen. There are many girls who marry at seventeen, and you have been so well taught that you can readily take your place at the head of a household. I need not be ashamed of you there, that's sure. And you will have your mother near you, for it is understood, of course, that you and Halfdan stay here with us. You will have your bridal now in the fall, and next spring you can take over the farm.

LJOT. But I scarcely know him at all!

SVEINUNGI. Your mother did not know me, and I can't see but that we two have lived happily together all these years. It is not always those who marry for what they call love who are happiest. Arne and I are friends from old times, and I have as good as given him my word.

[*Enter* JORUNN *from the house.*]

LJOT [*straightening herself*]. You should not have done that without speaking to me.

SVEINUNGI. What has come over you? Do you mean to go right against the will of your parents? I can tell you one thing, if it is this tramp you are thinking of, it shall never come to pass. Not as long as I live. [*Goes in.*]

JORUNN. Your father was angry. What were you talking about?

LJOT. He wants me to marry a man I don't know.

JORUNN. Does he? You cannot say of Halfdan that he is a man you don't know.

LJOT. We have never spoken a word to each other.

JORUNN. Yet he has been here several times. Once he stayed overnight. Besides you have heard him spoken of, and you know his people. Everybody knows the Hofstad people.

LJOT. Father has given his word without asking me. He had no right to do that.

JORUNN. You have worked yourself up, Ljot. I don't understand you. Can it really be that you have promised yourself to some one without letting your parents know it?

LJOT. I have not.

JORUNN. You need not hide anything from me. If you have given your word, you must keep it.

LJOT. I told you that I have not.

JORUNN. You could not tell your old mother a falsehood! But if you are free and not bound by any promise, this puzzles me. Halfdan is young and a capable man, and his father is one of the richest and most respected farmers in the countryside.

LJOT. But I don't care for him. You can't mean that I should marry a man I don't care for. [*Leans over the fence.*]

JORUNN. Once you are married you will come to care for him. [*Goes to her.*] It is a great step you are about to take. Weigh your words well, so that you may not rue them. Be careful not to thrust away happiness when she reaches out her hand to you, or there may come a day when you will repent. You must know that your parents wish nothing but what is good for you.

LJOT [*with tears in her voice*]. It seems to me you are against me, both you and father.

JORUNN [*stroking her hair*]. I believe you are hiding something from your mother. I think I know what it is. You were very much pleased with the bird's skin you got to-day. [LJOT *is silent.*] The winter your father asked me in marriage there came to my home a man who used to go from farm to farm doing odd carpenter jobs. One evening I carried his coffee to him where he was at work. He had a big chest standing there that he kept his tools in. I can remember it plainly; it was yellow. I stood waiting for him to finish his coffee so that I could take the cup back, when he took out of the chest a work-box — the prettiest thing I've ever seen. It was of dark brown wood, the lid round, with pictures of animals carved on it. He made me a present of it, and when I was about to go, he asked me for a kiss, but I would not give it to him.

LJOT. You never told me about this.

JORUNN. He was a good looking man, with big brown eyes. Well, when your father came, my father and mother both wanted me to become his wife. It was not altogether easy for me, but I would not go against their wishes. I thought it my duty to please them, and besides the other man had never asked me straight out.

LJOT. But he was the one you cared for.

JORUNN. Perhaps I thought so at the time. [*Silence.*] He went away on the night he heard that I was promised to your father. A year after I married your father, he was drowned — some thought he had taken his own life.

LJOT. Maybe that was your doing.

JORUNN. How can you say such a thing to your mother!

LJOT. Don't be angry with me, mother.

JORUNN. A man who cannot bear his fate is not worth much. I should not have been happy as his wife, and I could not wish for a better man than your father. When two people live together a whole lifetime and have an honest will to do what is right by each other, they will come to care for each other, as the years go by. [*Silence.*] I have told you this so that you may think it over, but if you feel in your own heart that it is right to go against the wishes of your parents, then

C

you will have to do so. [Ljot *is silent.*] You say
nothing, my child? I have tried as best I could, in
my poor way, to do what seemed my duty. I cannot
give my daughter any other or better advice. When
the hour of sorrow comes, as it must come to you too,
there is nothing else that can bring you peace.

Ljot. I will do as you wish.

Jorunn. I always knew that I had a good daughter.
[*Strokes her hair.*] How glad your father will be!
This will be a great day for him, and you will never re-
gret that you did as your parents wished. [*Goes in.*]

[Ljot *stands alone.*]

[*Enter* Einar *and* Frida *from the house.*]

Einar [*to* Frida]. You can start the bellows. I
hope the fire has not gone out. [*They go into the smithy.*]

[*Enter* Helgi *from the house. He goes into the smithy
and comes out again with a turf-spade in his hand.*]

Einar [*in the door*]. Shall you be home for dinner?

Helgi. No, the others will bring it to me. [*Exit
to the left.*]

[*Enter* Sveinungi.]

Sveinungi. Are you here? Won't you come in
and talk to your father? [*Patting her shoulder.*] This
is the happiest day in my life since the time I got your
mother. [*They go in. Enter* Jakobina *with a plate
of chicken-feed in her hand; goes to the door of the smithy.*]

Jakobina. Is Frida there? Can you spare her while
she runs over to the chickens for me with their food?

Einar. Yes, indeed. [Frida *goes with the chicken-
feed.*]

Jakobina [*sits down on the horse-block*]. I had such
a queer dream last night. I thought I was standing
out there in the yard, and I saw a giant come striding

across the *hraun*. I saw him stop right there — he stood with arms stretched out and bent down over the house.

ACT II

[*A grass-grown yard, some rocks partly sunk in the ground. In the foreground, farthest to the right, a tent. In the background, to the left, the farm-house. In the outskirts of the yard a sheephouse with the roof and part of the walls in ruins. Beyond it, the "hraun," a lava-field stretching for miles, studded with jutting rocks and lava formations.*]

[*It is the evening of the same day.*]

THE SERVANTS [*seated, singing*].

God, the power unending
Rests with Thee alone.
Cherubim are bending
Low before Thy throne.
From Thy Heaven hear me!
Weak and soiled am I,
Wounds and sorrows sear me,
Fainting I draw nigh.
Is there then another way?
Sorrow's rising hills may they
Not reach up to heaven, pray?
Help me — lest I die.

[*They cover their eyes in prayer. Silence.*]

JORUNN [*uncovers her eyes*]. The peace of God be with us. [*The Servants rise and shake hands.*]

JORUNN [*patting* FRIDA'S *cheek*]. Now you must not be afraid of the earthquake any more. When we trust in Him, no harm can befall us. [*Gathers the hymn-books.*] Please take the books back to the tent, Ljot; it's a little too early yet to go in. [LJOT *goes with the books.*] And you may fetch the shoes I was sewing. I left them in there.

[*Some sit on the rocks, others squat in the grass. Only* SVEINUNGI *remains standing.*]

LJOT [*coming from the tent*]. Here are the shoes, mother.

JORUNN. Thank you, daughter.

[LJOT *lies down in the grass, gazing out over the* "*hraun.*"]

INDRIDI. Did you hear the church-bells ringing?

EINAR. I did not hear them.

JORUNN. I did. They rang of themselves. [*Silence.*]

INDRIDI. Where were you, Thora, when the shock came?

THORA. In the kitchen.

INDRIDI. It's your week, isn't it?

THORA. I don't know how I ever got out, for the whole floor heaved under me, so that I was thrown right against the wall, and you should have seen me when I came out — all black from the falling soot.

JON. And the rest of you — where were you?

BJØRG. We were sitting in the *badstofa*, sorting wool.

RANNVEIG. It felt as if some one was shaking the roof and trying to pull up the whole house.

INDRIDI. We were just about to leave our work and run home to hear how you had fared, but then I thought they would be sure to send us word [*looking askance at* SVEINUNGI] if anything had happened. Besides, we wanted to get enough turf cut while we were at it so that we should not have to go back another time.

Jon. But I must say that when I began working again, it went against me. It was cutting into a living thing — like skinning a live animal.

Rannveig. Ugh, yes.

Jon. And the place where we'd cut turf last year looked like an ugly scar.

[*Silence.*]

Jorunn. Did you meet anybody when you came home from work?

Indridi. No.

Jorunn. And no outsider has been here this afternoon. They don't come when they are wanted. I ought to have sent one of you to the next farm to find out how things were there, anyway.

Jon. I can easily go yet, if mistress wants me to.

Jorunn. Oh, no, it's getting late. I hope we shall have no bad tidings from any one.

Indridi. I hope so, too.

Jon. I'm afraid the Vik farm-house has fallen. It is both old and poorly built — nothing like ours. [*Silence.*]

Einar. You should have seen the hawks, Jorunn, right after the shock. They kept flying back and forth, just as they do when they're warding off a foe from their nest.

Jorunn. They were frightened.

Einar. And no wonder. Great pieces of rock came tumbling down into the creek. The sheep out on the heath yonder huddled together in flocks, looking like old snow.

Jon. Then you were out hunting.

EINAR.   No, I was not hunting.   I was looking at the hawks, wondering whether one could get at them by going down in a rope.

[*Silence.*]

JORUNN.   What about the boy, Sveinungi?   Do you mean to let him stay with the sheep all night?

SVEINUNGI.   Certainly.   He can sleep to-morrow.

JORUNN.   I was only thinking he might be afraid to be alone.

SVEINUNGI.   He's no more afraid than grown people.

JORUNN.   I saw he took both the dogs with him. [*Silence.*]

HELGI.   There was a man walking across the *hraun* a little while ago.   Who can it be?

INDRIDI.   I saw him too.

JON.   It was Sølvi.   He carried his gun.   [*Silence.*]

LJOT.   How still it is on the *hraun.*

EINAR.   I thought you were listening for something, while you lay there quiet as a mouse.   I thought you were listening for the earthquake.

FRIDA.   Can one hear the earthquake when it is coming?

RANNVEIG.   Are you afraid?   Yes, sometimes it can be heard a little before the shock.   They say it sounds like the clatter of hoofs from many hundred horses.

BJØRG.   To me it sounded like the whistling of the wind.

JORUNN.   You should sit down, Sveinungi.   You'll get tired standing.

SVEINUNGI.   I am not tired.   [*Silence.*]

FRIDA.   What if the earth should open up right here where we are sitting?

RANNVEIG. It won't. Who told you that it might?

FRIDA. Jakobina said so.

RANNVEIG. You must not listen to all she says; she talks so much.

JAKOBINA. I say nothing but what is true. At the time of the last great earthquake the ground cracked and made a fissure many miles long; I saw it myself. The earth opened her mouth to breathe.

EINAR [*to* FRIDA]. Don't be afraid. I have a black lamb — do you remember it? — with white feet. When I get it home in the fall, I will give it to you.

JAKOBINA [*facing the "hraun"*]. Not one of you knows the *hraun* as I do. Can you tell me why the hollows out there are never filled with snow? Have you ever seen the snow falling fast enough to cover even the rims around them? It's the earth blowing her breath against it. The earth sets traps for men; the earth is a man-eater.

JORUNN [*to* JAKOBINA]. You must not frighten the child. [*Silence.*]

SVEINUNGI. Wasn't it you, Jakobina, who said that sometimes blood comes on the window-panes? It bodes ill, they say.

JAKOBINA. Why do you ask? There is no one here who has seen it, is there?

SVEINUNGI. Never mind why I ask.

JAKOBINA. Well, if I must say it, it is a sign that some one in the house is going to die soon.

SVEINUNGI. Or it might bode ill to the farm itself, maybe.

JAKOBINA. What do you mean?

SVEINUNGI. That it might be doomed.

JORUNN. Indeed, it means neither the one nor the other. It's nothing but a silly superstition.

SVEINUNGI. Not that I believe in it, but look at the windows. Don't they look as if they were wet with blood?

JORUNN. It's the sun shining on them.

SVEINUNGI. And see the gables, how white they are. They don't look whiter from the fields down yonder when you spread a cloth over them to call me home.

INDRIDI [*lowering his voice*]. Did you see the sheep-cot fall?

THORA. Yes, it happened just as we came out.

INDRIDI. What did Sveinungi say?

THORA. He said nothing.

INDRIDI. But he told us to move out here.

THORA. No, it was Jorunn who made us do it.

SVEINUNGI [*to* JORUNN]. I did not tell you that when I came into the *badstofa*, right after the shock, our old clock had stopped running.

JORUNN. Was it broken?

SVEINUNGI. No, when I touched the pendulum it started again, but the place was still as death when I entered. The grass on the roof cast a shadow over the skylight. It was as quiet as when my father lay dead.

JORUNN. I think we had better go and lie down. There's nothing gained by staying here any longer.

SVEINUNGI. I can't see that there was any need of moving out, but you had your way, Jorunn.

JORUNN. I feel sure that they have done the same on all the other farms. We must be thankful it is summer, so that we can stay outdoors.

SVEINUNGI. Must we be thankful? So you give thanks that my work is ruined.

JORUNN. We must take what comes, whether good or evil, and trouble may help us to remember all the things we have neglected to give thanks for.

SVEINUNGI. I don't know but that I have always done my duty. I have built all the sheep-cots; I have fenced in the land and looked after it as best I could. I demand justice of Him up there.

JORUNN [*rising*]. I won't listen to such talk. Did you buy the land from Him, perhaps? And what did you have to pay with that was not His already?

SVEINUNGI. You needn't mock me. You can walk all over the yard and cut your handful of grass with your scissors wherever you like; it grows thick as wool everywhere, and it's all my work.

JORUNN. Was it you who ruled the *hraun* for thousands of years so that it did not swallow up the bit of ground you are standing on, which you call yours? [*Goes into the tent.*]

SVEINUNGI. Which I call mine! [*Stamping his foot.*] It is mine! I bought the land from Him up there with my work. [*The Servants rise.*]

JON. I believe the worst is over and that we shall be let off with the fright.

INDRIDI. I hope so.

BJØRG. You can never tell. Remember what happened the time when more than threescore farm-houses fell in one night.

THORA. It must have been dreadful.

SVEINUNGI. Now you must all go into the tent. [*The Servants go in.*]

JAKOBINA. I shouldn't wonder if something dreadful were to happen to the farm. [*Goes into the tent.*
SVEINUNGI *stands quite still a little while, then walks a*

few steps, pauses, takes a few more steps, and again stops.]

[*Enter* LJOT *from the tent.*]

LJOT. Are you not coming, father? Mother told me to ask you to come in.

SVEINUNGI. Why doesn't she lie down? She need not wait for me.

LJOT. We are so frightened, father — all of us.

[*Enter* JORUNN *from the tent.*]

JORUNN. It's getting cold.

LJOT. Yes, it is cold.

JORUNN. The sun has set.

SVEINUNGI. Why are you coming out again, Jorunn? Can't you sleep?

JORUNN. No, I can't sleep.

SVEINUNGI. Do you remember the night you thought I was lost in the snowstorm? A light was burning in the upper window. To see it was better than meeting a human being, and when the dogs began to bark behind the door, it was just as if the house itself were speaking — calling out its joy. It sounded better to me than a human voice, and when I stepped into the hall, the darkness seemed to put its arms around me. Never have I had so sweet a welcome, not even when my daughter was a little child.

JORUNN. Ought we not to go in, Sveinungi? It's getting late. You too must go in now, Ljot.

LJOT. I am only waiting for father.

JORUNN. Do you hear that, Sveinungi? Ljot is waiting for you, and the servants can't sleep either before you go in.

SVEINUNGI. I am not going to stay in the tent to-night. I am going home.

JORUNN. You don't mean that!

LJOT. But, father dear!

SVEINUNGI. I won't let any foolish fear drive me out of my house, and it is nothing but a foolish fear. The earthquake will not come so suddenly but that I shall have time to get out. It's impossible. Besides, the *badstofa* will hold. It's well built, though it's old.

JORUNN. Do you think the *badstofa* will hold if there should come a big earthquake? You cannot mean that!

SVEINUNGI. It is not at all sure there will be another shock. It's only a fancy that the earthquake must needs keep on once it has begun. I believe it is over; I feel it. [*During the last speeches the Servants have been coming out of the tent.*] What are you running out for? Go in, all of you.

JAKOBINA. I must tell master about the dream I had. It was last night. I thought I was standing out in the yard and saw a giant coming across the *hraun*. He walked with long, unsteady strides [*she takes a few steps forward; her voice sounds distant and threatening*], and seemed to grope as if he were blind. Then I saw him standing right by the house — with arms stretched out; he bent down over the farm and stood there like a stone cross. [*Makes the sign of the cross with her arms.*]

SVEINUNGI. Did I ask you to tell me about your dream?

JORUNN. I beg of you, Sveinungi, that you do not stay at the house to-night. It would be tempting God.

SVEINUNGI. It's rather He who is tempting me. If I ran away, it would serve me right to have the house fall down. [*Pointing to the house.*] There it has stood waiting for me every evening as far back as I can remember; I have seen the windows flaming in the sun. I have seen them wet with rain. I have seen them white with frost. I've been with it ever since I was a child. I have climbed on the roof as I climbed on my father's shoulders. When I stood on the ridge, it seemed it had lifted me up to let me see better. No, Jorunn, even if I knew the earthquake to be coming, I should go home. Nor is it any wonder that I long to get into my own bed. I am old now, and I have waked up there almost every morning of my life. I have gone to bed so tired and worn out that I could barely stand on my feet and have waked up young and strong. I have been ill and have lain there watching the sunbeams flitting across the floor. [SVEINUNGI *walks homeward.*]

JORUNN. Are you going home? [*Following him hurriedly.*] Whatever happens, your fate shall be mine.

SVEINUNGI [*stops and looks back*]. Do you hear that? She is not afraid, my wife. [SVEINUNGI *and* JORUNN *walk homeward.*]

LJOT. How can you do it, father? [*Walks a few steps away from the others and remains standing there.*]

JAKOBINA. God be with you, Jorunn, and with you, Sveinungi. You have been good to me, these nineteen years. [*Goes into the tent.*]

[*Silence.*]

HELGI. There, they went in.

BJØRG. Yes, they are in there now.

JON. I think we had better go and lie down, since there is nothing we can do.

INDRIDI. No, we can do nothing.

THORA. It will be a long night.

RANNVEIG. Poor Ljot. [*The Servants walk slowly into the tent.*]

[EINAR *and* LJOT *remain. Silence.*]

EINAR [*goes to* LJOT]. I wish I could make you happy as easily now as when you were a little girl.

LJOT [*struggling with her tears*]. Father does not care for me at all. He does not think of me for a moment.

EINAR. Your father cares for you; no doubt of that, but he is beside himself with the earthquake.

LJOT. You don't know what I am talking about. [*In sudden fear.*] If only something dreadful does not happen!

EINAR. We must trust to the Lord to keep us all. Won't you too try to lie down?

LJOT. I can't sleep.

EINAR. Perhaps you would rather stay here a little while. Let me bring a shawl for you; it is getting cold. [*Goes into the tent.* LJOT *stands motionless looking out over the "hraun."*]

EINAR [*coming from the tent*]. They are asleep in there already. Won't you put the shawl around your shoulders?

LJOT. I am not cold.

EINAR. Then I'll spread it over one of the rocks for you to sit on. They are wet with dew. [*Spreads it over the stone.*] There! What did you have in mind when you stood there looking out over the *hraun?*

LJOT. I was thinking of an old tale Jakobina once told me. It was about a young girl. She went out on the *hraun* with bare feet to meet her sweetheart, and wherever she stepped the moss grew under her foot.

EINAR. That's a pretty story. I can tell you one,

too, if you care to hear it.   It might help to quiet you a little.

LJOT [*takes his hand*].   You are so good.

EINAR [*sits down; relates*].   In olden times, they say, there was an underground stream that ran straight through the country from south to north and was meant as a sign of truce between land and sea.   It happened that a cross-eyed, ill-natured shark was trying to tempt a young whale to swim that stream from end to end.   The whale's name was Spraytail.   He was the handsomest of all the young whales and could shoot three jets of water at once.   The shark boasted that he had swum through the stream himself, but of course it was only real fishes that could do it.   Spraytail felt stung on behalf of his kin, and as the shark had told him that there were openings here and there in the roof of this underground way, he made up his mind to try his luck, trusting that he could hold his breath from one opening to another.   But it fell out otherwise.   Spraytail never came back.   The last ever heard of him was that some swans, in their flight over the hills, had seen a jet of blood spurting out of the ground.

The whales were in a rage and, as they thought in their grief that the land had broken truce, they goaded the sea to wreak vengeance upon it.   Are you listening?   [LJOT *nods her head.*]

One night a dreadful storm broke.   The sea came rushing over the land, fell upon the rocks like a monster, and tore them to pieces.   The next morning thousands of seafowls' nests were wrecked, and where green fields had been there were black sands.   Now there was sore need of wise counsel.   A shrewd old raven said that the fire should be roused.   All the birds agreed that the raven had spoken well, but none dared do the deed. The raven was made judge, and decided that the spider should undertake the ticklish task, and that the eagle should carry her to the crater.

They gave the spider ten fat blue-flies to take with her. She spun herself well and firmly under some strong feathers, and off they went. They flew over deep dales, over dreary wastes, and over glaciers. In the evening they came to the fire-mountain, and there they rested overnight, but they did not sleep much, for the fire was snoring like a giant down below in the earth. Early the next morning the eagle flew to the top of the mountain. The spider made fast her thread and spun herself slowly down into the crater. It was dark down there, and the heat and sulphur made her eyes smart, but she could see enough to make out that the fire lay sleeping under a very thin black coverlet. The spider knew nothing but the finger-language, and she moved her legs incessantly, telling fully and truly all about the havoc that was wrought, and urging the fire to come to the rescue lest the whole land be swallowed up by the sea. Yet the fire did not stir. Then the spider bent her legs up under her and let herself fall all the way down to the fire. She stretched out one leg and poked the black coverlet. From that moment she couldn't remember anything till she was lying at the rim of the crater again. She peeped down and saw that the fire had thrown off the coverlet and was red and blazing. Then the spider understood that her task was done. Everybody knows how the fire had its reckoning with the sea and filled up whole fjords with lava and ashes. [Sølvi *is seen approaching from the hraun.*]

LJOT [*rising*]. You must tell me that story over again some time. I could not listen rightly.

EINAR [*rising*]. Who is that coming so late? [*Looking.*] Now I know him; it's Sølvi.

LJOT. I saw him awhile ago walking over the *hraun*.

EINAR. He may bring us news.

[*Enter* SØLVI *carrying a gun and with a game-bag on his back.*]

SØLVI. Good evening.

EINAR. Good evening.

SØLVI. How good it seems to meet people! You have moved out, of course?

EINAR. You are walking late.

SØLVI. You will have to take the earthquake as my excuse. This has been a bad day. What has happened here at your place?

EINAR. One of the outbuildings came down and a part of the yard fence.

SØLVI. At Hol one wall of the house fell. The folks barely got out. [*Lays down his gun.*]

EINAR. Was anybody hurt?

SØLVI. No. I could not stay there any longer. I saw your house standing, and that was a relief. [*Looking at* LJOT.] Yet I had to come.

EINAR. What do you think? Do you believe the earthquake is over? [SØLVI *fails to answer; looks at* LJOT.]

LJOT. My father and mother are sleeping in the house.

SØLVI. Why in the world are they doing that!

LJOT. We were ready to go to bed, but father would not come into the tent. Mother begged him to stay, but it was no use, and when father went back to the house, mother went with him.

Sølvi. But the buildings may fall at any moment if there should be another shock.

Einar. Sveinungi knows that as well as we do, but he would not let the house stand forsaken.

Sølvi. We must hope that no harm will come to them. So that is why you are still up. Have the others been in bed long?

Ljot. No, they went in a little while ago.

Einar. May I look at your gun?

Sølvi. As much as you like.

Einar. Is it loaded?

Sølvi. It is. [*To* Ljot.] You are not angry with me for coming so late? It seemed an eternity till Sunday.

Ljot. I knew you would come.

Sølvi. You knew it! Won't you sit down? I have something to show you. [Ljot *sits down.* Sølvi *opens the game-bag; takes from it a large fern.*] I found this out on the *hraun.* Is it not beautiful? [*Sits down.*] Look, the stem is no thicker than a hair, while the leaf can easily hide your whole face. [*Holds it up before her face.*] It trembles when your breath touches it.

Ljot. You have pulled it up by the roots. May I have the moss that came with it? [Sølvi *loosens the moss from the roots.* Ljot *lays it in her hand; smiles.*] When it withers, I'll keep it in my shoes.

Sølvi. Will you keep it in your shoes? See these two small ferns on one root. They look like two slim hands. [*Looks at* Ljot.]

Einar [*puts the gun aside*]. It's a fine one. It

D

must have cost a good deal. Perhaps you bought it yourself abroad?

SØLVI. I did. [*Lays down the fern. To* LJOT.] If you have time, you can plant it to-morrow. It won't hurt it to lie overnight in the wet grass.

EINAR [*goes to* SØLVI]. How long were you abroad?

SØLVI. Seven years.

EINAR. That's a long time. [*Sits down.*]

LJOT. My father was angry with me for keeping your bird's skin.

SØLVI. Was he? And I was thinking of asking you to visit me at Hol some day before I leave.

LJOT. I hardly think I dare to.

SØLVI. You could take Einar with you. It is not much more than an hour's ride, and I have a number of things I should like to show you, — petrified tree-trunks that I have dug out of the earth, in which you can see plainly every bud and shoot, and stone slabs with impressions of flowers and leaves that lived thousands of years ago. Should you like to see them?

LJOT. I should like it ever so much.

SØLVI. I have some rocks, too, baked by fire and furrowed by ice. If you knew all the tales they tell me! They lay bare to me things that are hidden from every one else. [*A whirring of wings is heard far away.*]

EINAR [*stands up, pointing with his finger*]. Look, there is a flock of ducks flying over the *hraun*. [*Stands gazing.*]

SØLVI [*in a low voice*]. It made me so happy to see you. This evening, when the sun was setting, I reached out toward it. I did the same when I saw you.

EINAR [*rising*]. They're flying unusually low. There they alight — I'll get my gun.

Sølvi [*rising*]. I'll lend you mine. [*Hands him the gun.*] It will carry a distance of a hundred and thirty feet.

Einar. What size shot have you?

Sølvi. Duck-shot.

Einar. Ljot, you don't mind, do you? I shall not be gone long. If they rise, I'm not going after them. [*Exit.*] [Ljot *rises.*]

Sølvi [*goes to her*]. My star must be in the heavens to-night.

Ljot. You must not think that I was sitting up so late because I was waiting for you — I saw you walking over the *hraun* — but we shan't talk about that.

Sølvi. Shall I tell you why I came home from abroad? It was for your sake.

Ljot [*sits down*]. That is not true.

Sølvi [*sits down*]. One night, the last winter I was away, I must have been dreaming, but it seemed to me that I was awake. I had come back home and was walking on the *hraun*. The *hraun* was covered with ashes. As I walked, I suddenly fell into a deep cleft and kept on falling and falling. At last I found myself lying on the bottom, unable to stir. Death came and sucked the life out of my eyes and held it in her hand like a tiny flame. Suddenly a woman stood beside me dressed in moss. She pleaded for me so long that death gave her my life. She looked like you. It was you. Don't you know that you hold my life in your hands? [*They rise.*]

Ljot. I think I shall go in. It is hard to tell when Einar will be back. When he is out hunting he forgets everything.

Sølvi. I love you, Ljot! You have not been out

of my thoughts since the first time I saw you. Everything reminds me of you — the sun, the sky —

LJOT. I too have been happy in seeing you and talking with you. [*Stands still as death.*] This morning,
right after you had gone, my father told me that on
his way home from town he had seen his old friend, —
and my father wanted me to promise myself to the
son of his old friend, but I would not, because I was
thinking of you. Then my mother came and talked
to me — and I gave in. I could not do anything else.

SØLVI. Why did I not speak before! You won't
feel hurt at what I say, Ljot? You must not let your
parents decide your life. That is for you to do.

LJOT. You don't know my father. If he thought
I was standing here talking to you, I can't tell what
he would do.

SØLVI. I am convinced your parents have but one
wish, and that is for your happiness.

LJOT. I don't know. My mother does not say much
about happiness; she does her duty — and I know
mine. [*Turns toward the tent.*]

SØLVI. Are you going?

LJOT. It is better that we two should not meet
again — it would only cause us suffering. [*Moves
away.*]

SØLVI [*following her*]. You don't realize what you
are about to do! You will be committing a terrible
crime — against all the wonderful days that life meant
us two to have together. For you do care for me, Ljot,
don't you? [LJOT *is silent.*] I thought you cared for
me. When you spoke to me this morning you blushed,
and I thought it was your heart that gave me its promise. The joy of it overwhelmed me.

Ljot. It matters little whom I care for. I have given my word.

Sølvi. You think it your duty to keep your word, but there is another duty that is far greater, and that is to open your arms to happiness when it comes. There is no greater duty. It is the meaning of our existence. You must feel that, you who have grown like a flower out of the earth!

Ljot. It is not only that I have given my word. If I had neither father nor mother, I should break my promise, but I know that it would grieve my parents. This morning father said to me that it was the happiest day of his life since he got my mother, and I know it was true.

Sølvi. You must tell your parents that you cannot keep your word. You must do it for my sake. [*Kneeling.*] You are the only one I care for in all the world.

Ljot. I can't deal such a blow to my father. No other living being has been so good to me as my father.

Sølvi [*rising*]. You do not care for me at all.

Ljot. You think it is easy for me! [*With tears in her eyes.*] I own a spring — I cleanse it every Saturday. I have told it your name. [*Goes into the tent.*]

Sølvi. You are going! [*Turns away from Ljot, sits down on one of the rocks, covers his face.*]

Ljot [*stands silent for a long time, then goes over to him and takes his hands from his face*]. I love you. [Sølvi *takes her face between his hands and kisses her.*] [*Enter* Jakobina.]

Jakobina [*coming slowly from the tent*]. We are not all asleep in there. [Sølvi *and* Ljot *rise.*]

Sølvi [*holding* Ljot *by the hand*]. Let us go out on the *hraun* and look for Einar.

LJOT [*runs to* JAKOBINA, *puts her arms around* JAKO-BINA'S *neck and holds her close*]. I know that you care for me. [*Goes to* SØLVI *and takes his hand.*] Come!

[*They go toward the "hraun."* JAKOBINA *stands still, following them with her eyes, then shakes her head and turns toward the tent.*]

ACT III

[*The farm-house is in ruins. Only the farther side of the "badstofa" is standing. It looks like a dark cavern. The servants have gathered near the wreckage; they are bare-headed, the men in their shirt-sleeves.* SVEINUNGI *is standing near the dark opening. It is night.*]

SVEINUNGI [*to* JON]. You dare not go in.

JON [*peering in the gloom*]. I don't know. There's only one post that holds the roof, and it may snap at any moment.

SVEINUNGI. It won't. It is drift-timber, which never rots.

JON. And besides, it stands aslant; the slightest push would make it go with a crash, and there would be no getting out alive if the heavy roof came down.

SVEINUNGI. You are afraid. Is there anybody else who dares?

JORUNN. You cannot ask any man to go in there.

SVEINUNGI [*to* JON]. It would take you but a moment to bring out those few things. There's my tall chest — you know where it stands — and my old clock; you can unscrew it from the wall with your knife.

JON. I am not going in there.

SVEINUNGI. Get drunk and brag — that you know how to do, all of you. [*Starts into the ruins.*]

JON. Is master going in there?

SVEINUNGI. Do you think I will let my things be ruined, because you are a coward?

JON. Then I will go with you. It's easier for two. [SVEINUNGI *and* JON *disappear from view.*]

JORUNN. No matter what happens to that man, he will never learn to bend. [*Goes to the ruins; looks in.*] Can you see anything in there? Is it not too dark? [*Silence.*]

[SVEINUNGI *and* JON *appear, carrying the tall chest.*]

SVEINUNGI. Indridi and you, Helgi, come here and take it from us. Set it over there.

[SVEINUNGI *and* JON *disappear again.*]

INDRIDI [*to* JORUNN, *as the men carry the chest out into the open*]. Can we leave it here?

JORUNN. Yes. [*She peers into the ruins again.*]

[*Enter* JAKOBINA *from the direction of the tent.*]

JAKOBINA [*goes to* JORUNN, *lays her hand on* JORUNN's *shoulder*]. I must feel that you are indeed safe and sound. [*Stroking her arm.*] When you went home, I was afraid that you would never come out of that house again. I thought your husband must be struck with blindness.

JORUNN. You don't know where Einar and Ljot have gone?

JAKOBINA. I saw Ljot going out on the *hraun.*

[SVEINUNGI *and* JON *appear carrying the clock.*]

SVEINUNGI. You will have to be a little careful, the glass is broken. [*Steps out into the open. To* JON.] I dare say you have had enough of this.

JON. I can't say it was any too cheerful in there.

SVEINUNGI [*to the men*]. You can carry the clock into the tent; the dampness here might be bad for it. And you, Bjørg, go and get a blanket to spread over the chest.

[*Exeunt Servants*, BJØRG *running*, INDRIDI *and* HELGI *carrying the clock*, JAKOBINA *following them.*]

JORUNN. You are lucky, Sveinungi, that you have not come to grief with your foolhardiness.

SVEINUNGI. It is nothing but my duty to care as best I can for what is mine. I have risked my life before in a good deal worse dangers than this. But I must send some one to look after the boy. He may have lost all the sheep. Will you go, Jon?

JON. I will.

SVEINUNGI. You had better drive the sheep home.

JORUNN. And if you should see Ljot and Einar, tell them to hurry.

JON. I will. [*Exit.*]

SVEINUNGI. Where are they?

JORUNN. They are out on the *hraun.*

[*Enter* BJØRG, *carrying a blanket.*]

BJØRG. Here is the blanket.

SVEINUNGI. Why did they go out there? [*Takes the blanket, goes to the chest, and runs his hand over it.*] Here it's been bruised. [*Throws the blanket over it.*] I did not think you would have all this to go through. [*Takes a long breath.*] It is pretty hard when one has grown as old as I am to see one's work destroyed.

JORUNN. That is true.

SVEINUNGI. My only comfort is that I shall have a capable man to help me put up the buildings again. [*Gazing over the "hraun."*] What can it be that is keeping Ljot out there? Has she been gone long?

RANNVEIG. I don't know.

SVEINUNGI. I hope she has not gone down into one of the fissures. One can't tell what may happen. The walls might cave in, or they might close overhead.

[*Enter* INDRIDI *from the direction of the tent.*]

INDRIDI. Einar and Ljot are coming now. We could see them from the tent.

SVEINUNGI. Are they coming? [*Goes toward the background.*] Yes, Ljot has seen us; she is running.

JORUNN. She must have thought we were buried under the ruins.

SVEINUNGI [*looking*]. There is a third person with them. Who can it be?

RANNVEIG. So there is.

INDRIDI. I believe it's Sølvi.

SVEINUNGI. What business has he out there at night?

INDRIDI. It's hard to tell!

SVEINUNGI. I do hope that Ljot has not been talking to that fellow.

[*Enter* HELGI *from the direction of the tent.*] [*Silence.*]

[*Enter* LJOT, *running.*]

LJOT [*puts her arms around her mother*]. I was so frightened!

JORUNN. Were you frightened? You are quite out of breath with running.

SVEINUNGI [*smiling*]. Have you no greeting for your father?

LJOT. Dear, dear father! [*Embraces him.*]

SVEINUNGI. You were glad when you saw us?

LJOT. I was so glad that I don't know yet what I am saying. I was afraid you had been caught under the ruins. I thought that was to be my punishment.

SVEINUNGI [*stroking her hair*]. Have you done anything you should be punished for?

LJOT [*taking his hand*]. Be fond of me, father. Be very, very fond of me! [*Enter* EINAR *and* SØLVI.]

EINAR. Thank God, you are safe! Then you had time to get out?

JORUNN. No, we were in there.

LJOT. Were you in there? [*Goes to the ruins.*] How weird it looks!

SVEINUNGI [*goes to the ruins*]. It is only the one post that holds it all. If that had snapped, you would never have laid eyes on us again.

EINAR [*looks into the ruins*]. It's a miracle it didn't break.

JORUNN. Yes, if it had not been God's will, we should not be here now.

EINAR [*turns from the ruins*]. It was not any too cheerful out on the *hraun* either. The place seemed suddenly to have become alive.

SVEINUNGI. What in the world made you go out there?

EINAR. There was a flock of ducks flying over the *hraun*, and I wanted to try a shot at them.

SVEINUNGI [*to* LJOT]. And why did you go with him?

LJOT. I was not with him. Sølvi and I stayed behind.

SVEINUNGI. Do you sit alone with a stranger in the middle of the night? [*To* SØLVI.] And you, why are you here at this time? I will not have you go hunting on my land without asking my leave.

SØLVI. I was not hunting on your land.

SVEINUNGI. But you are picking up stones, and I

forbid you to take as much as a single pebble from my land. Now you know that.

LJOT. Why do you say that, father?

SVEINUNGI. You can go into the tent, Ljot. You have nothing to do here.

LJOT. I have something to say to you.

SVEINUNGI. What is it? [LJOT *is silent. To the Servants.*] You can go. To-morrow I shall have a talk with you, Einar, which you will remember.

EINAR. It was not my fault.

SVEINUNGI [*to the Servants*]. Go! What are you waiting for? [*Exeunt Servants.*]

SVEINUNGI [*to* LJOT]. Now, what is it you have to say to me?

SØLVI. I have come here to ask for the hand of your daughter.

SVEINUNGI. Has not my daughter told you that she is betrothed?

LJOT. I have told him everything. I never cared for Halfdan — you know that, father, and I will not be his wife.

JORUNN. Ljot, it has never happened yet that one of my kin has broken faith. If you do it, you will be the first.

SVEINUNGI. And you have not reckoned with your father. It does not lie altogether with yourself to break your word. Do you think you can make a fool of me? [*To* SØLVI.] It does not make you my son-in-law that you have trifled with my daughter.

SØLVI. It was no mere chance that we two found each other. Only for Ljot's sake have I stayed so long in these parts. I came here to-night to find out how you had fared; I could not help it.

SVEINUNGI. You feel proud that you have coaxed a young girl to break her word. You think yourself very brave, and you have taken advantage of her when she was beside herself with fear. You have come like a thief in the dead of the night.

SØLVI. I love your daughter. There is nothing wrong in that, and I am proud and happy that she has given me her heart.

SVEINUNGI [*to* LJOT]. So that is what you have done. I dare say you have met him before and more than once behind my back.

LJOT. Not once.

SVEINUNGI. And straightway you are ready to break your word. You knew that Halfdan's father is the best friend I have.

LJOT. You must forgive me, father!

SVEINUNGI. And you knew I had sent him word that everything was settled.

LJOT [*takes his hand*]. Do you remember, father, when I was so little that I had to put my arms around your knee? Then you never said no when I asked for anything. I am still your little girl.

SVEINUNGI. Let me go!

LJOT. You do care for me, father. I know of no one who has been so good to me as you. You have given me everything that I call my own. You must give me my happiness!

SVEINUNGI. Let go my hand!

JORUNN. I understand that Sølvi is very dear to you, my child, but this comes upon us unawares, and it has been a terrible night for us all. [*To* SØLVI.] Could you not have waited before speaking to Sveinungi?

Sølvi. I cannot help it that it has come in this way. I would have waited if I could.

Jorunn. I might perhaps have seen my way to put in a good word for you two. [*To* Sveinungi.] You won't be hard on your daughter! If we had been lying under the ruins now, she would have had no need to ask us. To-night we must not be merciless.

Sveinungi. Who is this man? I don't know him, nor do I know his people.

Sølvi. My father was a farmer like yourself. Had he been living, you two might have become friends.

Sveinungi [*interrupting*]. The only thing I know about you is that you go about picking up stones like the children.

Sølvi. You speak slightingly of my stones, but the knowledge I gain from them can bring me more money than you ever made on your farm, and it can bring me fame.

Sveinungi. What kind of knowledge is that?

Sølvi. Those stones teach me to know my country and how it has been built by fire and water and ice. They give me an opportunity of finding out new links in laws that are eternal and mightier than all mankind.

Sveinungi. Indeed! Since you are so passing wise, you ought to have told me days ago that a great earthquake would come to-night. *That* I could have understood; but it seems that you knew as little there as the rest of us. I believe old Jakobina is wiser than you.

Sølvi. I don't know how wise she is, but I do know of people who go through life as if they were blind. They may have been living in the same place all their lives, and yet they have never seen the landscape they live with—neither its beauty nor its peculiar character.

SVEINUNGI. They haven't? [*Points toward the "hraun."*] I have been out there in a snowstorm so heavy that I could scarcely see a hand before me, and shall I tell you how I found my way? I knew where I was by feeling before me with my hands. [*Laughs.*] No, I have never seen the *hraun!*

SØLVI. I did not say that you were among the blind, and I am sure you are human enough not to force your daughter to marry against her will. It would not give you much joy to feel that you had made her unhappy for her whole life. If you think you do not know me well enough, you can find out all you wish from myself or from others.

SVEINUNGI. I have no desire to learn anything about you, and you need not worry about my daughter. She will stay here with me.

SØLVI. Ljot is not a child any longer. She can decide for herself.

SVEINUNGI. Perhaps you think she can't live without you. [*To* LJOT.] If you care as much for him as he imagines, I will let you prove it. I will let you choose between him and me. If you choose him, then I have no daughter any more.

LJOT. You don't mean to force me to such a choice!

SVEINUNGI. Can you for a single moment be in doubt about whom to choose of us two — him or your old father?

LJOT [*kneeling*]. He is so unutterably dear to me.

SVEINUNGI. Get up! I don't want to see you lying like a dog at my feet.

LJOT [*rising*]. Then you have no daughter.

SØLVI. I knew you would not fail me!

JORUNN. You had better give your consent, Sveinungi, since it cannot be otherwise. I cannot do without my only child.

SVEINUNGI [*goes to* LJOT]. You are quite free, Ljot; I will not try to force you, but when you have thought it over, you will not leave your father and mother for the sake of a stranger. You are my only child, and you have been the light of my eyes since you were a little tot. When I came home from work I was never too tired to listen to what you had to say. When you stroked my cheek it was like warm summer rain falling on my face. It will be lonely and empty here if you go. You cannot do it.

LJOT. Father, it is you who drive me away.

SVEINUNGI. You must listen to me. It has always been my intention that you should take the farm, and yesterday when you promised to marry Halfdan it seemed to me that all my wishes had been fulfilled. I was happy, and not only for your sake, but fully as much for the farm. Yet you would leave it now in the midst of misfortune. Look about you! Not a single building standing. Can you let your old father sit here alone and forsaken? You might as well kill your father. And for whom should I build it up again if you are not to have it? It might as well be left to rot on the ground.

LJOT. You don't know, father, how much I care for him. I used to dream often that the mountains fell so that I could see the land beyond. To-night it seemed to me that the mountains fell.

SVEINUNGI. You are a willful girl. [*To* SØLVI.] Could you think of taking over my farm, perhaps?

SØLVI. I could not —

SVEINUNGI [*interrupting*]. Do you two believe that

you can cow me? [*Pointing to the ruins.*] There is a chest of drawers in there that Ljot keeps her clothes in. I will have nothing of hers in my house. [*To* Sølvi.] Will you go in there with me and bring it out?

Sølvi. I have nothing to do in there.

Sveinungi. You can go, Ljot. I can't bear to see you. [*Goes over to the ruins; stands resting his hands on the walls.*]

Sølvi [*takes* Ljot *by the hand quietly*]. It is better that we leave your parents alone for a little while. [*Exeunt.*]

Jorunn. You will have to give your consent, Sveinungi. You say yourself that all you have done has been for your daughter.

Sveinungi [*turns to* Jorunn, *passing his earth-stained hand over his forehead*]. Did you understand what I was about to do? I wanted to get him into the ruins, and then I meant to give the post a shove.

Jorunn. God forgive you, man!

Sveinungi. Now we two must hold together. If we two are of one mind, I believe Ljot will give in. You must try to bring her to her senses.

Jorunn. They are very fond of each other. It warmed my heart to see them. It brought back the days of my own youth. I feel sure it would be a sin to try to part those two.

Sveinungi. And you say that!

Jorunn. I think it was her fate to meet this man. She has always been a good and dutiful daughter.

Sveinungi. And it was you who went with me into the house! Have you turned against me — you too?

Jorunn [*goes to him*]. You must not make the evil

worse than it really is. The man looks as if he came of good people, and we have every reason to believe that he is a capable man. Even if we can't keep Ljot here, as we had hoped to do, she will certainly find time to come and see us once in a while, and we shall have that to look forward to.

SVEINUNGI. You think only of your daughter. It is nothing to you if my life work is wasted. I could name you many farms that have been an ornament to the neighborhood as long as they have been handed down from man to man in the same family, but once they have passed into other hands, they have been tended in a makeshift way or left to go to rack and ruin altogether. You have seen those old forlorn places, where the site is overgrown with grass, and the heather has been allowed to spread all over the yard. They remind me of graves. I tell you the truth : if such a fate were in store for my farm, I should wish for nothing but to be lying under the ruins myself.

JORUNN. Who says that your farm will not be re-built! You are not so old that you cannot do it without help. If I know you rightly, you always grow younger and stronger whenever there is anything that needs all your powers. In a year or two you will have the buildings up again every bit as fine as before.

SVEINUNGI. Spare your wheedling! What would be the use, even though I got the houses up again? When my days are over, everything will pass into the hands of careless people. And to think that this should happen only because of a fleeting fancy!

JORUNN. Did it seem to you like a passing whim when Ljot was begging for your consent? To me it seemed that she was pleading for her life.

E

SVEINUNGI. Even though this should mean more to my daughter than I think it does, that can alter nothing. It is my right to care for my home and keep it intact even after I am gone. When I am standing out in the *hraun* and looking toward home, the green yard looks like a spot of sunshine.

JORUNN. You take it for granted that none of your kin will ever reap the benefit of your work, but your daughter is not dead, though she has chosen another man than the one you wanted her to marry. Why should not those two have children? They are both strong and healthy, and there is, after all, a chance that some day one of their sons may take over the farm.

SVEINUNGI. I dare say a son of his would be the right man!

JORUNN. A daughter's son is often more like his grandfather than his father. You know that as well as I.

SVEINUNGI. You are like a child playing with soap-bubbles. When one breaks, you are straightway ready to blow a new one. You can't make me play at that game. Even though they should have children, do I know how they would turn out? And you see it the same way yourself, but you are trying to fool me into giving my consent.

JORUNN. What do you gain even if you have your way and part those two? You may bring it about that your daughter becomes one of those sour old maids; for you cannot mean to drag her to the altar against her will.

SVEINUNGI. I didn't expect you to be against me. You wouldn't mind leaving the farm, you could live with your daughter. You care more for her than for me.

JORUNN [*her voice growing husky*]. Why do you say this, Sveinungi? I have never weighed my feelings for you two, nor do I intend to do it. I only know that where you are, there I stay too.

SVEINUNGI. Even this very earth upon my hand is dear to me. I care for it as the old house-leek would if she could feel. As for the young man whom you think so much of, I should have grudged him even to have the earth to fall on his face. But you were not born here, as I was. You have not lived here as a child. You are an outsider.

JORUNN. Am I an outsider! I am grown too old to kneel before you as your daughter did, but if you send her away, I know that even though you build your house both larger and finer, the room will seem less light to me, and the smile will be gone from my face. Can you not spare me the sorrow of losing my only child?

SVEINUNGI. I thought you knew me well enough not to tease me with your bootless prayers. What I have said stands.

JORUNN. I don't know what gives you the right to be so heartless. You were tempting God when you went into the house, but He had mercy on you and spared your life, and the very first thing you do is an act of cruelty. [*Bursts out sobbing.*]

SVEINUNGI. Don't take to crying, wife.

JORUNN [*weeping; sits down on one of the stones that have been torn from the wall by the earthquake*]. I don't see how I am going to live through it if you send her away.

Sveinungi [*stands puzzled for a moment, then goes to her*]. I understand that you take this very much to heart. Do go into the tent now and lie down. We must try to get over this as best we can.

Jorunn [*rising*]. I am sure I have lost my daughter forever. [*Weeps.*]

Sveinungi [*takes her hands and kisses her on the cheek*]. I have always said good night to you with a kiss. You have been a good wife to me. I little thought, when you went with me into the house that you should cry yourself to sleep this very night because of me. [Jorunn *clings to him, weeping.* Sveinungi *releases himself suddenly.*] Listen to what I say. You shall not leave me this way. Now you can go to the young folks and tell them that I give my consent. [*Moves a little away.*] But it will be on one strict condition. [Jorunn *wipes her eyes on her apron.*] They must promise me that if they have a son, he shall be brought up here with us.

Jorunn [*her face lighting up*]. I believe this thought was sent you by Him who showed mercy upon you this night.

Sveinungi. Even if it should be their only child. [*Goes to* Jorunn.] And you can tell them that it is only for your sake I yield. Now you won't cry any more?

Jorunn. God bless you! How happy Ljot will be! [*Turns to go.*]

Sveinungi. You needn't be in such a hurry. I don't care to have the young folks see that you have been crying. And one thing more; Sølvi must not come here until I send him word. I want to explain to my old friend how all this has come about.

JORUNN. Sølvi will understand. [*Sits down, very still, with her hands in her lap, gazing straight before her.*] And the boy is to be named Sveinungi. [*Unconsciously she passes her right hand back and forth over the edge of the stones.*]

SVEINUNGI. Yes, they can well be used again, the old stones. Now you had better go to Ljot.

JORUNN [*rising, puts his arm*]. Yes, yes, I am going, and I am happy. [*Exit.* SVEINUNGI *stands for a moment looking after her, then bends down over the stones, examining them closely. He turns over one stone — and one more —*]

THE MERRY MERRY CUCKOO[1]

BY

JEANNETTE MARKS

"The Merry Merry Cuckoo" is one of three exquisite plays dedicated to the Welsh National Theater by this American author. It vividly portrays the almost ultradramatic quality of the Welsh mind, its deep emotionalism, and its love of song, all of which the author has so inimitably caught. If "The Deacon's Hat" and "Welsh Honeymoon" are read in connection with the present play, they will show how justifiable was the bestowal of a prize upon the author in 1911 by the Welsh National Theater. These compositions have been presented in various Little Theaters, colleges, and clubs in New York, Boston, Minneapolis, and elsewhere.

THE MERRY MERRY CUCKOO

CHARACTERS

ANNIE, *the wife of David*
DAVID
LOWRY PRICHARD ⎫ *two neighbors*
GUTO PRICHARD ⎭
MORRIS, *a young minister*

ACT I

[*A garden. Cottage at back running from right to center. A group of three windows in the shape of a bay, showing a bed inside and an old man lying on it. A door leads into cottage. A gate in fence on the right side leads to the road and village beyond. All of the left side of stage a garden and orchard, with a path through it to a gate in wall at back; garden wall to left, at back over it village chapel from which the church music comes.*

A thatched cottage with whitewashed walls. Ivy is growing about the doorway, and hanging from the thatch above the door; fuchsia bushes on either side of door; trees to the left in the garden, including holly and yew; green grass; mountains beyond cottage and garden and chapel. In the foreground, to right by cottage door, is a washtub.

*It is about six o'clock, the first Monday in April.
Towards end of act the sun sets.*

*At rise of curtain, windows of the cottage closed, and
Annie, old, very plump, with sparse gray hair
escaping from under her white cap and damp on
her forehead from her work, and wearing a short
skirt, apron, fichu over shoulders, clogs on her feet,
is washing. Church music off left continues a
minute after rise of curtain. David calls out.
Annie leaves the tub and hurries to the windows
to open them from the outside. David, a very old
man, with white hair and thin face, is seen lying in
bed.]*

DAVID [*calling*]. Annie, Annie!

ANNIE [*opening windows*]. Aye, lad dear, I was
listenin' for ye; yiss, yiss, an' expectin' ye to call.

DAVID [*sleepily*]. I was dreamin' an' — dear, dear,
what a dream! It seemed like fifty years ago when we
were married an', you remember, we stood out there
in the garden that first night. Are there any violets
bloomin' yet?

ANNIE. Not yet, Davy lad.

DAVID. An' the marsh marigolds?

ANNIE. I'm thinkin' they're sure to be out.

DAVID. An' that same night, Annie, do ye remember
we heard the cuckoo singin'?

ANNIE. Aye, lad darlin', fifty years ago this comin'
week, an' a cuckoo singin' to us every spring since
then. [ANNIE *takes a tumbler from the sill and gives
him a spoonful of medicine.*] Take this, dear; there,
'twill be makin' ye better.

DAVID [*taking medicine*]. An' well?

ANNIE. Yiss, yiss, better.

DAVID. But the cuckoo, will the cuckoo be singin'
soon ?

ANNIE [*words inconclusive*]. Lad, dear, no more,
or ye'll be havin' an attack an' — Dear people, chapel
is out, an' I hear them on the road !

DAVID [*plaintively*]. The Monday meetin'. Why
have ye not been ?

ANNIE. Work is keepin' me home, lad.

DAVID. But, Annie, ye've not said a word of the
cuckoo.

ANNIE [*sending her voice up as cheerfully as she can*].
Aye, the cuckoo ; yiss, the cuckoo —

DAVID [*clasping and unclasping his hands*]. Has it
come ? Did ye hear it ?

ANNIE [*gulping*]. David, dear, if ye'd but listen to
what I was a-goin' to say. I was a-goin' to say that
I've not heard the cuckoo yet, but that everythin's
over-early this spring in Wales, an' I'm expectin' to
hear one any time now. 'Tis so warm there might
be one singin' at dusk to-day — there might be !

DAVID [*brightening*]. Might there be, Annie ?

ANNIE [*smoothing his head with her hand*]. Aye,
lad. Hush, lad, they're singin' in the chapel !

[*She stands there with one hand resting on his forehead, listening to the singing of Penlan, a hymn by David
Jenkins. When the music stops, she moves away.*]

DAVID. 'Tis over-early, an', Annie —

ANNIE. Davy dear, be still ! Pastor Morris says
— Tut, tut, I'll close the window, for there comes that
Lowry Prichard and her man.

[ANNIE *closes windows hastily and goes back to her
washing. Enter from right* LOWRY *and her husband*

GUTO, *coming from the Monday prayer meeting and carrying hymnals.* LOWRY *dressed in Welsh costume, clogs, short full skirt, striped apron, white sleeves from elbow to wrist, tight bodice, shawl over her shoulders, white cap, and tall, Welsh beaver hat.* GUTO, *Welsh beaver hat on like his wife's, striped vest, brass buttons on lapels of black cloth coat, long, somewhat tight trousers. At sight of washtub and* ANNIE *busy over it,* LOWRY *and* GUTO *make gestures of shocked dismay to each other.*]

LOWRY. Good evenin', Annie Dalben.

ANNIE [*wiping her wet hand on her apron*]. Good evenin', Lowry Prichard, an' to you, Guto.

GUTO. Good evenin', mum.

LOWRY. How is your man?

ANNIE. He's no better.

LOWRY. Is he worse?

ANNIE. Nay.

LOWRY. We missed ye, Annie Dalben.

GUTO. Aye, we did. Why were ye not at meetin'?

ANNIE. I've my man to mind these days.

LOWRY [*triumphantly*]. But ye said he was no worse, ye did.

ANNIE. Aye, I did, but I cannot leave him alone.

GUTO. But ye're neglectin' chapel an' forgettin' the Lord, Annie Dalben. Ye'll go quite on the downfall, like this.

LOWRY. Aye, ye've not been to meetin's an' 'tis bad when he's dyin' for ye to forget your Lord. Is he in there?

ANNIE [*moving protectingly nearer the closed window*]. Yiss.

LOWRY. Why were ye washin'?

ANNIE. Ye've no cause to ask that — ye know.

Except I did the washin', what would there be for me to care for David with — now that he needs me?

GUTO. Yiss, but ye could do it on some other day.

ANNIE. Nay, for the ladies are waitin' now for what they've given me to do — an' they so kind.

LOWRY. I see Pastor Morris comin' in.

ANNIE. Aye, he's comin' every day an' some days bringin' me the food from his own table for my man.

[*Enter* PASTOR MORRIS, *young, earnest, and rather severe because of his youth.*]

LOWRY [*the inquisitional look on her face deepening, and her voice growing more shrill, pointing to* ANNIE]. Ye see, sir, what Annie Dalben's been doin' while we were in meetin'. She's needin' a sermon, aye, that she is.

GUTO. She's goin' quite on the downfall, sir.

ANNIE. Lowry Prichard, ye've no cause to speak so about me. When was I ever absent when my man was well? But now, sir [*turning to* MORRIS], as ye know, he's ill an' needin' me an' all the s'illin's I can earn. I cannot go away from him.

LOWRY [*speaking to* PASTOR MORRIS]. She's needin' your advice, sir. 'Tis that she is needin' whatever. Warn her well.

GUTO. Yiss, an' rebuke her.

LOWRY. Ye're young, sir, but ye're the instrument of the Lord whatever. 'Tis your duty to bring her back to her conscience.

GUTO. Amen.

[LOWRY *and* GUTO *go off very self-righteous and looking triumphantly at* ANNIE, *who, quiet, her face pale and weary, turns to her washing and rubs and rinses diligently while the minister is talking.*]

MORRIS [*gently*]. I've been troubled, for I knew that it would come to this, Annie. I should have spoken with you before about going to chapel. Some one could be found to stay with David while you were at meeting. You have not been to chapel for a month, Annie.

ANNIE [*continuing her work but in her voice the attitude of the older woman towards the young man*]. Ye're very kind, sir, to take the interest, but I'm thinkin' ye cannot understand. There's been no occasion, sir, for ye to understand through what I've been goin' these days. [*She rubs her sleeve across her tear-filled eyes and continues washing sturdily.*]

MORRIS. Yes, but, Annie, what is David thinking? Does he want you to stay away from the meetings where you have always been together?

ANNIE. Nay, sir.

MORRIS. Has he spoken of your staying away?

ANNIE [*reluctantly*]. Aye, sir, he asked this evenin' why I was not in meetin'.

MORRIS [*reflectively*]. He did. Well, I am thinking that —

ANNIE [*dropping her work and speaking as if worried*]. Nay, sir, I've no cause to excuse myself to ye — ye're naught but a lad. 'Tis past your knowledge how my man is everythin' to me — everythin', he is. He's been such a husband as no one but myself can know, thinkin' of me all the time, livin' for me, as gentle an' tender to me as if I had been a child, an' now, sir, he's ill — he may be dyin', an' I can think of nothin' but doin' everythin' for — [DAVID *taps on window and* ANNIE *turns to open it.*] Aye, lad dear. 'Tis the Pastor comin' to see ye again.

DAVID [*smiling, and holding out one weak old hand*]. Good evenin', sir, such a grand day, with spring everywhere. We've been expectin' the cuckoo, sir — the wife and I. Have ye heard the cuckoo, yet, Annie?

MORRIS [*starting to speak*]. 'Twill be a fortnight be—

ANNIE [*interrupting hurriedly*]. Nay, lad dear, I've been busy, but I'm thinkin' I'm likely to hear it now any moment — aye, any moment.

MORRIS. But, Annie, the cuckoo doesn't —

ANNIE. Tut, sir, I could almost promise the cuckoo would be singin' at sundown whatever — aye, indeed, lad darlin'. Now I'll —

DAVID [*interrupting*]. Annie, ye mind that baby cuckoo we saw the skylark a-feedin' that first spring in Blaen Cwm? It all comes back so clear now an' clearer every moment. I'd not once thought of it, sir, since then.

MORRIS. But, David, the —

ANNIE [*speaking to DAVID and closing the windows*]. Lie down, lad darlin', an' be quiet. I'll call ye, if the cuckoo sings.

[*In the distance the choir can be heard practising Cariad, a revival hymn, in the chapel. Continues until* ANNIE *is alone and talking to herself.*]

MORRIS [*severely*]. But, Annie, you know the cuckoo will not sing at least for another fortnight. It is mid-April before the cuckoo sings.

ANNIE [*wearily*]. Aye, sir.

MORRIS. Why did you say that to David?

ANNIE. He's achin', sir, to hear the cuckoo sing, an' I'm wantin' to comfort him.

MORRIS. But, Annie, it is a lie to say what you did to him.

ANNIE [*vigorously*]. Aye, sir, but I'm not carin' whatever.

MORRIS [*severely*]. Not caring about telling a lie?

ANNIE. Nay, sir, I'm not carin' about anythin' but makin' him happy.

MORRIS [*rebukingly*]. Annie! [ANNIE *continues washing and does not reply.*] Annie! Well, indeed, Annie, if there is nothing I can do for you, and you will not listen to me, I must be going to choir practice. I promised to be there this evening.

ANNIE [*without turning from the tub*]. Aye, sir. [PASTOR MORRIS *off through garden path to choir practice. Goes to left.* ANNIE *continues washing until he is well out of sight. She stands up straight and looks about the garden.*] He's wantin' to hear the cuckoo more nor anythin' else, dear, dear! Everywhere 'tis green now, an' the lilies will be here before long — but lad, lad, the cuckoo, will it come? [*She goes to left into garden, the wet clothes in a basket under her arm, and stands there looking about.*] 'Twas over there it laid its egg in the robin's nest this year ago in May — aye, an' one poor little bird pushed the other out, an' ye picked it up, lad dear, an' were so tender with it. An' they're not wantin' ye, Davy, my old lad darlin', to think the cuckoo will be singin' soon. Dear God, is there to be no cuckoo singin' for the lad again? Just once more, dear God, to sing to him and comfort him? Aye! just the one song? No cuckoo? Aye, there will be a cuckoo singin', there shall be a cuckoo singin'! [*She looks towards the closed windows behind which* DAVID *lies, and puts down her basket of clothes.*] He's asleep! Hush, I'll be the cuckoo! He'll wake an' think the spring has really come. Here by this tree. They're in the chapel, an' they'll never know. [*Throughout this scene, until* LOWRY *speaks, a cuckoo song is being played very softly. And it is into a few notes of this, several times repeated, that* ANNIE *swings when she actually sings her cuckoo song. She opens her mouth to begin, a look of appealing misery on her face.*] 'Twas somethin' like this: *Coo-o. Coo-o!* Tut, that sounds like a hen. I know, it goes over an' over again, sing-song, sing-song, like this: *cu-cu, cu-cu.* Aye, that's better. [*She rocks herself backwards and forwards, practising it and repeating cu-cu, cu-cu.*] 'Tis growin' better, but lad, lad, I'm plannin' to deceive ye whatever. [*Brushes tears away impatiently and begins song again.*] *Cucu-cu, cucu-cu, cucucu-cu, cu!* Aye, that's fair; aye, 'tis fine! He'll not know me from a real cuckoo. I'll try loud now, for ye've no long, dearie.

[*She holds eagerly on to tree beside her, so lost in cuckoo music that she is not aware of a head popping up behind the garden wall and down again. She draws a long breath and begins, softly, slowly, the song sounding as if it came from a distance. She waits a moment, — the heads are well above the wall now in amazement, — and then sings more loudly, making the song sound as if it came from the garden where she is standing.*]

DAVID [*calling*]. Annie!

ANNIE [*hurrying to open his windows*]. Aye, lad dear, I'm comin'.

DAVID [*ecstatically*]. Annie, Annie, dear, I heard the cuckoo singin'; I was dreamin' again, an' all at once I heard the cuckoo singin' in the garden, loud and clear. It sang three times; first, it sounded like somethin' else, 'twas so breathless; then it sang

F

quiet an' sweet, like a cuckoo; an' the third time it seemed comin' from the old mill wheel.

ANNIE. But, lad darlin', ye've heard it, an' I'm that glad! Three times; yiss, yiss, 'tis a real fine cuckoo. Now ye're happy, darlin', an' ye'll sleep well upon it.

DAVID [*disappointedly*]. Did ye no hear it?

ANNIE. I'm thinkin' I did an' thinkin' I didn't.

DAVID. Where were ye?

ANNIE. Out in the garden, hangin' out the clothes.

DAVID [*still more disappointedly*]. An' ye didn't hear it?

ANNIE. I'm no certain, darlin'; I heard somethin' — I did, indeed.

DAVID [*proudly*]. 'Twas the cuckoo, Annie dear; I'm hearin' it first every year; ye must be growin' deaf.

ANNIE. Yiss, yiss. Now go to sleep, an' I'll call ye if I hear the cuckoo sing.

DAVID. Will it sing again?

ANNIE. Aye, darlin', if ye heard it once, 'tis sure to sing again.

DAVID. I'll be gettin' well, Annie, is it not so?

ANNIE [*turning away suddenly*]. Indeed, lad dear, ye'll be about among the heather 'fore long.

DAVID [*speaking quietly, almost to himself*]. To think the cuckoo's singin' — singin' for me!

ANNIE. Aye, aye; now go to sleep.

[*He lies back and closes his eyes obediently. ANNIE, drying her eyes on her apron, goes to left towards her basket of clothes. She stands by the tree where she had sung the cuckoo song for DAVID, unconscious that two people are head and shoulders above the garden wall, looking at her.*]

Lowry [*in a loud voice*].   So ye've come back, Annie Dalben, to sing the cuckoo again.

Guyo.   Aye, we heard ye singin' the cuckoo.

Lowry.   Pooh, 'tis a pretty cuckoo ye make, an old woman like you, an' a pretty song!

Annie.   Lowry Prichard, have a care!

Guto.   'Tis over-early for the cuckoo, is it not?

Annie.   Yiss.

Guto.   An' what are ye singin' in your garden for, an' David dyin'?

[Annie *does not reply but stoops to her basket of clothes and begins to hang them out.*]

Lowry.   So ye'll give no answer?   Well, indeed, maybe ye'll answer Pastor Morris.   Aye, Guto, go fetch the Pastor.

[Guto *goes off to left, through garden gate in garden wall.*]

Lowry [*going toward the windows behind which* David *lies*].   'Tis a godly song ye've sung, Annie, an' a tale for the chapel, eh?

Annie [*following and stepping in front of* Lowry].   Ye may go out of this garden, an' that this minute!

Lowry [*making her way nearer and nearer the window*]. Nay, nay, I'm a-goin' to speak with David an' tell him he's a cuckoo for a wife.   Tut, ye look fair crazy, Annie, crazy with wrath!   Your hair is all rumpled, an' your smock is dirty.   David, bein' a cuckoo is — [*But the taunt is left unfinished, for at that moment young* Morris *comes in hastily,* Guto *following.*]

Morris [*authoritatively*].   Annie! Lowry! Annie, is this I hear true?   Have you been imitating the cuckoo?

Annie.   Aye, sir.

MORRIS [*turning to* LOWRY *and* GUTO]. You may go. Leave this to me.

[GUTO *and* LOWRY *go off right, through front gate, staring in at* DAVID *as they pass.*]

MORRIS [*sternly*]. So, Annie, you have been acting the cuckoo — acting a lie. With this lie upon you, how will it be with salvation?

ANNIE [*hotly*]. Salvation, sir? I've no mind to your salvation; no, nor to heaven's, if the Lord makes this singin' a lie! I'm thinkin' of David as I've thought of him these fifty years, years before ye were born, sir, an' if a lie will make him happy when he's dyin', then I'm willin' to lie, an' do it every minute of the day.

MORRIS. That means you are willing to sin?

ANNIE. Aye, sir, to sin. I'm a willin' sinner!

MORRIS [*more gently*]. You are overwrought, Annie.

ANNIE [*wearily*]. Ye're all against me, sir.

MORRIS. Nay, nay, but wouldn't it be better if I were to tell David about the cuckoo?

ANNIE [*sobbing*]. Oh, no, no, no, sir! Not that!

MORRIS [*stretching out his hand to comfort her*]. Annie, there, there, you mustn't cry so.

ANNIE. 'Tis all the happiness he's got, an' he's goin'. Oh, my lad, my lad!

MORRIS. There, there, Annie!

ANNIE. We've been married fifty years this spring, an' every spring we've listened for the cuckoo an' not one missed. An' now he's a-dyin' an' a-wantin' to hear it so, an' 'twas over-early, an' then I thought of bein' the cuckoo myself. Oh, Davy, Davy darlin'!

MORRIS [*altogether forgetting his pastoral severity*]. There, Annie, there, dear, tell me about it! We'll see, Annie.

ANNIE. There's no more. Only he kept askin' about the spring, the violets an' marsh marigolds, an' I knew all the time he was thinkin' of the cuckoo an' not askin' because he was goin' an' mightn't hear it. An' then he did. An' I said I thought he'd hear one this evenin', that everythin' was over-early whatever. After that he seemed happier than I'd seen him, an' I closed his windows an' went off into the garden to practise it. I worked at it till I could do it fair. Oh, Davy, Davy lad!

MORRIS. Now, Annie dear, don't cry, just tell me more.

ANNIE. Then, sir, I sang the song here by this tree, an' when he called me to him, there was such a look of joy on his face as has not been there this long time. 'Tis the last happiness I can give him, sir.

DAVID [*calling*]. Annie, Annie!

ANNIE. He's callin'. Aye, lad dear, I'm comin'.

[*She goes into cottage and, after opening all the windows, stands by the foot of* DAVID'*s bed.*]

DAVID. Have ye heard the cuckoo singin'?

ANNIE. No, not yet. It must be singin' again soon.

DAVID [*anxiously*]. Ye're sure 'tis goin' to sing?

ANNIE [*gathering him up and turning his pillow*]. Indeed, yiss, an' with the windows all open, ye'll be hearin' it fine an' clear, ye will. I'll go back up into the garden to see is the cuckoo there.

DAVID. Will it be singin' over an' over again, the way it did that first time?

ANNIE. Aye, I'm thinkin' so, lad darlin'. Ye must listen quietly.

DAVID. 'Twas so beautiful singin'. I'd like hearin' it with ye here beside me.

ANNIE [*kissing him*]. I'll come back, lad.

DAVID. Aye, I'll be waitin' for ye.

[ANNIE *goes out of the cottage door and back into garden where* PASTOR MORRIS *is standing, his hat off, while* ANNIE *and* DAVID *are talking together. He can see them both, but* DAVID *cannot see him.* ANNIE *and* MORRIS *converse in whispers. The cuckoo song begins to be played softly.*]

MORRIS. Is he worse?

ANNIE [*looking at* MORRIS *beseechingly*]. I cannot tell, sir, but he's longin' to hear the cuckoo sing again.

MORRIS. I see, and you are wishing to do it again?

ANNIE. Yiss, an' with the lad dyin', can ye tell me not to do what Davy is askin' for? Each time might be his last, sir.

MORRIS [*after a moment's hesitation*]. Nay, go sing for him. I will stand guard for you, and no one shall disturb you.

ANNIE [*a deep sigh of relief*]. Oh, sir, thank you! 'Tis sure to be a comfort. But ye're harmin' your conscience for me, sir, are ye?

MORRIS [*humbly*]. I'm not saying, Annie; I'm over-young to have a conscience in some things.

ANNIE [*taking his hand to kiss it*]. May God bless ye, sir, for bein' kind to an old woman!

[*The sun has set behind the chapel, and it is rapidly growing dark as the music grows louder.* MORRIS *steps back to the garden gate to keep watch.* ANNIE *stands by the tree and, dropping her hands by her side, lifting her head, and swaying her old body to and fro, sings the cuckoo song over and over again three times.* DAVID *has risen in bed, an expression of rapturous delight upon his face as he leans against the casement, listening. The lights are being lighted in the chapel, and the chapel bell begins to ring.*]

DAVID [*calling faintly*]. Annie, Annie darlin', come quickly, the cuckoo's singin'!

ANNIE [*hastening towards him*]. Yiss, lad, I'm comin'.

DAVID [*stretching out his hands towards her*]. Annie, sweetheart, did ye hear the cuckoo singin'?

ANNIE. Yiss, dearie, loud and clear.

DAVID [*trying to imitate its song while his voice grows fainter*]. It sang over an' over like this —

ANNIE [*within the cottage and beside* DAVID]. Yiss, dear, I see.

DAVID [*sinking back into her arms*]. An' — it — was — quiet — but — Annie —

ANNIE [*holding him to her and crying out*]. Lad, lad dear, Davy, can ye not speak to me?

[*The bell for chapel stops ringing. The organ, playing "Jesus, Lover of My Soul," is heard.* MORRIS *is standing by the gate, facing towards the old people, his hat off, his head bowed.*]

CURTAIN

THE LOCKED CHEST [1]

A PLAY IN ONE ACT

(From a Tale in the Laxdaelasaga.)

JOHN MASEFIELD

[1] Reprinted by permission of the author and by special arrangement with The Macmillan Company, Publishers.

For permission to perform this play application must be made to the author in care of the publisher.

The Laxdaelasaga, from which the incident told in this play is taken, describes events from the years 886 to 1030. It is one of the longest sagas and is remarkable for its skillful delineation of character.

In this play we have an instance illustrating the statement of William Lyon Phelps that "putting new wine into old bottles has been the steady occupation of John Masefield." Mr. Phelps likens Mr. Masefield's sincerity and catholicity to Chaucer. Certainly the author has the art of the perfect dramatist; his characters are never described, they do the talking; and there is no hesitation on the author's part in regard to the language employed when there is a need for effect.

THE LOCKED CHEST

Persons

Thord Goddi, *A Farmer*
Thorolf
Ingiald, *A Lord*
Soldiers, *Adherents of Ingiald*
Vigdis Goddi, *Wife of Thord*

Scene: Iceland

[Scene: *A room. A chest used as a bench, a table, etc.*]
[Vigdis *embroidering a cloth.*]

Vigdis [*singing*]. My love is drowned in the Low-
lands,
Away. Heigho.
My love is drowned in the Low-
lands,
Lowlands no more.

[*Enter* Thord Goddi.]
Well, Thord. I hope you had a good market.
[*Sings.*] His hair is cold with the seaweed,
Away. Heigho.
His hair is cold with the seaweed,
Lowlands no more.

Come and sit down by the fire, won't you?
[*Sings.*] O my love is drowned in the Low-
lands,
Away —
Thord. For Heaven's sake, stop it.

75

VIGDIS. Stop what?

THORD. That caterwauling.

VIGDIS. Caterwauling?

THORD. I'm not going to have that howling when I've got a headache —

VIGDIS. I'm sorry I sang when you had a headache. I didn't know.

THORD. I've always got a headache.

VIGDIS. I'm sorry, Thord.

THORD. O, don't "sorry" me. If you're so sorry as all that there'd have been a nice supper ready. But there. It's always the way.

VIGDIS. Let me get you your supper.

THORD. O, I don't want it now, thanks, I couldn't eat it. Why wasn't it ready for me, the moment I came in?

VIGDIS. But, Thord. My dear man.

THORD. How many more times am I to tell you I won't be "my deared" when I've a headache?

VIGDIS. I'm sorry, Thord.

THORD. If you knew how much it aggravated. But there. You only do it to drive me mad.

VIGDIS. I don't, Thord.

THORD. Contradict me. Do. That's right. Contradict me. I suppose you'll say next — But there, it's always the way.

VIGDIS. Thord!

THORD. Now, why wasn't supper ready the moment I came in?

VIGDIS. You said you'd be home late, Thord, and that supper wasn't to be till half-past seven.

THORD. You might have known the fair would be a bad one.

VIGDIS. Was the fair a bad one?

THORD. O, use your sense.   Use your sense, woman.

VIGDIS. But I do, Thord.

THORD. Would I be here at this time if the fair had been a good one?   You know perfectly well I shouldn't.

VIGDIS. I'm so sorry, Thord.

THORD [*growling*]. Yes, so that you might have more money to spend on jewelry.   [*He sits down.*] I'm tired.

VIGDIS. Let me help you pull your boots off. [*She pulls a boot and drops it.*]

THORD. O, for Heaven's sake. Didn't I tell you I'd got a headache? But there. No, I'll take off the other myself. I'm tired to death.

VIGDIS. Let me give you a nip of brandy.

THORD. Brandy? With a headache? You know brandy nearly kills me. Now do for Heaven's sake leave me alone.

VIGDIS. You're tired, Thord. You're tired. Lie down on the chest, and rest till supper. You're tired to death.

THORD. I wouldn't be tired if I wasn't driven half mad by your tongue. A plague take all wives and fairs.

VIGDIS. Tell me about the fair, Thord, if you're not too tired.

THORD. I've already told you about the fair.

VIGDIS. Were there many people?

THORD. Enough to fill a graveyard. I'd be glad to have the burying of some of them.

VIGDIS. What's the news?

THORD. News? What d'ye want with news?

VIGDIS. But I like to hear what's going on.   What were they talking of?

THORD. What were who talking of?

VIGDIS. The people at the fair.

THORD. None of their business. That's what they were talking of. They were talking of a murder.

VIGDIS. A murder!

THORD [*shouting*]. A murder. Can't you pay attention when I'm talking to you? I said a murder. Why don't you listen?

VIGDIS. Who has been murdered?

THORD. I didn't say any one had been murdered.

VIGDIS. But you said —

THORD. But I said nothing of the sort. There was a fight down on the beach and a man was killed.

VIGDIS. What man?

THORD. That big swaggering fellow Hall.

VIGDIS. Hall? Brother of Ingiald?

THORD. Yes. Brother of Ingiald. A lout he was, too.

VIGDIS. Who killed him?

THORD. Does it matter to you who killed him?

VIGDIS. No. Only I would like to know.

THORD. You're always wanting to know. You want to know too much. What was Hall to you?

VIGDIS. Nothing. My cousin was his partner. That's all I know about him. And they used to quarrel all day, as though they were man and wife.

THORD. I suppose that's meant for me. Well, I don't know who killed him. But I know this.

VIGDIS. What?

THORD. I pity the man who did it.

VIGDIS. Why?

THORD. Have you any sense at all, woman?

VIGDIS. I don't see why he should be pitied.

THORD. Well, I do. D'you suppose a great man like Ingiald will let his brother's murderer escape?

VIGDIS. But you said it was a fight on the beach.

THORD. I said. I said. I said. Nag. Nag. Nag. Even if it were, d'you suppose a man like Ingiald would let the man escape? Ingiald'll hunt him down. That murderer's a doomed man.

VIGDIS. Poor fellow, I say.

THORD. Serve him right, I say. Serve him right.

VIGDIS. I wonder who it was.

THORD. It isn't known who it was. Two or three are suspected.

VIGDIS. I hope it wasn't cousin Thorolf.

THORD. Well, if it was he must take the consequences.

VIGDIS. That man Hall was a sad man to work with. I hate to speak ill of a dead man; but he had a bad name.

THORD. He was a drunken boor.

VIGDIS. He went for Thorolf with an axe once.

THORD. Well, I pity the man who went for *him* with an axe. Is supper ever going to come at all? Or am I to stay talking here all night?

VIGDIS. Won't you go in and lie down, Thord? Supper will be ready in a moment.

THORD. How can I go in and lie down? You know perfectly well I've got to see to the chores. I can't trust the hired men.

VIGDIS. I'll run out and see to the chores, Thord.

THORD. You? I can't trust you to get supper, let alone do the chores. No. I must sacrifice myself. I've got a headache and I'm half dead. But there, it's always the way. I must do a thing myself if I want it done. Give me my boots.

VIGDIS. Let me go, Thord. I'll see the cows driven in and milked.

THORD. Give — me — my — boots. Don't I tell you? Don't tell me what you'll do and what you'll not do. There [*puts on boots*], I thought when I came in I'd have time to rest myself. But there. It's always the way. [*Turns to go out.*] What are you glowering there for? Go — and — get — the supper ready. When you've worn me to my grave I suppose you'll be glad. You do make me so mad.

VIGDIS. I'll have supper directly, Thord.

THORD. You do make me so mad. But there. It's always the way. [*He goes out.*]

VIGDIS. It's a pity we've no child, Thord and I. They say a child is a great sweetener in a house. If we'd a child, perhaps he wouldn't take on so. Ah well. It wasn't like this when we were courting. I must get this table clear. If I'd had a child now, he'd have been different. That's what a wife must expect. Nothing but "O my headache," and "O if I'm not tired." I only wanted to hear about the murder. It's not so often we get a murder to talk about. The way he talks you'd think we had one every day. So Hall is murdered. I never liked that man. I wonder who killed him. Well. There's one comfort. My cousin Thorolf wouldn't go for to kill a man. Not even Hall, he wouldn't. He wouldn't kill a fly, my cousin Thorolf wouldn't. He's like a blessed babe. [*The door at the back is knocked violently.*] Bless us and save us.

VOICE. Let me in. Let me in. Vigdis. Thord.

VIGDIS. Who's there?

VOICE. Open. Open. For God's sake let me in.

VIGDIS. Enter. If you be of God.

Voice. Open.

Vigdis [*running to door*]. Come in. Who's there? [*Enter* Thorolf.] Thorolf. Cousin Thorolf. How are you?

Thorolf. Stand back. Don't kiss me.

Vigdis. What's the matter, Thorolf?

Thorolf. Stand back. You keep your hands off.

Vigdis. But I'm your cousin, Thorolf.

Thorolf. Yes. But perhaps you won't be quite so glad to be my cousin when you hear the news.

Vigdis. What news, Thorolf?

Thorolf. About Hall.

Vigdis. He's dead. What d'ye mean, Thorolf?

Thorolf. I killed him, Vigdis.

Vigdis. You, Thorolf?

Thorolf. He cheated me. O, but I can't go into that. So we fought, and I killed him. It was a fair fight. I didn't want to kill him. God knows.

Vigdis. Men have no sense when they have swords in their hands.

Thorolf. It was a fair fight.

Vigdis. I'm not blaming you, Thorolf. It seems men must kill each other from time to time. But what are you going to do now?

Thorolf. What indeed?

Vigdis. You know what it means. You must know what it means. Do they know you did it?

Thorolf. Ingiald will know by this.

Vigdis. But you know what Ingiald is. He'll be after you to-night, now. Now. What will you do? What will you do, Thorolf?

Thorolf. You're my cousin, Vigdis?

Vigdis. Of course I'm your cousin.

THOROLF. You wouldn't cast me off. You don't think worse of me. I mean it was a fair fight. It was fair and square.

VIGDIS. Of course I won't cast you off. You're my cousin. Men have no sense at any time. But when they have swords in their hands — it might happen to any one.

THOROLF. Vigdis. Will you stand by me?

VIGDIS. You're my cousin, Thorolf. There's my hand. But don't waste time like this. Where will you hide? Who can shelter you against Ingiald? The King himself could hardly do it. It's death to shelter you. Where will you go? Think. Think. Where will you go?

THOROLF. I was thinking perhaps you would shelter me.

VIGDIS. I, Thorolf?

THOROLF. You and Thord.

VIGDIS. And Thord?

THOROLF. I was thinking perhaps you would.

VIGDIS. Against Ingiald?

THOROLF. Until I could get a ship. Only till I could get a ship.

VIGDIS. Against a man like Ingiald?

THOROLF. I know it's a risk, dear, I know it's a risk.

VIGDIS. You know, Thorolf, my man Thord isn't much of a warrior.

THOROLF. It wouldn't be for long, dear. If I could lie low a night or two —

VIGDIS. What should we be, against Ingiald?

THOROLF. If we could just put him off the track, dear, then I could slip down to Broadfirth and get a ship. It would only be a night or two.

VIGDIS. Thord is Thord. And I'm only a woman, and women aren't much good in a case of this sort.

THOROLF. Let me stay, Vigdis. Will you?

VIGDIS. I wish I could think of a plan.

THOROLF. Where else can I go?

VIGDIS. Go? You won't go anywhere. You'll just stay here, where you are. Don't worry yourself about that. It's Ingiald and Thord I'm thinking of.

THOROLF. My God, Vigdis, you're good. I'll kiss you for that.

VIGDIS. Oh, none of your nonsense, now. This is no kissing matter. No, you can't stay in here. Let go my hand, or I'll box your ears. Come this way, now. I'll shut you up in the sheep-fold. Quickly, now, before my husband comes. [*Goes out at side door.*]

THOROLF. I've only got to put Ingiald off the track, dear. Old Hrut will get me a ship.

VIGDIS. Put Ingiald off the track first, my friend. We'll think of the ship later. Come along. [*Exeunt.*] [*The other side door opens, and reënter* THORD.]

THORD. Vigdis. Vigdis. Is supper ready yet? Now if that isn't too bad. What's the woman thinking of? Vigdis, I say. It's not enough that I have a headache, and get fairly fratted to death, but I'm to be kept waiting for my supper. Vigdis. Vigdis, I say. [*Enter* VIGDIS.]

VIGDIS. What is it, Thord?

THORD. What is it? Supper. Where's supper? Why on earth isn't supper ready?

VIGDIS. I've had a visitor, Thord. A guest.

THORD. A guest, eh. Who invited him?

VIGDIS. No one invited him. He's a sort of a relation of mine.

THORD. So it is a he. How long am I to be tortured with him?

VIGDIS. I'd like him to stay for some time. If you don't mind, Thord.

THORD. You know I mind. You know as well as I do I can't abide strangers in the house. They make this house just like an inn. Except that they never pay for what they have. I will not put up with it. It's enough that I'm half mad with headache, but I must have a stranger in the house. But there. It's always the way. Who is this stranger? Is he respectable?

VIGDIS. He's a sort of relation of mine. I told you just now.

THORD. A relation. If it had been a stranger I wouldn't have minded; but to have a relation. And I shall have to be civil to him. Vigdis, I do think you might have had a little thought of me. But there. You think of no one but yourself. It's always the way with you women.

VIGDIS. It won't be for long, Thord.

THORD. I tell you what is it, Vigdis. If he's respectable he may stay the night and go on before breakfast. If he's one of these rowdy fellows, or if he's in trouble, I'll not have him near the place. I'll put the dogs on him myself.

VIGDIS. You cannot, Thord. I've already taken him in. I can't go back on my word. I've promised him shelter now.

THORD. Shelter?

VIGDIS. You see he's in trouble.

THORD. What trouble? Who is he, once for all?

VIGDIS. Cousin Thorolf.

THORD. Thorolf! What's he been doing? He's an idle blackguard, Thorolf.

VIGDIS. He's not.

THORD. He is, I say. Don't contradict. What's he been doing?

VIGDIS. There was . . . It was . . . It was a fair fight, Thord.

THORD. A — fair — fight. You — don't — mean —

VIGDIS. Down on the beach.

THORD. Not . . . No . . . Not Hall?

VIGDIS. Yes. He killed Hall.

THORD. Ingiald's brother.

VIGDIS. Ingiald's brother.

THORD. And you've been such a fool as to take him in. To take in Hall's murderer. Ingiald's brother's murderer.

VIGDIS. It was a fair fight, Thord.

THORD. It — was — a — fair fight. A — fair — fight. Ingiald's brother. A fair fight.

VIGDIS. They fought with swords.

THORD. In my house. Here. Ingiald's brother's murderer. And you've let him in. Where is he?

VIGDIS. In the sheep-fold at the back of the house, for the present. That's a good place. They'd never look among the sheep.

THORD. My head is like the seven mills of Milltown. In my house. O, my head. O miserable man. It'll be my death. It's not enough that I must have a headache, and come home tired out, but I must have Ingiald down on me. He'll burn the house. He will. He will. I know Ingiald. He'll burn the house. He's sure to find out. And if he doesn't burn the house he'll put a blood-fine on me. He'll fine me a flock of sheep. It's not enough that I'm fratted to death and find no supper ready, but I must lose my cattle and be murdered in my bed. But there, it's always the way.

VIGDIS. You'll be nothing of the sort. Have pity on poor Thorolf.

THORD. Pity. Let poor Thorolf show a little pity on me. I'm a ruined man. Ingiald will drag me up and down by the hair. He'll hit me in the ribs with his great fists. He will. He will. I know Ingiald. And you go and take in a murderer. A murderer. If it had been a murderer of some common man I wouldn't have minded. But the murderer of Ingiald's brother.

VIGDIS. I tell you it was not a murder. Thorolf's no murderer. He's like a woman in most things, Thorolf is. I tell you it was not a murder. It was a fair fight.

THORD. So Ingiald'll say. Yes, he'll say. I'll take your sheep, he'll say. And them nice cows too, Thord, he'll say. It was a nice fair fight, he'll say, so now I'll burn you in your bed. I know Ingiald. Ahoo. Ahoo.

VIGDIS. Well. I wouldn't be a cry baby. There's worse things than being burned in our beds. Come. Be a man, Thord. One would think you were afraid of dying.

THORD. O hold your nagging tongue, for God's sake. Ahoo. Ahoo.

VIGDIS. It will all come right, Thord. Look. I'll get you some nice supper.

THORD. You'll drive me mad in another minute. Supper, Ingiald's knife'll be the only supper I shall have. Hold your nagging tongue, and let me die in peace.

VIGDIS. It's very likely that we'll have Ingiald

here before long. He's not a man to wait on the road. He comes like an eagle, Ingiald does.

THORD. O what shall I do? What shall I do?

VIGDIS. Do? Put a bold face on it. There's no danger where there's no fear. Look him in the face and tell him to walk out of here.

THORD. He may be coming now. Look out at the door, Vigdis. Is he coming?

VIGDIS. There's some one coming. It's a party of men. A dozen, quite.

THORD. O, I'm not fit to die. I'm not.

VIGDIS. Be a man. They're coming quickly. They'll be here in a minute. Yes. It's Ingiald. There's his red cloak. He's walking ahead of the rest. Be a man now, Thord. It'll be all right.

THORD. O! O!

VIGDIS. Can you think of any better plan than the sheep-fold?

THORD. O!

VIGDIS. O, why didn't I marry a man? You don't think he'd look in the sheep-fold, with all the sheep in it? I'm sure he wouldn't.

THORD. O, Thorolf's all right. It's myself I'm thinking of. It's myself. O!

VIGDIS. I wonder you aren't ashamed.

THORD. I was getting on so well. I'd have been able to buy Rapp's field next year —

VIGDIS. Think of poor Thorolf. Brace up, man. Ingiald'll suspect at once if he sees you like that. What's your life? What's my life? It's our guest's life that matters.

THORD. An idle vagrant's life better than mine? If it had been the King, now.

VIGDIS. Thord, brace yourself. Thorolf's safe in the sheep-fold. Ingiald can prove nothing. Your guest's life depends on the way you look. Don't flop there like a done-out old gather-up of a bachelor. Swell your chest out. Put a scowl on, like a Viking. That's better. Here they are. [*A knock at the door.*]

THORD. O, I'm a dead man.

VIGDIS. O, I could shake you. For Thorolf's sake, perk yourself. [*A knock.*] Come in. Go and open the door, Thord.

THORD. I can't. How can you ask me to open the door?

[*A knock.*]

VIGDIS. Go on, Thord. Go. Open, man.

THORD. Vigdis. You don't mind. You open. Your nerves aren't like mine.

VIGDIS. Quick, Thord. It's for the host to open.

VOICES. Open within there. Open in the name of the law.

VIGDIS. I must open, then. [*Goes to the door.*] Come in, come in. [*Enter* INGIALD *and Men-at-arms.*]

INGIALD. God save all here. Thank you, Vigdis.

VIGDIS. My man's not quite himself, to-night, Lord Ingiald.

INGIALD. I'm sorry to hear that. What pin pricks now, Thord?

THORD. Ah. Oh.

INGIALD [*looking keenly at both of them*]. I should have thought life was pretty quiet up here. No fighting. No gambling. No anxiety —

VIGDIS. My man gets run down, Lord Ingiald. It's going to these fairs that does it. I've known him come home in a way of speaking, and he'd be all cold,

like a dead man. It's the nerves and that on the brain.
[*A pause.*] What could I do for you, Lord Ingiald?
Will you not sit down? Is there anything you would
like to take? It's not often we see you up here. Why,
I don't think I've seen you, not since last October
twelve month.

INGIALD. No. I daresay not. [*He goes over to*
THORD *and bangs him on the shoulder.*]

THORD. Ow. What is it, Ingiald? Don't.

INGIALD. I want to have a talk with you, my friend.

THORD. A — a talk. O yes. Yes, that. Yes.
Very nice.

INGIALD [*to his Men*]. Go out and stand by the
door. Don't budge till I tell you.

MEN. Ay, ay, sir. [*Exeunt.*]

VIGDIS. Wouldn't your men be pleased to take a
drop of something? You've surely not come all the
way fom Sheep Isles. What is it we could do for you,
Lord Ingiald? Perhaps you would let me hear it.
My man's not himself to-night. Were you wanting
any hands to help get your harvest in? Tell me what
it is.

INGIALD. Thank you, Vigdis. I want to have a
talk with Thord, here.

THORD. I — I'm so ill, Ingiald. It's the weather.
Vigdis will do any business. My head. My head is
bad. I'm a martyr to my head in wet weather.

INGIALD. I know what it is. My own head gives
me tortures. But I must have a talk with you. Perhaps you would ask your wife to mull me a little ale?

VIGDIS. You must let me mull it in here, then.
The kitchen fire's out.

INGIALD. I should be delighted; but my nerves

can't bear the smell of ale being mulled. It always upsets me. [*To* THORD.] Perhaps you would ask your wife to — to look at the sunset. Most beautiful sunset, outside.

VIGDIS. Yes, we were looking at it this last half hour.

INGIALD. I see. Well, Vigdis, I must talk to Thord here privately. Will you go into the next room? I won't keep you long.

VIGDIS. Certainly, Lord Ingiald. Now, I won't have you telling my man about any of those naughty baggages at Reykjavik. He knows quite enough, already.

INGIALD. I won't mention a single baggage. [*He calls to a Soldier.*] Erik, just attend the lady for a moment. [*Aside to Soldier.*] See she doesn't leave the room.

VIGDIS. I know you men. [*She tries to catch* THORD'S *eye.*] I'll make him repeat every word you say. [*She goes out unconcernedly.*]

INGIALD [*aside*]. Well. If you're not a wonder. [*Sharply.*] Now Thord, my friend, I've got only one thing to say to you. Where's Thorolf?

THORD. Thorolf.

INGIALD. Well?

THORD. Which Thorolf would that be?

INGIALD. You know quite well which Thorolf.

THORD. O, you mean old Thorolf of the Ridge? Ah yes. A fat man. He —

INGIALD. Now, Thord. [*Glares at him.*]

THORD. O, young Thorolf. Koll o' Dales' lad. He goes to school, now.

INGIALD [*rapping the table*]. Thord.

THORD. Don't, Ingiald. You put a fellow out so.

INGIALD. Where's Thorolf? Vigdis's cousin. Your cousin, Thorolf.

THORD. Ha, ha, ha! *That* Thorolf. Yes. An idle blackguard. Yes.

INGIALD. Yes. That Thorolf. Where is he?

THORD. I've not seen him, Ingiald.

INGIALD. I suppose you've not heard about him, either?

THORD. No.

INGIALD. Not? Sure?

THORD. No. I mean yes. Of course I've heard about him.

INGIALD. About what he has done to-day?

THORD. I didn't know he did anything to-day.

INGIALD. You heard about my brother?

THORD. Your poor brother, Hall? Yes, I was truly grieved. I was quite upset.

INGIALD. That's what Thorolf did.

THORD. Thorolf?

INGIALD. Now where is he?

THORD. Your brother?

INGIALD. I see. You won't answer.

THORD. Now don't be hasty, Ingiald. You're so hasty. You don't give me a chance. What is it you want to know?

INGIALD. Where is Thorolf?

THORD. I've not seen him, Ingiald. How should I know where Thorolf is?

INGIALD. He was seen coming towards this house.

THORD. Towards this house?

INGIALD. Only an hour ago.

THORD. Thorolf?

INGIALD. No more talk, my friend. Where is he?

THORD. I don't know, Ingiald. I don't know.

INGIALD. You lying knave. You creeping worm. You dog of —. I'll ram this scabbard down your throat. You say you don't know. Where is he? Any more of your lies and I'll squeeze your lying tongue off.

THORD. Don't, Ingiald. Don't. You're hurting. Don't, man.

INGIALD. Well. No more of your lies, then.

THORD. Now you've hurt me. I shall have a sore throat for a week.

INGIALD. Do you good. [*A pause.*] Now then, Thorolf's here. Isn't he? Hey?

THORD. Yes, Ingiald.

INGIALD. I thought we should come to it sooner or later. See what comes of being patient. So he's here. Hidden somewhere?

THORD. Yes, Ingiald.

INGIALD. Where is he hidden?

THORD. O, but I couldn't tell you that. If I told you that I'd have to leave the country. No one would speak to me, if I told you that.

INGIALD. That's nothing to do with me. Now then. Where is he?

THORD. O, I couldn't.

INGIALD. Hey?

THORD. I'd have to leave this farm. Have mercy, Ingiald.

INGIALD. Mercy, eh?

THORD. I couldn't bear it. I'm not strong, Ingiald. My head.

INGIALD. D'ye see this little knife of mine?

THORD. O, don't, Ingiald. Ingiald, you don't mean. Ingiald, I'd have to leave the country if I told you.

INGIALD. Look here, Thord. I'm going to get Thorolf before I go. Let's understand each other.

THORD. O, yes, Ingiald. I'll do anything. I'll say anything. But I can't tell you where he is. I can't. I'd have to leave the country.

INGIALD. Well. You needn't tell me where he is. Not in so many words. D'ye understand?

THORD. O, Ingiald.

INGIALD. Let's come to some arrangement. You don't want your neighbours to call you a traitor. I understand that. You don't want me to burn your house down, or to stick this knife into you. I understand that, too. Well. You give up Thorolf to me quietly.

THORD. I can't, Ingiald. They'd know. They'd know. Vigdis would tell them.

INGIALD. I don't say "betray him," you silly gowk.

THORD. But what then, Ingiald?

INGIALD. Give me some hint where he is, so that I can find him. I'll pretend to search the house, and light on him, as it were, by chance. Come now.

THORD. But —

INGIALD. Come now. D'ye see this bag? [*Produces a purse.*]

THORD. Yes.

INGIALD. D'ye hear it? Eh? Chink. Eh? Chink? Where is he?

THORD. I couldn't.

INGIALD. Come now. Hark? Three silver marks. Eh? Just whisper. Where? Come now.

THORD. Three silver marks.

INGIALD. Three silver marks. You needn't say it right out. Hear it jingle.

THORD. It's a lot of money.

INGIALD. You could do with it, eh? Come now, old man, where is he?

THORD. Let me weigh it in my hand.

INGIALD. Certainly. Here you are. Now then. Whisper here. Where is he? Tell me where he is. Where is he? Is he in the chest here?

THORD. No, not in the chest.

INGIALD. No? What is in the chest?

THORD. Things of Vigdis's.

INGIALD. Is he upstairs, then? Eh? Upstairs?

THORD. No. He's not upstairs.

INGIALD. Outside? Eh?

THORD [*putting the bag on the table*]. Ingiald.

INGIALD. Yes. Well. What is it?

THORD. You won't take it to heart my hiding him?

INGIALD. No. No. Of course I won't.

THORD. Swear you won't. You won't fine me? Nor take my cattle?

INGIALD. Not if you tell me where he is.

THORD. You'll search the house first, Ingiald. In pretence?

INGIALD. Yes. I'll pretend to search the house. And then?

THORD. You see that door there?

INGIALD. Yes. Yes. What then?

THORD. You must go through that door. No. No. Go through *this* door, and then round the house.

INGIALD. Yes? Where to? Among the ricks?

THORD. No. Not among the ricks.

INGIALD. In the dairy?

THORD. You might look in the dairy.

INGIALD. Where else, eh?

THORD. Just to the left of the dairy.

INGIALD. The cowbyre, eh?

THORD. No. No. You might look in the cowbyre, though.

INGIALD. Where else?

THORD. Ingiald.

INGIALD. Yes.

THORD. Swear you won't tell any one. Swear you won't say I told you.

INGIALD. Of course I won't tell any one.

THORD. You might count the sheep. You understand?

INGIALD. To the left of the dairy, eh?

THORD. To the left of the dairy.

INGIALD. I'll see them counted. Thank'ee, Thord.

THORD. Now, you'll pretend to look upstairs?

INGIALD. Yes. We'll let in Vigdis, now.

THORD. No, not Vigdis, no.

INGIALD. Yes, man. Hey there. Erik!

ERIK. Sir.

INGIALD. Tell the lady to come in.

ERIK. Tell the lady to come in, sir. You may go in now, mum. [*Enter* VIGDIS.]

VIGDIS. Well. Have you had a nice talk?

INGIALD. No. Not so nice as I could have wished, perhaps. Your husband's very low to-night. Excuse me a moment. Hi there, Hrapp, Hoskuld.

SOLDIERS [*entering*]. Sir. Sir.

INGIALD. I'm sorry, Vigdis. But I must search the house. Your husband has given me permission. I must look through all the rooms.

VIGDIS.   Search my house, indeed.

INGIALD.   I won't disarrange it more than can be helped.

VIGDIS.   Search my house, indeed.   For what will you search my house?

INGIALD.   For your cousin, Thorolf.

VIGDIS.   My — cousin — Thorolf.   And why should you want my cousin Thorolf, I should like to know?

INGIALD.   Come, Vigdis, I'm sorry.   Now don't let's have a scene.

VIGDIS.   A scene, indeed.   And why should you have a scene?   I'm not going to have my house pulled to pieces.

INGIALD.   They won't do any harm, Vigdis.

VIGDIS.   Harm or no harm, I won't have any one spying around my house.   I never heard of such impudence.   This is *my* house.   It isn't Thorolf's house. What d'ye want Thorolf for?

INGIALD.   You know perfectly well, Vigdis, what I want Thorolf for.

VIGDIS [*to* THORD].   And I'm to be insulted in my own house!   I wonder you sit there and let your wife be insulted.   As for you, Ingiald, for all your lordship, you never had more manners than one brought up in a pigsty.   It is what I might expect from you.   But as for you, Thord, I'm ashamed of you.   Defend your wife, man.   Don't let these louts throw the whole house overboard.

INGIALD [*to his* Men].   Upstairs with you.   Search every room in the house.

VIGDIS.   How dare you insult a woman so!   You great captains want humbling.   If I were a man now, you wouldn't dare.

ERIK [*to* INGIALD]. Beg pardon, captain.

INGIALD. What is it?

ERIK. That box, captain. [*Points to the chest.*]

INGIALD. Well. What about it?

ERIK. I was thinking he might be in that box.

INGIALD. O, nonsense. Upstairs with you. [*They all run upstairs.*] [*To* THORD.] You come, too, Thord. If anything's missing you'll blame my men.

THORD [*aside*]. Let Vigdis go, Ingiald. Take Vigdis.

INGIALD [*glancing at her*]. No. She suspects nothing. You come.

THORD. No. I don't think she suspects. No, she suspects nothing.

VIGDIS. Where are you going, Thord?

THORD. Upstairs with Ingiald.

VIGDIS. Am I married to a man or to a bleating old sheep with the staggers? Do you call yourself a human being, Thord? [*Aside.*] What's Ingiald going to do?

INGIALD. Come, Thord. Come on, now.

THORD [*to* VIGDIS]. Get supper ready. Don't stand there. [*Exit with* INGIALD.]

VIGDIS. Get supper ready. Get supper ready. What's he going to do? Why didn't Thord give me a hint? He'll search the sheep-fold. Of course he'll search the sheep-fold. He'll be going to the fold in another minute. Why did I leave him in the sheep-fold? Why did I let him stay at all? What can I do? What can I do? He'll be down in a minute. What's this bag of money? What's this bag of money? Thord's sold him. It's blood money, I know it. What can I do? O, God. What can I do?

THORD [*above*]. Vigdis.

VIGDIS.   Yes, Thord.

THORD.   All right.   Nothing.   I only wanted to know if you were there.

VIGDIS.   What can I do?   I know.   I know.   It's a bare chance.   It's a bare chance.   [*She runs softly and swiftly from the room.   In two seconds she returns with* THOROLF.]   [*Noise above, and shouts.*]

VIGDIS.   Quiet.   Quiet.   Not a whisper.

THOROLF.   What shall I do?

VIGDIS.   Not a whisper.

THORD [*above*].   Vigdis.   Are you there still?

VIGDIS.   I'm still here, Thord.   What's the matter with you?   Into the chest, Thorolf.   Get into the chest.   [*She opens chest.*]

THOROLF [*kissing her*].   Good-bye, in case, Vigdis.

VIGDIS.   O, you silly boy.   Get in.   I must lock you in.   Don't sneeze, for God's sake.   Press your upper lip if you want to sneeze.   It's a bare chance, Thorolf.   [*She locks the chest on him and takes key.   Then she hurriedly and softly puts bread and beer upon the table as for supper.*]   [*Reënter* INGIALD, THORD, *and Soldiers.*]

VIGDIS.   Well, my lord.   Did you find my cousin Thorolf by any chance?

INGIALD.   I've not finished looking yet.

VIGDIS.   Haven't you?   You might look on the dresser there.   I would if I were you.   Or in the oven. Yes, look in the oven, Ingiald.   Show him the oven, Thord.

INGIALD [*to some of his Men*].   Step into the kitchen and look in the oven.   You.   Come with me, the rest of you.   We must look through the farmyard.

VIGDIS.   Don't disturb your elder brother, Ingiald.

INGIALD. What elder brother?

VIGDIS. The donkey.

INGIALD. Ah, you're funny, Vigdis. Well, he laughs best who laughs last, *I* say. [*Exit with Men.*]

VIGDIS. Thord. Thord Goddi.

THORD. Yes, Vigdis.

VIGDIS. What's this bag of money here?

THORD. Bag of money?

VIGDIS. This bag of money here. What is it?

THORD. It's what I brought from market.

VIGDIS. It's nothing of the sort.

THORD. Oh, no. Nor it is.

VIGDIS. Well?

THORD. Well? I suppose Ingiald left it there when he came in.

VIGDIS. Did you see Ingiald leave it there? O what am I thinking of? [*Aside.*]

THORD. Now for Heaven's sake stop nagging. Hark!

VIGDIS. What is it?

THORD. I thought I heard a noise in the yard. A cry.

VIGDIS. My God. A cry. [*They go to the door.*]

THORD. I hope they won't find him.

VIGDIS. Thank God I did what I could for him. O, may Heaven blind them.

THORD. I'm afraid they're sure to find him. What was that?

VIGDIS. My God. They're brave, aren't they, thirteen to one?

THORD. Didn't you hear a sort of groan then?

VIGDIS. Poor Thorolf. Poor Thorolf.

THORD. We did our best, Vigdis.

VIGDIS.   Yes.   May God always help you, Thord, as well as you helped Thorolf!

THORD.   Yes, I shall always be glad I did my best for him.

VIGDIS.   Yes, Thord.   I suppose you will be.   I hope you will be.

THORD.   Poor fellow.

VIGDIS.   Poor Thorolf.

THORD.   Don't take on, Vigdis.   We must all die. Ah.   Ah.   Come away from the door.   Come.   [*Cries without.*]

VIGDIS [*covering her eyes*].   O, my dear, my dear. O Thorolf, little brown-haired Thorolf.

THORD.   There.   There.   It's all over now.

VIGDIS.   O, my Thorolf, my cousin Thorolf.

THORD.   There.   There.   Now don't take on. Don't take on; you get on my nerves when you cry like that.

VIGDIS.   O, you had brown hair, Thorolf.   Bonny hair you had.   O, my boy, my poor cousin.   [*Cries without.*]

THORD [*aside*].   They've got him.   They've got him. [*He rubs his hands.*]   We all owe Heaven a death.   Poor Thorolf.   Poor fellow.   And him so young.

VIGDIS.   It was a sight for sore eyes on a sunny morning to see him going over the hills.   O Thorolf, you were the joy of a woman's eyes.   You were as stately as a stag.   You were as comely as a king's darling.   O, my boy, my poor cousin, my own dear, my heart's darling, Thorolf!

THORD.   And him so young.   And such a promising young fellow.   To be cut short.   Life is but a span.   And him so young.   Idle, vicious, drunken blackguard, it's a good job you are cut short.   [*More noise without.*]

VIGDIS. He had soft brown hair with threads of gold in it like the bright bird's feathers. Now it's dabbled with blood, dabbled with blood, dabbled with blood.

THORD. Dabbled with blood. O! O me!

VIGDIS. O young man, O treasure of the west, O white, comely, handsome Thorolf! Yours will be a cold bride bed under the winter grass.

THORD. O do for Heaven's sake be quiet.

VIGDIS. A cold bed, a lonely bed, a white bed.

THORD. You'll waste none of our sheets, laying of him out. Let me tell you that.

VIGDIS. Three white lonely candles in a draught, three flames guttering, but you will lie still beneath them, Thorolf.

THORD. Vigdis. Do you want to drive me mad? Have done now.

VIGDIS. O bonny Thorolf. Swimming and rowing and going among young men, you were like a king. None could sail a boat like you. No queen ever loosed her hair about a lovelier lover than you. You were courteous, you were kind, you had strength and beauty, you were brave; now you will lie in the ground, and the sheep will crop the grass there.

THORD. Here. Vigdis. A little of that goes a long way. Thorolf's dead. Here's Ingiald coming back. Hold your noise now, for Heaven's sake. [*Re-enter* INGIALD *with Men.*]

INGIALD. I've a bone to pick with you, Thord.

VIGDIS. Bring me my dead. Give me my dead, you butchers, you bloody men.

INGIALD. D'ye hear?

VIGDIS. Thirteen to one. Thirteen to one. You

butchers. You bloody men. Bring me my dead. Bring me my dead darling. You cowards. You cowards.

INGIALD. What's wrong with *you*, Vigdis?

VIGDIS. Let me look upon the boy's dead face. You butchers. O fair, white face. O white face with the red blood upon it. O my boy, my dear boy, Thorolf.

INGIALD. He'll be a white face when I get him and that's a fact, Vigdis. I'll promise you that much. Thord, I'll wring your ears off.

VIGDIS. Where is my dead lad? You dogs. You butchers. Take me to his corpse.

INGIALD. Your dead lad? There's no dead lad.

VIGDIS. Not dead, O, Heaven! [*Pretends to swoon.*]

THORD. What?

INGIALD. I'll tell you what, you creeping rot. You cur. You Judas. What have you done with him?

THORD. Done with him?

INGIALD. With Thorolf. Eh? Where is he? Eh? What have you done with him?

THORD. I've done nothing, Ingiald. Nothing.

INGIALD. Don't tell me you've done nothing.

THORD. I didn't do anything with him.

INGIALD. You lying knave. D'ye dare to sit there and say you haven't got him off?

THORD. I haven't got him off.

INGIALD. You lie.

THORD. How could I have got him off?

INGIALD. How? How do I know how? But I'll know how. I'll flay you alive. I'll skin you and salt you. I'll — I'll — I'll —

THORD. O don't. Ingiald, I swear — I swear I thought you'd get him.

INGIALD. I tell you, you've got him off.

THORD. I haven't, Ingiald.

INGIALD [*to his Men*]. Look at him. Look at that liar, here. I come here to this liar and tell him I want Thorolf. And he cringes and whines and licks my boots. So I just speak to him kindly, like a father. I'm always kindly and like a father. I'm too kind. And he cringes and whines, and begs me not to hit him. Only spare my precious hide, he says, and I'll tell you where Thorolf is.

THE MEN. Hear that now. He betrayed him, etc. Then he wants a little money, for saying where Thorolf is. The money on the table there. Three marks of silver, no less. He'd sell his own mother for a little money. Wouldn't you, eh?

THORD. I wouldn't.

INGIALD. You would, you know it. Three marks of silver you begged. And then you told me to look in the sheep-fold.

THE MEN. Treacherous swine. His own cousin. His own cousin.

INGIALD. And then he sneaks his man off while we're rummaging in the wrong place. And now he expects me to be out three marks of silver.

THE MEN. Tie him to the bull's tail, master; and let's hunt him.

INGIALD. So you'd sell your cousin, would you, and then try to go back on your bargain? [*Going to him.*] Where have you taken Thorolf to? Eh?

THORD. He was in the sheep-fold where I told you, Ingiald. He was. Indeed he was.

INGIALD. O. Was he? And where is he now? Gone to Olaf's, I suppose.

THORD.   He may have gone to Olaf's.

THE MEN.   Olaf's is a likely place.   We'd better go on there at once.

INGIALD.   Lord help you, Thord, if we don't get him. Understand?   I mean it.   Come on there.

A MAN.   You never looked in that chest yet, captain.

INGIALD.   O yes, that chest.   [*He tries lid.*]   Where's the key, Thord?

THORD.   Ask Vigdis.

INGIALD.   Where's the key of this chest, Vigdis?

VIGDIS.   Key of the chest, indeed.   Who are you to ask for my keys?   I'm not going to have you spying in my chests.   You and your gang have done harm enough here.   You'll get no key.   Let that be enough.

INGIALD.   Come now.   The key.

VIGDIS.   I tell you, you shall not have the key.

THE MEN.   Break it open, captain.

A MAN.   O let the chest alone.   Thorolf'll be safe at Olaf's if we don't hurry.

INGIALD.   Give me the key.

THORD.   Give up the key at once.

VIGDIS.   I tell you, you shall not have the key. You've thrown the house overboard as it is.   Get out now.   Go.

INGIALD.   Give me that key at once, Vigdis.

VIGDIS [*flinging key on the floor*].   Take it then, and bad luck go with it.   Here it is.   Now open.

INGIALD [*giving it back*].   Thank you.   That's all I wanted.   Now, Thord.   Give back that bag of money.

THORD.   O, Ingiald, you gave it to me.

INGIALD.   Now you will give it back.

THORD.   O, Ingiald.

VIGDIS.   Give it, Thord.   Give it, you Judas, you. D'ye think I'll have blood money in the house?   Give it up at once.   [*The Men go out and linger at the door.*]

INGIALD.   Come on now.

VIGDIS [*taking money bag*].   I've only one thing to say to you, Ingiald.   I say, take your money and get out of my house, now.   [*She makes him back to the door.*]   Take your dirty blood money.   [*She smites him over the face with the money bag and drives him out.   She watches them go.*]   Go on to Olaf's with you, and try some other Judas.   That's all I've to say to you, my lord.   [*She turns and unlocks chest.   Then, instead of opening, she turns and looks at* THORD.   THORD *goes to the door and looks out, comes back, and sits on chest.* VIGDIS *backs away from him.*]

THORD.   Well.   They've gone.   [*A pause.*]   They've gone.   [*No answer.*]   Can't you answer when I speak to you?

VIGDIS.   Yes.   I can answer.   Listen to me, Thord Goddi.   You and I will part from now.   You took money to betray Thorolf, your guest and my cousin. I always knew you for a mean man.   Now I know you are base, and a dastard, and a dog.   God forgive me, I once loved you.   Pah.   I let you kiss me.   I held you in my arms.   There.   There.   There.   Take it.   [*She flings her wedding ring at him.*]   Now we'll part, my sir.   I thank God I never bore you a child.

THORD [*laughing nervously*].   I've got a headache. I can't — Ow — [*The chest lid rises.* THORD *leaps from it.* THOROLF *appears.*]   Thorolf!

THOROLF.   Thorolf!

THORD.   Thorolf, I didn't mean — I swear I didn't. I didn't mean.   It was only a joke.   I'll explain.

THOROLF. Thord. Pah. You're not worth it.

THORD. O Thorolf. You shall have — I'll give you my money. All of it —

THOROLF. Pah. Vigdis, my dear, where are they?

VIGDIS. They've gone, Thorolf. We can slip away to Broadfirth now. It's quite safe. Come. Come. We'll go together, my friend. [*They turn to go.*]

THORD. I'll change my religion.

CURTAIN

THE POST OFFICE[1]

BY

RABINDRANATH TAGORE

[1] Reprinted by permission of the author and by special arrangement with The Macmillan Company, Publishers.

For permission to perform this play application must be made to the author in care of the publisher.

The whole literary world rejoiced with Tagore's native India when in 1913 he received the Nobel prize for "idealistic literature." Tagore, born in 1861, has had back of him generations of intellectuality, and has lived a life of ease, yet his loving and lovable soul has made him a spokesman for world-wide humanity. There has been with him both opportunity and inclination to develop and adorn every department of literature with idealism, imagery, beauty, and a spiritual zeal. These qualities of style have been expressed in a hundred or more volumes of poems, essays, and stories ebullient with joy of life, the love of truth, and reverence for humanity.

There is in Tagore's thought a kinship to Burns' unconcern for rank, and Whitman's distinction of common things. Blake taught the meaning in the Christian thought of spirituality in the child; and other poets, having a deep sense of the divinity of childhood, have reverentially expressed it in many memorable lines. But the very soul of Tagore bears fruit in "The Post Office," a simple little play full of imagery carrying lofty thought.

THE POST OFFICE

Dramatis Personæ

Madhav
Amal, *his adopted child*
Sudha, *a little flower girl*
The Doctor
Dairyman
Watchman
Gaffer
Village Headman, *a bully*
King's Herald
Royal Physician

ACT I

[Madhav's House]

Madhav. What a state I am in! Before he came, nothing mattered; I felt so free. But now that he has come, goodness knows from where, my heart is filled with his dear self, and my home will be no home to me when he leaves. Doctor, do you think he —

Physician. If there's life in his fate, then he will live long. But what the medical scriptures say, it seems —

Madhav. Great heavens, what?

Physician. The scriptures have it: "Bile or palsey, cold or gout spring all alike."

MADHAV. Oh, get along, don't fling your scriptures at me; you only make me more anxious; tell me what I can do.

PHYSICIAN [*taking snuff*]. The patient needs the most scrupulous care.

MADHAV. That's true; but tell me how.

PHYSICIAN. I have already mentioned, on no account must he be let out of doors.

MADHAV. Poor child, it is very hard to keep him indoors all day long.

PHYSICIAN. What else can you do? The autumn sun and the damp are both very bad for the little fellow — for the scriptures have it:

"In wheezing, swoon or in nervous fret,
    In jaundice or leaden eyes —"

MADHAV. Never mind the scriptures, please. Eh, then we must shut the poor thing up. Is there no other method?

PHYSICIAN. None at all: for, "In the wind and in the sun —"

MADHAV. What will your "in this and in that" do for me now? Why don't you let them alone and come straight to the point? What's to be done then? Your system is very, very hard for the poor boy; and he is so quiet too with all his pain and sickness. It tears my heart to see him wince, as he takes your medicine.

PHYSICIAN. The more he winces, the surer is the effect. That's why the sage Chyabana observes: "In medicine as in good advices, the least palatable ones are the truest." Ah, well! I must be trotting now. [*Exit.*]

[GAFFER *enters*]

MADHAV. Well, I'm jiggered, there's Gaffer now.

GAFFER. Why, why, I won't bite you.

MADHAV. No, but you are a devil to send children off their heads.

GAFFER. But you aren't a child, and you've no child in the house; why worry then?

MADHAV. Oh, but I have brought a child into the house.

GAFFER. Indeed, how so?

MADHAV. You remember how my wife was dying to adopt a child?

GAFFER. Yes, but that's an old story; you didn't like the idea.

MADHAV. You know, brother, how hard all this getting money in has been. That somebody else's child would sail in and waste all this money earned with so much trouble — Oh, I hated the idea. But this boy clings to my heart in such a queer sort of way —

GAFFER. So that's the trouble! And your money goes all for him and feels jolly lucky it does go at all.

MADHAV. Formerly, earning was a sort of passion with me; I simply couldn't help working for money. Now, I make money and as I know it is all for this dear boy, earning becomes a joy to me.

GAFFER. Ah, well, and where did you pick him up?

MADHAV. He is the son of a man who was a brother to my wife by village ties. He has had no mother since infancy; and now the other day he lost his father as well.

GAFFER. Poor thing: and so he needs me all the more.

MADHAV. The doctor says all the organs of his little body are at loggerheads with each other, and there isn't much hope for his life. There is only one way to save him and that is to keep him out of this autumn wind and sun. But you are such a terror! What with this game of yours at your age, too, to get children out of doors!

GAFFER. God bless my soul! So I'm already as bad as autumn wind and sun, eh! But, friend, I know something, too, of the game of keeping them indoors. When my day's work is over I am coming in to make friends with this child of yours. [*Exit.*]

[AMAL *enters*]

AMAL. Uncle, I say, Uncle!

MADHAV. Hullo! Is that you, Amal?

AMAL. Mayn't I be out of the courtyard at all?

MADHAV. No, my dear, no.

AMAL. See, there where Auntie grinds lentils in the quirn, the squirrel is sitting with his tail up and with his wee hands he's picking up the broken grains of lentils and crunching them. Can't I run up there?

MADHAV. No, my darling, no.

AMAL. Wish I were a squirrel! — it would be lovely. Uncle, why won't you let me go about?

MADHAV. Doctor says it's bad for you to be out.

AMAL. How can the doctor know?

MADHAV. What a thing to say! The doctor can't know and he reads such huge books!

AMAL. Does his book-learning tell him everything?

MADHAV. Of course, don't you know!

AMAL [*with a sigh*]. Ah, I am so stupid! I don't read books.

MADHAV. Now, think of it; very, very learned people are all like you; they are never out of doors.

AMAL.   Aren't they really?

MADHAV.   No, how can they? Early and late they toil and moil at their books, and they've eyes for nothing else.   Now, my little man, you are going to be learned when you grow up; and then you will stay at home and read such big books, and people will notice you and say, "he's a wonder."

AMAL.   No, no, Uncle, I beg of you by your dear feet — I don't want to be learned, I won't.

MADHAV.   Dear, dear; it would have been my saving if I could have been learned.

AMAL.   No, I would rather go about and see everything that there is.

MADHAV.   Listen to that! See! What will you see, what is there so much to see?

AMAL.   See that far-away hill from our window — I often long to go beyond those hills and right away.

MADHAV.   Oh, you silly! As if there's nothing more to be done but just get up to the top of that hill and away! Eh! You don't talk sense, my boy. Now listen, since that hill stands there upright as a barrier, it means you can't get beyond it. Else, what was the use in heaping up so many large stones to make such a big affair of it, eh!

AMAL.   Uncle, do you think it is meant to prevent your crossing over? It seems to me because the earth can't speak it raises its hands into the sky and beckons. And those who live far and sit alone by their windows can see the signal. But I suppose the learned people —

MADHAV.   No, they don't have time for that sort of nonsense.   They are not crazy like you.

I

AMAL. Do you know, yesterday I met some one quite as crazy as I am.

MADHAV. Gracious me, really, how so?

AMAL. He had a bamboo staff on his shoulder with a small bundle at the top, and a brass pot in his left hand, and an old pair of shoes on; he was making for those hills straight across that meadow there. I called out to him and asked, "Where are you going?" He answered, "I don't know, anywhere!" I asked again, "Why are you going?" He said, "I'm going out to seek work." Say, Uncle, have you to seek work?

MADHAV. Of course I have to. There's many about looking for jobs.

AMAL. How lovely! I'll go about, like them too, finding things to do.

MADHAV. Suppose you seek and don't find? Then —

AMAL. Wouldn't that be jolly? Then I should go farther! I watched that man slowly walking on with his pair of worn-out shoes. And when he got to where the water flows under the fig tree, he stopped and washed his feet in the stream. Then he took out from his bundle some gram-flour, moistened it with water and began to eat. Then he tied up his bundle and shouldered it again; tucked up his cloth above his knees and crossed the stream. I've asked Auntie to let me go up to the stream, and eat my gram-flour just like him.

MADHAV. And what did your Auntie say to that?

AMAL. Auntie said, "Get well and then I'll take you over there." Please, Uncle, when shall I get well?

MADHAV. It won't be long, dear.

AMAL. Really, but then I shall go right away the moment I'm well again.

MADHAV. And where will you go?

AMAL. Oh, I will walk on, crossing so many streams, wading through water. Everybody will be asleep with their doors shut in the heat of the day, and I will tramp on and on seeking work far, very far.

MADHAV. I see! I think you had better be getting well first; then —

AMAL. But then you won't want me to be learned, will you, Uncle?

MADHAV. What would you rather be then?

AMAL. I can't think of anything just now; but I'll tell you later on.

MADHAV. Very well. But mind you, you aren't to call out and talk to strangers again.

AMAL. But I love to talk to strangers!

MADHAV. Suppose they had kidnapped you?

AMAL. That would have been splendid! But no one ever takes me away. They all want me to stay in here.

MADHAV. I am off to my work — but, darling, you won't go out, will you?

AMAL. No, I won't. But, Uncle, you'll let me be in this room by the roadside.

[*Exit* MADHAV.]

DAIRYMAN. Curds, curds, good nice curds.

AMAL. Curdseller, I say, Curdseller.

DAIRYMAN. Why do you call me? Will you buy some curds?

AMAL. How can I buy? I have no money.

DAIRYMAN. What a boy! Why call out then? Ugh! What a waste of time.

AMAL. I would go with you if I could.

DAIRYMAN. With me?

AMAL. Yes, I seem to feel homesick when I hear you call from far down the road.

DAIRYMAN [*lowering his yoke-pole*]. Whatever are you doing here, my child?

AMAL. The doctor says I'm not to be out, so I sit here all day long.

DAIRYMAN. My poor child, whatever has happened to you?

AMAL. I can't tell. You see I am not learned, so I don't know what's the matter with me. Say, Dairyman, where do you come from?

DAIRYMAN. From our village.

AMAL. Your village? Is it very far?

DAIRYMAN. Our village lies on the River Shamli at the foot of the Panch-mura hills.

AMAL. Panch-mura hills! Shamli river! I wonder. I may have seen your village. I can't think when, though!

DAIRYMAN. Have you seen it? Been to the foot of those hills?

AMAL. Never. But I seem to remember having seen it. Your village is under some very old big trees, just by the side of the red road — isn't that so?

DAIRYMAN. That's right, child.

AMAL. And on the slope of the hill cattle grazing.

DAIRYMAN. How wonderful! Aren't there cattle grazing in our village! Indeed, there are!

AMAL. And your women with red sarees fill their pitchers from the river and carry them on their heads.

DAIRYMAN. Good, that's right. Women from our

dairy village do come and draw their water from the river; but then it isn't everyone who has a red saree to put on. But, my dear child, surely you must have been there for a walk some time.

AMAL. Really, Dairyman, never been there at all. But the first day doctor lets me go out, you are going to take me to your village.

DAIRYMAN. I will, my child, with pleasure.

AMAL. And you'll teach me to cry curds and shoulder the yoke like you and walk the long, long road?

DAIRYMAN. Dear, dear, did you ever? Why should you sell curds? No, you will read big books and be learned.

AMAL. No, I never want to be learned — I'll be like you and take my curds from the village by the red road near the old banyan tree, and I will hawk it from cottage to cottage. Oh, how do you cry — "Curd, curd, good nice curd!" Teach me the tune, will you?

DAIRYMAN. Dear, dear, teach you the tune; what an idea!

AMAL. Please do. I love to hear it. I can't tell you how queer I feel when I hear you cry out from the bend of that road, through the line of those trees! Do you know I feel like that when I hear the shrill cry of kites from almost the end of the sky?

DAIRYMAN. Dear child, will you have some curds? Yes, do.

AMAL. But I have no money.

DAIRYMAN. No, no, no, don't talk of money! You'll make me so happy if you have a little curds from me.

AMAL. Say, have I kept you too long?

DAIRYMAN. Not a bit; it has been no loss to me at all; you have taught me how to be happy selling curds. [*Exit.*]

AMAL [*intoning*]. Curds, curds, good nice curds — from the dairy village — from the country of the Panch-mura hills by the Shamli bank. Curds, good curds; in the early morning the women make the cows stand in a row under the trees and milk them, and in the evening they turn the milk into curds. Curds, good curds. Hello, there's the watchman on his rounds. Watchman, I say, come and have a word with me.

WATCHMAN. What's all this row you are making? Aren't you afraid of the likes of me?

AMAL. No, why should I be?

WATCHMAN. Suppose I march you off then?

AMAL. Where will you take me to? Is it very far, right beyond the hills?

WATCHMAN. Suppose I march you straight to the King?

AMAL. To the King! Do, will you? But the doctor won't let me go out. No one can ever take me away. I've got to stay here all day long.

WATCHMAN. Doctor won't let you, poor fellow! So I see! Your face is pale and there are dark rings round your eyes. Your veins stick out from your poor thin hands.

AMAL. Won't you sound the gong, Watchman?

WATCHMAN. Time has not yet come.

AMAL. How curious! Some say time has not yet come, and some say time has gone by! But surely your time will come the moment you strike the gong!

WATCHMAN. That's not possible; I strike up the gong only when it is time.

AMAL. Yes, I love to hear your gong. When it is midday and our meal is over, Uncle goes off to his work and Auntie falls asleep reading her Rāmayana, and in the courtyard under the shadow of the wall our doggie sleeps with his nose in his curled-up tail; then your gong strikes out, "Dong, dong, dong!" Tell me why does your gong sound?

WATCHMAN. My gong sounds to tell the people, Time waits for none, but goes on forever.

AMAL. Where, to what land?

WATCHMAN. That none knows.

AMAL. Then I suppose no one has ever been there! Oh, I do wish to fly with the time to that land of which no one knows anything.

WATCHMAN. All of us have to get there one day, my child.

AMAL. Have I too?

WATCHMAN. Yes, you too!

AMAL. But doctor won't let me out.

WATCHMAN. One day the doctor himself may take you there by the hand.

AMAL. He won't; you don't know him. He only keeps me in.

WATCHMAN. One greater than he comes and lets us free.

AMAL. When will this great doctor come for me? I can't stick in here any more.

WATCHMAN. Shouldn't talk like that, my child.

AMAL. No. I am here where they have left me — I never move a bit. But when your gong goes off, dong, dong, dong, it goes to my heart. Say, Watchman?

WATCHMAN. Yes, my dear.

AMAL. Say, what's going on there in that big house on the other side, where there is a flag flying high up and the people are always going in and out?

WATCHMAN. Oh, there? That's our new Post Office.

AMAL. Post Office? Whose?

WATCHMAN. Whose? Why, the King's, surely!

AMAL. Do letters come from the King to his office here?

WATCHMAN. Of course. One fine day there may be a letter for you in there.

AMAL. A letter for me? But I am only a little boy.

WATCHMAN. The King sends tiny notes to little boys.

AMAL. Oh, how lovely! When shall I have my letter? How do you guess he'll write to me?

WATCHMAN. Otherwise why should he set his Post Office here right in front of your open window, with the golden flag flying?

AMAL. But who will fetch me my King's letter when it comes?

WATCHMAN. The King has many postmen. Don't you see them run about with round gilt badges on their chests?

AMAL. Well, where do they go?

WATCHMAN. Oh, from door to door, all through the country.

AMAL. I'll be the King's postman when I grow up.

WATCHMAN. Ha! ha! Postman, indeed! Rain or shine, rich or poor, from house to house delivering letters — that's very great work!

AMAL. That's what I'd like best. What makes you smile so? Oh, yes, your work is great too. When it is silent everywhere in the heat of the noonday, your gong sounds, Dong, dong, dong, — and sometimes when I wake up at night all of a sudden and find our lamp blown out, I can hear through the darkness your gong slowly sounding, Dong, dong, dong!

WATCHMAN. There's the village headman! I must be off. If he catches me gossiping with you there'll be a great to do.

AMAL. The headman? Whereabouts is he?

WATCHMAN. Right down the road there; see that huge palm-leaf umbrella hopping along? That's him!

AMAL. I suppose the King's made him our headman here?

WATCHMAN. Made him? Oh, no! A fussy busybody! He knows so many ways of making himself unpleasant that everybody is afraid of him. It's just a game for the likes of him, making trouble for everybody. I must be off now! Mustn't keep work waiting, you know! I'll drop in again to-morrow morning and tell you all the news of the town. [*Exit.*]

AMAL. It would be splendid to have a letter from the King every day. I'll read them at the window. But, oh! I can't read writing. Who'll read them out to me, I wonder! Auntie reads her Rāmayana; she may know the King's writing. If no one will, then I must keep them carefully and read them when I'm grown up. But if the postman can't find me? Headman, Mr. Headman, may I have a word with you?

HEADMAN. Who is yelling after me on the highway? Oh, you wretched monkey!

AMAL. You're the headman. Everybody minds you.

HEADMAN [*looking pleased*]. Yes, oh yes, they do! They must!

AMAL. Do the King's postmen listen to you?

HEADMAN. They've got to. By Jove, I'd like to see —

AMAL. Will you tell the postman it's Amal who sits by the window here?

HEADMAN. What's the good of that?

AMAL. In case there's a letter for me.

HEADMAN. A letter for you! Whoever's going to write to you?

AMAL. If the King does.

HEADMAN. Ha! ha! What an uncommon little fellow you are! Ha! ha! the King indeed, aren't you his bosom friend, eh! You haven't met for a long while and the King is pining, I am sure. Wait till to-morrow and you'll have your letter.

AMAL. Say, Headman, why do you speak to me in that tone of voice? Are you cross?

HEADMAN. Upon my word! Cross, indeed! You write to the King! Madhav is devilish swell nowadays. He'd made a little pile; and so kings and padishahs are everyday talk with his people. Let me find him once and I'll make him dance. Oh, you snipper-snapper! I'll get the King's letter sent to your house — indeed I will!

AMAL. No, no, please don't trouble yourself about it.

HEADMAN. And why not, pray! I'll tell the King about you and he won't be very long. One of his footmen will come along presently for news of you.

Madhav's impudence staggers me. If the King hears of this, that'll take some of his nonsense out of him. [*Exit.*]

AMAL. Who are you walking there? How your anklets tinkle! Do stop a while, dear, won't you?

[*A Girl enters*]

GIRL. I haven't a moment to spare; it is already late!

AMAL. I see, you don't wish to stop; I don't care to stay on here either.

GIRL. You make me think of some late star of the morning! Whatever's the matter with you?

AMAL. I don't know; the doctor won't let me out.

GIRL. Ah me! Don't then! Should listen to the doctor. People'll be cross with you if you're naughty. I know, always looking out and watching must make you feel tired. Let me close the window a bit for you.

AMAL. No, don't, only this one's open. All the others are shut. But will you tell me who you are? Don't seem to know you.

GIRL. I am Sudha.

AMAL. What Sudha?

SUDHA. Don't you know? Daughter of the flower-seller here.

AMAL. What do *you* do?

SUDHA. I gather flowers in my basket.

AMAL. Oh, flower gathering! That is why your feet seem so glad and your anklets jingle so merrily as you walk. Wish I could be out too. Then I would pick some flowers for you from the very topmost branches right out of sight.

SUDHA. Would you really? Do you know more about flowers than I?

AMAL. Yes, I *do*, quite as much. I know all about Champa of the fairy tale and his seven brothers. If only they let me, I'll go right into the dense forest where you can't find your way. And where the honey-sipping humming-bird rocks himself on the end of the thinnest branch, I will flower out as a champa. Would you be my sister Parul?

SUDHA. You are silly! How can I be sister Parul when I am Sudha and my mother is Sasi, the flower-seller? I have to weave so many garlands a day. It would be jolly if I could lounge here like you!

AMAL. What would you do then, all the day long?

SUDHA. I could have great times with my doll Benay the bride, and Meni the pussycat and — but I say it is getting late and I mustn't stop, or I won't find a single flower.

AMAL. Oh, wait a little longer; I do like it so!

SUDHA. Ah, well — now don't you be naughty. Be good and sit still and on my way back home with the flowers I'll come and talk with you.

AMAL. And you'll let me have a flower then?

SUDHA. No, how can I? It has to be paid for.

AMAL. I'll pay when I grow up — before I leave to look for work out on the other side of that stream there.

SUDHA. Very well, then.

AMAL. And you'll come back when you have your flowers?

SUDHA. I will.

AMAL. You will, really?

SUDHA. Yes, I will.

AMAL. You won't forget me? I am Amal, remember that.

SUDHA. I won't forget you, you'll see. [*Exit.*]

[*A Troop of Boys enter*]

AMAL. Say, brothers, where are you all off to? Stop here a little.

BOYS. We're off to play.

AMAL. What will you play at, brothers?

BOYS. We'll play at being ploughmen.

FIRST BOY [*showing a stick*]. This is our ploughshare.

SECOND BOY. We two are the pair of oxen.

AMAL. And you're going to play the whole day?

BOYS. Yes, all day long.

AMAL. And you'll come back home in the evening by the road along the river bank?

BOYS. Yes.

AMAL. Do you pass our house on your way home?

BOYS. You come out to play with us, yes, do.

AMAL. Doctor won't let me out.

BOYS. Doctor! Suppose the likes of you mind the doctor. Let's be off; it is getting late.

AMAL. Don't. Why not play on the road near this window? I could watch you then.

THIRD BOY. What can we play at here?

AMAL. With all these toys of mine lying about. Here you are, have them. I can't play alone. They are getting dirty and are of no use to me.

BOYS. How jolly! What fine toys! Look, here's a ship. There's old mother Jatai; say, chaps, ain't he a gorgeous sepoy? And you'll let us have them all? You don't really mind?

AMAL. No, not a bit; have them by all means.

Boys. You don't want them back?

Amal. Oh, no, I shan't want them.

Boys. Say, won't you get a scolding for this?

Amal. No one will scold me. But will you play with them in front of our door for a while every morning? I'll get you new ones when these are old.

Boys. Oh, yes, we will. Say, chaps, put these sepoys into a line. We'll play at war; where can we get a musket? Oh, look here, this bit of reed will do nicely. Say, but you're off to sleep already.

Amal. I'm afraid I'm sleepy. I don't know, I feel like it at times. I have been sitting a long while and I'm tired; my back aches.

Boys. It's only early noon now. How is it you're sleepy? Listen! The gong's sounding the first watch.

Amal. Yes, dong, dong, dong, it tolls me to sleep.

Boys. We had better go then. We'll come in again to-morrow morning.

Amal. I want to ask you something before you go. You are always out — do you know of the King's postmen?

Boys. Yes, quite well.

Amal. Who are they? Tell me their names.

Boys. One's Badal, another's Sarat. There's so many of them.

Amal. Do you think they will know me if there's a letter for me?

Boys. Surely, if your name's on the letter they will find you out.

Amal. When you call in to-morrow morning, will you bring one of them along so that he'll know me?

Boys. Yes, if you like.

CURTAIN

THE POST OFFICE

ACT II

[Amal in bed]

AMAL. Can't I go near the window to-day, uncle? Would the doctor mind that too?

MADHAV. Yes, darling, you see you've made yourself worse squatting there day after day.

AMAL. Oh, no, I don't know if it's made me more ill, but I always feel well when I'm there.

MADHAV. No, you don't; you squat there and make friends with the whole lot of people round here, old and young, as if they are holding a fair right under my eaves — flesh and blood won't stand that strain. Just see — your face is quite pale.

AMAL. Uncle, I fear my fakir'll pass and not see me by the window.

MADHAV. Your fakir, whoever's that?

AMAL. He comes and chats to me of the many lands where he's been. I love to hear him.

MADHAV. How's that? I don't know of any fakirs.

AMAL. This is about the time he comes in. I beg of you, by your dear feet, ask him in for a moment to talk to me here.

[GAFFER enters in a fakir's guise]

AMAL. There you are. Come here, Fakir, by my bedside.

MADHAV. Upon my word, but this is —

GAFFER *[winking hard]*. I am the fakir.

MADHAV. It beats my reckoning what you're not.

AMAL. Where have you been this time, Fakir?

FAKIR. To the Isle of Parrots. I am just back.

MADHAV. The Parrots' Isle!

FAKIR. Is it so very astonishing? Am I like you, man? A journey doesn't cost a thing. I tramp just where I like.

AMAL [*clapping*]. How jolly for you! Remember your promise to take me with you as your follower when I'm well.

FAKIR. Of course, and I'll teach you such secrets too of travelling that nothing in sea or forest or mountain can bar your way.

MADHAV. What's all this rigmarole?

GAFFER. Amal, my dear, I bow to nothing in sea or mountain; but if the doctor joins in with this uncle of yours, then I with all my magic must own myself beaten.

AMAL. No. Uncle shan't tell the doctor. And I promise to lie quiet; but the day I am well, off I go with the Fakr and nothing in sea or mountain or torrent shall stand in my way.

MADHAV. Fie, dear child, don't keep on harping upon going! It makes me so sad to hear you talk so.

AMAL. Tell me, Fakir, what the Parrots' Isle is like.

GAFFER. It's a land of wonders; it's a haunt of birds. There's no man; and they neither speak nor walk, they simply sing and they fly.

AMAL. How glorious! And it's by some sea?

GAFFER. Of course. It's on the sea.

AMAL. And green hills are there?

GAFFER. Indeed, they live among the green hills; and in the time of the sunset, when there is a red glow on the hillside, all the birds with their green wings flock back to their nests.

AMAL. And there are waterfalls!

GAFFER. Dear me, of course; you don't have a hill without its waterfalls. Oh, it's like molten diamonds; and, my dear, what dances they have! Don't they make the pebbles sing as they rush over them to the sea. No devil of a doctor can stop them for a moment. The birds looked upon me as nothing but a man, quite a trifling creature without wings — and they would have nothing to do with me. Were it not so I would build a small cabin for myself among their crowd of nests and pass my days counting the sea waves.

AMAL. How I wish I were a bird! Then —

GAFFER. But that would have been a bit of a job; I hear you've fixed up with the dairyman to be a hawker of curds when you grow up; I'm afraid such business won't flourish among birds; you might land yourself into serious loss.

MADHAV. Really this is too much. Between you two I shall turn crazy. Now, I'm off.

AMAL. Has the dairyman been, Uncle?

MADHAV. And why shouldn't he? He won't bother his head running errands for your pet fakir, in and out among the nests in his Parrots' Isle. But he has left a jar of curd for you saying that he is rather busy with his niece's wedding in the village, and he has got to order a band at Kamlipara.

AMAL. But he is going to marry me to his little niece.

GAFFER. Dear me, we are in a fix now.

AMAL. He said he would find me a lovely little bride with a pair of pearl drops in her ears and dressed in a lovely red *saree;* and in the morning she would

K

milk with her own hands the black cow and feed me with warm milk with foam on it from a brand new earthen cruse; and in the evenings she would carry the lamp round the cowhouse, and then come and sit by me to tell me tales of Champa and his six brothers.

GAFFER. How delicious! The prospect tempts even me, a hermit! But never mind, dear, about this wedding. Let it be. I tell you when you wed there'll be no lack of nieces in his household.

MADHAV. Shut up! This is more than I can stand. [*Exit.*]

AMAL. Fakir, now that Uncle's off, just tell me, has the King sent me a letter to the Post Office?

GAFFER. I gather that his letter has already started; but it's still on the way.

AMAL. On the way? Where is it? Is it on that road winding through the trees which you can follow to the end of the forest when the sky is quite clear after rain?

GAFFER. That's so. You know all about it already.

AMAL. I do, everything.

GAFFER. So I see, but how?

AMAL. I can't say; but it's quite clear to me. I fancy I've seen it often in days long gone by. How long ago I can't tell. Do you know when? I can see it all: there, the King's postman coming down the hillside alone, a lantern in his left hand and on his back a bag of letters; climbing down for ever so long, for days and nights, and where at the foot of the mountain the waterfall becomes a stream he takes to the footpath on the bank and walks on through the rye; then comes the sugarcane field and he disappears into the narrow lane cutting through the tall stems of sugarcanes; then he reaches the open meadow where the cricket chirps and where there is not a single man to be seen, only the snipe wagging their tails and poking at the mud with their bills. I can feel him coming nearer and my heart becomes glad.

GAFFER. My eyes aren't young; but you make me see all the same.

AMAL. Say, Fakir, do you know the King who has this Post Office?

GAFFER. I do; I go to him for my alms every day.

AMAL. Good! When I get well, I must have my alms too from him, mayn't I?

GAFFER. You won't need to ask, my dear, he'll give it to you of his own accord.

AMAL. No, I would go to his gate and cry, "Victory to thee, O King!" and dancing to the tabor's sound, ask for alms. Won't it be nice?

GAFFER. It would be splendid, and if you're with me, I shall have my full share. But what'll you ask?

AMAL. I shall say, "Make me your postman, that I may go about lantern in hand, delivering your letters from door to door. Don't let me stay at home all day!"

GAFFER. What is there to be sad for, my child, even were you to stay at home?

AMAL. It isn't sad. When they shut me in here first I felt the day was so long. Since the King's Post Office I like it more and more being indoors, and as I think I shall get a letter one day, I feel quite happy and then I don't mind being quiet and alone. I wonder if I shall make out what'll be in the King's letter?

GAFFER. Even if you didn't wouldn't it be enough if it just bore your name?

[MADHAV *enters*]

MADHAV. Have you any idea of the trouble you've got me into, between you two?

GAFFER. What's the matter?

MADHAV. I hear you've let it get rumored about that the King has planted his office here to send messages to both of you.

GAFFER. Well, what about it?

MADHAV. Our headman Panchanan has had it told to the King anonymously.

GAFFER. Aren't we aware that everything reaches the King's ears?

MADHAV. Then why don't you look out? Why take the King's name in vain? You'll bring me to ruin if you do.

AMAL. Say, Fakir, will the King be cross?

GAFFER. Cross, nonsense! And with a child like you and a fakir such as I am. Let's see if the King be angry, and then won't I give him a piece of my mind.

AMAL. Say, Fakir, I've been feeling a sort of darkness coming over my eyes since the morning. Everything seems like a dream. I long to be quiet. I don't feel like talking at all. Won't the King's letter come? Suppose this room melts away all on a sudden, suppose —

GAFFER [*fanning* AMAL]. The letter's sure to come to-day, my boy.

[DOCTOR *enters*]

DOCTOR. And how do you feel to-day?

AMAL. Feel awfully well to-day, Doctor. All pain seems to have left me.

DOCTOR [*aside to* MADHAV]. Don't quite like the

look of that smile. Bad sign that, his feeling well! Chakradhan has observed —

MADHAV. For goodness' sake, Doctor, leave Chakradhan alone. Tell me what's going to happen?

DOCTOR. Can't hold him in much longer, I fear! I warned you before — This looks like a free exposure.

MADHAV. No, I've used the utmost care, never let him out of doors; and the windows have been shut almost all the time.

DOCTOR. There's a peculiar quality in the air today. As I came in I found a fearful draught through your front door. That's most hurtful. Better lock it at once. Would it matter if this kept your visitors off for two or three days? If some one happens to call unexpectedly — there's the back door. You had better shut this window as well, it's letting in the sunset rays only to keep the patient awake.

MADHAV. Amal has shut his eyes. I expect he is sleeping. His face tells me — Oh, Doctor, I bring in a child who is a stranger and love him as my own, and now I suppose I must lose him!

DOCTOR. What's that? There's your headman sailing in! — What a bother! I must be going, brother. You had better stir about and see to the doors being properly fastened. I will send on a strong dose directly I get home. Try it on him — it may save him at last, if he can be saved at all. [*Exeunt* MADHAV *and* DOCTOR.]

[THE HEADMAN *enters*]

HEADMAN. Hello, urchin! —

GAFFER [*rising hastily*]. 'Sh, be quiet.

AMAL. No, Fakir, did you think I was asleep?

I wasn't. I can hear everything; yes, and voices far away. I feel that mother and father are sitting by my pillow and speaking to me.

[MADHAV *enters*]

HEADMAN. I say, Madhav, I hear you hobnob with bigwigs nowadays.

MADHAV. Spare me your jests, Headman, we are but common people.

HEADMAN. But your child here is expecting a letter from the King.

MADHAV. Don't you take any notice of him, a mere foolish boy!

HEADMAN. Indeed, why not! It'll beat the King hard to find a better family! Don't you see why the King plants his new Post Office right before your window? Why there's a letter for you from the King, urchin.

AMAL [*starting up*]. Indeed, really!

HEADMAN. How can it be false? You're the King's chum. Here's your letter [*showing a blank slip of paper*]. Ha, ha, ha! This is the letter.

AMAL. Please don't mock me. Say, Fakir, is it so?

GAFFER. Yes, my dear. I as Fakir tell you it *is* his letter.

AMAL. How is it I can't see? It all looks so blank to me. What is there in the letter, Mr. Headman?

HEADMAN. The King says, "I am calling on you shortly; you had better arrange puffed rice offerings for me. — Palace fare is quite tasteless to me now." Ha! ha! ha!

MADHAV [*with folded palms*]. I beseech you, Headman, don't you joke about these things —

GAFFER. Cutting jokes indeed, dare he!

MADHAV. Are you out of your mind too, Gaffer?

GAFFER. Out of my mind, well then I am; I can read plainly that the King writes he will come himself to see Amal, with the state physician.

AMAL. Fakir, Fakir, 'sh, his trumpet! Can't you hear?

HEADMAN. Ha! ha! ha! I fear he won't until he's a bit more off his head.

AMAL. Mr. Headman, I thought you were cross with me and didn't love me. I never could think you would fetch me the King's letter. Let me wipe the dust off your feet.

HEADMAN. This little child does have an instinct of reverence. Though a little silly, he has a good heart.

AMAL. It's hard on the fourth watch now, I suppose — Hark the gong, "Dong, dong, ding," "Dong, dong, ding." Is the evening star up? How is it I can't see —

GAFFER. Oh, the windows are all shut, I'll open them.

[*A knocking outside.*]

MADHAV. What's that? — Who is it? — what a bother!

VOICE [*from outside*]. Open the door.

MADHAV. Say, Headman — Hope they're not robbers.

HEADMAN. Who's there? — It's Panchanan, the headman, calls. — Aren't you afraid of the like of me? Fancy! The noise has ceased! Panchanan's voice carries far. — Yes, show me the biggest robbers! —

MADHAV [*peering out of the window*]. I should think the noise has ceased; they've smashed the door.

[*The King's* HERALD *enters.*]

HERALD. Our Sovereign King comes to-night!

HEADMAN. My God!

AMAL. At what hour of the night, Herald?

HERALD. On the second watch.

AMAL. When from the city gates my friend the watchman will strike his gong, "ding dong ding, ding dong ding" — then?

HERALD. Yes, then. The King sends his greatest physician to attend on his young friend.

[STATE PHYSICIAN *enters.*]

STATE PHYSICIAN. What's this? How close it is here! Open wide all the doors and windows. [*Feeling* AMAL's *body.*] How do you feel, my child?

AMAL. I feel very well, Doctor, very well. All pain is gone. How fresh and open! I can now see all the stars twinkling from the other side of the dark.

PHYSICIAN. Will you feel well enough to leave your bed with the King when he comes in the middle watches of the night?

AMAL. Of course, I'm dying to be about for ever so long. I'll ask the King to find me the polar star. I must have seen it often, but I don't know exactly which it is.

PHYSICIAN. He will tell you everything. [*To* MAD-HAV.] Will you go about and arrange flowers through the room for the King's visit? [*Indicating the* HEAD-MAN.] We can't have that person in here.

AMAL. No, let him be, Doctor. He is a friend. It was he who brought me the King's letter.

PHYSICIAN. Very well, my child. He may remain if he is a friend of yours.

MADHAV [*whispering into* AMAL's *ear*]. My child,

the King loves you. He is coming himself. Beg for a gift from him. You know our humble circumstances.

AMAL. Don't you worry, Uncle. — I've made up my mind about it.

MADHAV. What is it, my child?

AMAL. I shall ask him to make me one of his postmen that I may wander far and wide, delivering his message from door to door.

MADHAV [*slapping his forehead*]. Alas, is that all?

AMAL. What'll be our offering to the King, Uncle, when he comes?

HERALD. He has commanded puffed rice.

AMAL. Puffed rice! Say, Headman, you're right. You said so. You knew all we didn't.

HEADMAN. If you send word to my house then I could manage for the King's advent really nice —

PHYSICIAN. No need at all. Now be quiet, all of you. Sleep is coming over him. I'll sit by his pillow; he's dropping into slumber. Blow out the oil-lamp. Only let the starlight stream in. Hush, he slumbers.

MADHAV [*addressing* GAFFER]. What are you standing there for like a statue, folding your palms? — I am nervous. — Say, are they good omens? Why are they darkening the room? How will starlight help?

GAFFER. Silence, unbeliever.

[SUDHA *enters*.]

SUDHA. Amal!

PHYSICIAN. He's asleep.

SUDHA. I have some flowers for him. Mayn't I give them into his own hands?

PHYSICIAN. Yes, you may.

SUDHA. When will he be awake?

PHYSICIAN.   Directly the King comes and calls him.

SUDHA.   Will you whisper a word for me in his ear?

PHYSICIAN.   What shall I say?

SUDHA.   Tell him Sudha has not forgotten him.

CURTAIN

SIX WHO PASS WHILE THE LENTILS BOIL [1]

BY

STUART WALKER

[1] Reprinted by special permission from " Portmanteau Plays " by Stuart Walker, published by Stewart & Kidd Company, Cincinnati. Professional and amateur stage rights strictly reserved by the author.

Probably the most popular play of Stuart Walker, the inventor and director of the Portmanteau Theater, is "Six Who Pass." It is a fanciful bit of action carried out by six persons who pass a pot of boiling lentils. They are on their way to the execution of a Queen who is condemned to die before the clock strikes twelve. Her crime is having stepped upon the ring-toe of the King's great aunt.

If the reader wishes, he may read symbolism into the action, but the content, the vigor, and the grace are sufficient for the reader apart from any such addition.

"Trimplet," "Nevertheless" and "Medicine Show" are three other one-act plays by this author, which with "Six Who Pass" comprise an evening's performance.

SIX WHO PASS WHILE THE LENTILS BOIL

CHARACTERS

THE BOY
THE QUEEN
THE MIME
THE MILKMAID
THE BLINDMAN
THE BALLAD-SINGER
THE DREADFUL HEADSMAN
YOU [*in the audience*].

The Scene is a kitchen.
The Period is when you will.

[*Before the opening of the curtains the* PROLOGUE *enters upon the fore-stage and summons the* DEVICE-BEARER, *who carries a large copper pot.*]

PROLOGUE. This is a copper pot. [*The* DEVICE-BEARER *shows it to the audience carefully.*] It is filled with boiling water. [*The* DEVICE-BEARER *makes the sound of bubbling water.*] It is on the fire. See the flames. [*The* DEVICE-BEARER *sets the pot in the center of the fore-stage and blows under it with a pair of bellows.*] And see the water boiling over. [*The* DEVICE-BEARER *again makes the sound of bubbling water and then withdraws to where he can see the play from the side of the fore-stage.*]   We are looking into the kitchen of the Boy whose mother left him alone.   I do not know where she has gone but I do know that he is gathering lentils now.

You.   What are lentils?

PROLOGUE.   A lentil?   Why a lentil, don't you see, is not a bean, nor yet a pea; but it is kin to both . . . You must imagine that the Boy has built the fire and set the water boiling.   He is very industrious but you need not feel sorry for him.   His mother is very good to him and he is safe.   Are you ready now? . . .   Very well.   Be quiet.   [*The* PROLOGUE *claps his hands twice. The curtains open and a kitchen is disclosed.   There are a bench, a stool and a cupboard.   A great door at the back opens into a corridor.   There are also two windows — one higher than the other, looking upon the corridor.   At the right a door opens into the bedroom of the* BOY'S *mother. A great pewter spoon lies upon the shelf in the cupboard.   A large* BUTTERFLY *comes in through the doorway, flits about, and looks off stage.   The song of the* BOY *is heard from the garden.   The* BUTTERFLY *goes to the door, poises a moment, then alights on the cupboard.   The* BOY *enters with a great bowl filled with lentils.   The* BUTTERFLY *flies to the bowl and satisfied returns to the cupboard.   The* BOY *smiles at the* BUTTERFLY *but he does not touch him. Then he empties the lentils into the pot and water splashes on his careless hand.   A moan is heard in the distance. The* BOY *and the* BUTTERFLY *go to the door.   The* QUEEN'S *voice is heard calling*]

Butterfly, butterfly, where shall I hide?

[*Enter the* QUEEN.]

QUEEN.   Boy, Boy — oh, I am distraught!

You.   What is distraught?

PROLOGUE. Distraught means distracted, perplexed, beset with doubt, worried by some fear.

BOY [*pityingly*]. Why are you distraught?

QUEEN. Oh — Oh — Oh — They are going to behead me!

BOY. When?

QUEEN. Before mid-day.

BOY. Why are they going to behead you? Is it a story? Tell it to me.

QUEEN. I was guilty of a breach of etiquette.

BOY. What is that?

QUEEN. I did something that was considered bad manners and the law says the punishment is decapitation.

YOU. What is decapitation?

PROLOGUE. Decapitation is beheading; cutting off one's head.

BOY. Why, only kings and queens can be decapitated.

QUEEN. Oh, I know — I know —

BOY [*disappointed*]. Are you a queen?

QUEEN. Yes.

BOY. I thought all queens were big. My mother says they are always regal. And my mother knows.

QUEEN. Oh, I *am* the Queen. I *am* the Queen; but I am so unhappy.

BOY. My mother told me kings and queens knew no fear. Why, you're afraid.

QUEEN. Oh, Boy, Boy, I *am* your Queen and I am afraid and unhappy. And queens are just like other people when they are afraid and unhappy.

BOY [*disappointed*]. Aren't they always regal?

QUEEN. No — no. Oh, little Boy, hide me, hide me from the Dreadful Headsman!

Boy. I haven't any place to hide you. You couldn't get under the bench and you couldn't get into the cupboard.

Queen. Little Boy, can't you see that I shall lose my head if I am found?

Boy. You might have hidden in the pot if I hadn't put it on the fire.

Queen. Oh — Oh — Oh —

Boy. I'm sorry.

Queen. I am distraught.

Boy. Well, I'll hide you, because you are distraught; but — I am not sure you are a queen. . . . Where's your crown? You can't be a queen without a crown!

[*She reaches up to her head.*]

Queen. Oh, I was running so fast that it must have slipped from my head. [*Sees the* Butterfly.] Butterfly, tell him I am your Queen. [*The* Butterfly *flies to her head and lights on her disheveled locks like a diadem.*]

Boy. Oh, I have talked to the Queen! . . . You can hide in my mother's bedroom in there; but first please tell me a story.

Queen. They will find me here. I'll tell you a story afterward.

Boy. I want you to tell me now.

Queen. Well, you watch at the door and warn me when you see some one coming. [*The* Butterfly *brushes her ear.*] But stay, the Butterfly says he'll watch.

[*The* Butterfly *goes to the door.*]

Boy. Will he know?

Queen. Oh, yes. He is a wonderful Butterfly — wise beyond his years.

Boy. Sit down and tell me your story. [*He places a*

black pillow for the QUEEN *on the step and an orange pillow for himself.*]

QUEEN. Last night we celebrated the second year of peace with the neighboring kingdom. We were dancing the minuet just after the banquet, when I stepped on the ring-toe of my husband the King's great-aunt.

BOY. Didn't you say excuse me?

QUEEN. It was useless. The law says that if a Queen steps on the ring-toe of the King's great-aunt or any member of her family the Queen must be beheaded while the King's four clocks are striking twelve at mid-day.

BOY. Oh, that means to-day?

QUEEN. Yes.

BOY. Why, it's almost mid-day now. See, I've just set the lentils boiling.

QUEEN. If you can hide me until after the King's four clocks strike twelve I shall be safe.

BOY. Why are there four clocks?

QUEEN. Because the law allows only one clock for each tower in the castle.

BOY. Then I hear all the King's clocks every day! There's a big clock, and two clocks not so big, and a tiny little clock.

QUEEN. Yes, those are the four.

BOY. Why will you be safe *after* the four clocks strike twelve?

QUEEN. Because that is the law.

BOY. Aren't laws funny?

QUEEN. Funny? This one is very sad, I think.

BOY. Mightn't it be twelve any mid-day?

QUEEN. No; the Prime Minister of my grand-

L

father who passed the law decided that it meant only the following mid-day.

BOY [*rising and rushing to the door*]. They'll find you here.

QUEEN [*rising calmly*]. Oh, no, this is the short cut to the beheading block. Through that corridor.

BOY. Why didn't you run the other way?

QUEEN. Because they always search for escaped people in that direction. So I ran through your garden and into this room. They'll never search for me so close to the castle.

BOY. How did you escape?

QUEEN. I —

[*The* BUTTERFLY *seems agitated.*]

BOY. You —

QUEEN. Some one is coming. Hide me!

BOY. In here — in my mother's room. 'Sh! 'sh!

[*The* QUEEN *goes out. Enter the* MIME. *He pokes his head in the lower window and peeps around the door. The* BOY *turns.*]

BOY [*weakly*]. Are you the Dreadful Headsman?

MIME. *What?*

BOY. Are you the Dreadful Headsman?

MIME. Do I look like a headsman?

BOY. I don't know; I've never seen one.

MIME. Well, suppose I am.

BOY. Are you?

MIME. Maybe I am.

BOY. Oh!

MIME. Booh!

BOY. I'm — I'm — not afraid.

MIME. Bah!

BOY. And my mother isn't here.

MIME. Br-r-r-r!

[*The* BOY *reaches for his knife.*]

MIME. Bing!

BOY. I wasn't going to hurt you!

MIME. 'Sh!... 'Sh!... 'Sh!...

BOY. I'll give you my knife if you'll go 'way.

MIME. Ah, — ha!

BOY. It's nearly mid-day and you'd better go.

MIME. Well, give me the knife.

BOY. Promise me to go.

MIME [*laughs, turning away*]. Aren't you going to the beheading?

BOY. No. I have to boil the lentils for our mid-day meal.

MIME. May I come back and eat some?

BOY. You'll have to ask my mother.

MIME. Where is she?

BOY. She's over that way. She went to the market to buy a bobbin.

YOU. What is a bobbin?

PROLOGUE. A bobbin is a spool upon which thread is wound, and it is sharp at one end so that it can be easily passed backward and forward, to and fro, through the other threads in making lace.

MIME [*starting off*]. Well, I'll be back to eat some lentils.

BOY [*too eagerly*]. You'd better hurry.

MIME. You seem to want to get rid of me.

BOY [*allaying suspicion*]. Well, I think you'd better go or you'll be late — and it's very wrong to be late.

MIME [*going toward the door*]. I think I'll [*changing his mind*] sit down.

BOY [*disappointed*]. Oh!

Mime. What would you say if I wasn't the Headsman?

Boy. But you said you were.

Mime. I said *maybe* I was.

Boy. Aren't you?

Mime. Maybe I'm not.

Boy. Honest?

Mime. Um, hum.

Boy [*relieved*]. Oh! . . .

Mime. You *were* afraid.

Boy. No . . . I wasn't.

Mime. Would you fight?

Boy. You bet I would.

Mime. It wouldn't take me a minute to lick you.

Boy. Maybe it wouldn't, but I wouldn't give up right away. That would be cowardly . . . Who are you?

Mime. I'm a mime —

Boy. What's a mime?

Mime. A mime's a mime.

Boy. Go on and tell me.

Mime. A mime's a mountebank.

Boy. What's a mountebank?

Mime. A mountebank's a strolling player.

Boy. Are you going to perform for me?

Mime. Not to-day — I'm on my way to the decapitation.

Boy. Do you want to see the decapitation?

Mime. Well, yes. But most of all I want to pick up a few coins.

Boy. How?

Mime. Why, I'll perform after the Queen has lost her head.

Boy. Won't you be too sorry?

Mime. No. You see, I'll be thinking mostly about what I'm going to do. I have to do my best because it is hard to be more interesting than a decapitation. And after it's all over the crowd will begin to talk and move about; and I'll have to rush up to the front of them and cry out at the top of my lungs, "Stop — Ho, for Jack the Juggler! Would you miss him? In London where the king of kings lives, all the knights and ladies of the Court would leave a crowning to watch Jack the Juggler toss three golden balls with one hand or balance a weathervane upon his nose." Then a silence will come upon the crowd and they will all turn to me. Some one will say, "Where is this Jack the Juggler?" And I shall answer, "Jack the Juggler, the greatest of the great, the pet of kings, entertainer to the Pope, and the joy of Cathay stands before you." And I'll throw back my cloak and stand revealed. So! Some one will then shout, "Let us have it, Jack." So I'll draw my three golden balls from my pouch — like this — and then begin. [*The* Boy *is watching breathlessly and the* Butterfly *is interested too. Their disappointment is keen when* Jack *does nothing.*]

Boy. Aren't you going to show me?

Mime. No, I must be off.

Boy. Aren't you ever coming back?

Mime. Maybe, yes; perhaps, no.

Boy. I'll give you some lentils if you'll juggle the balls for me.

Mime [*sniffs the pot*]. They aren't cooked yet.

Boy. Let me hold your golden balls.

Mime [*takes a gold ball from his pouch and lets the* Boy *hold it*]. Here's one.

BOY. And do they pay you well?

MIME [*taking the ball from the* BOY]. Ay, that they do. If I am as interesting as the beheading I'll get perhaps fifteen farthings in money and other things that I can exchange for food and raiment.

BOY. I'm going to be a mime and buy a castle and a sword.

MIME. Maybe so and maybe not. Who knows? . . . Good-bye. [*He goes out.*]

BOY [*to the* BUTTERFLY]. If he had been the Dreadful Headsman I would have slain him. So! . . ."Ah, wicked headsman, you shall not behead the Queen! . . . Cross not that threshold or I'll run you through." [*Throughout this the* BUTTERFLY *shows great interest and enters into the spirit of it, being absorbed at times and frightened at others.*]

[*Enter the* MILKMAID *at door.*]

MILKMAID. Pst! . . . Pst!

BOY [*startled*]. Oh!

MILKMAID. Are you going to the decapitation?

BOY. No. Are you?

MILKMAID. That I am.

BOY. Will your mother let you go?

MILKMAID. She doesn't know.

BOY. Did you run away?

MILKMAID. No. I went out to milk the cow.

BOY. And did you do it?

MILKMAID. Yes.

BOY. Why didn't you wait until you came back?

MILKMAID. My mother was looking and I had to let her see me doing something.

BOY. How did you get away when you took the milk pails into the house?

MILKMAID. I didn't take them in. As soon as my mother turned her back I hid the pails and I ran through here to take a short cut.

BOY. Where did you hide the milk?

MILKMAID. In the hollow tree.

BOY. Won't it sour?

MILKMAID. Maybe.

BOY. Won't your mother scold you?

MILKMAID. Yes, of course, but I couldn't miss the beheading.

BOY. Will you take the sour milk home?

MILKMAID. Yes, and after my mother scolds me I'll make it into nice cheese and sell it to the King's Cook and then mother will forgive me.

BOY [*sniffing the pot*]. You'd better hurry. It's nearly mid-day. Don't you smell the lentils?

MILKMAID. The headsman hasn't started yet.

BOY [*giggling*]. He'd better hurry.

MILKMAID. They can't find the Queen.

BOY [*so innocently*]. Did she escape?

MILKMAID. Yes.

BOY. Are they hunting for her?

MILKMAID. Yes, and they've offered a big reward to the person who finds her.

BOY. How much?

MILKMAID. A pail of gold and a pair of finger rings.

BOY. That's a good deal . . . with a pail of gold I could buy my mother a velvet dress and a silken kerchief and a bonnet made of cloth of gold — and I could buy myself a milk-white palfrey.

MILKMAID. And you'd never have to work again.

BOY. But she's such a gentle Queen. Where are they hunting her?

MILKMAID. Everywhere.

BOY. Everywhere! . . . Maybe she's waiting at the beheading block.

MILKMAID. Silly goose! She wouldn't try to escape this way. She'd go in the opposite direction.

BOY. Do people always run in the opposite direction?

MILKMAID. Of course, everybody knows that.

BOY. I wish I could go.

MILKMAID. Come on.

BOY. Um-uh. The lentils might burn.

MILKMAID. Pour some cold water on them.

BOY. Um-uh. I promised I wouldn't leave the house.

MILKMAID. Oh, it will be wonderful!

BOY. The Mime will be there.

MILKMAID. The one with the long cloak and the golden balls?

BOY. Um-uh.

MILKMAID. Ooh!

BOY. How did you know?

MILKMAID. I saw him on the way to the market one day — and when my mother wasn't looking at me I gave him a farthing.

BOY. Is he a good juggler?

MILKMAID. He's magic! Why, he can throw three golden balls in the air and catch them with one hand and then keep them floating in the air in a circle.

BOY. And can he balance a weathervane on his nose while it's turning?

MILKMAID. Yes, and he can balance an egg on the end of a long stick that is balanced on his chin!

BOY. Oh — I wish I could see him. [*Looks at the pot to see if the lentils are done.*]

MILKMAID. Come on!

BOY. Well — [*Begins to weaken and just as he is about to start, the* BUTTERFLY *flits past him into the* QUEEN'S *room.*]

MILKMAID. Oh — what a lovely Butterfly!

BOY. No — no — I can't go. But you had better hurry.

MILKMAID. Well, I'll try to catch the Butterfly first.

BOY. Oh, no, you mustn't touch that Butterfly.

MILKMAID. Why?

BOY. Because — because he's my friend.

MILKMAID. Silly!

BOY. He *is* a good friend and he's the wisest Butterfly in the world.

MILKMAID. What can he do?

BOY. He can almost talk.

MILKMAID. Almost? . . . Oh, I know. I'm a goose. You want to play a trick on me so I'll miss the beheading.

BOY. You'd better hurry.

MILKMAID. I wish you'd come.

BOY [*sadly*]. I can't. . . . I've a duty to perform.

MILKMAID. Aren't duties always hard? [*Both sigh.*] [*She takes up her milk pail.*]

BOY. What are you going to do with that pail?

MILKMAID. I'm going to stand on it. . . . Good-bye. [*She goes out.*]

BOY. Good-bye. [*He watches for a moment, then goes to the pot and tries the lentils; then whispers through door to the* QUEEN.] The lentils are getting soft.

[*There is a fumbling in the passage and a voice is heard,* Help the blind. Help the blind. *The* BUTTERFLY *re-*

turns to the top of the cupboard. The BLINDMAN *appears at the door.*]

PROLOGUE. He's blind, but he'll show you how the blind can see.

BLINDMAN [*sniffing*]. Cooking lentils?

BOY. Yes.

BLINDMAN. Cook, which way to the beheading?

BOY. Keep straight ahead — the way you are going, old man.

BLINDMAN. Don't you want to take me with you?

BOY. I'm not going.

BLINDMAN. Not going to the beheading?

BOY. No, I have to cook the lentils.

BLINDMAN. Come on and go with me and maybe I'll give you a farthing.

BOY. I can't.

BLINDMAN. Yes, you can. Who else is here?

BOY [*swallowing; it's hard to fib*]. No one.

BLINDMAN. Can't you run away? Your mother won't know you've gone.

BOY. It's my duty to stay here.

BLINDMAN. It's your duty to help a poor blindman, little Boy.

BOY. Are you stone blind?

BLINDMAN. Yes.

BOY. Then how did you know I was a *little* boy?

BLINDMAN. Because you *sound* like a little boy.

BOY. Well, if you're stone blind why do you want to go to the beheading?

BLINDMAN. I can see with my ears.

BOY. Aw —

BLINDMAN. Didn't I know you were a little boy?

BOY. Yes, but you had to guess twice. First you thought I was a cook.

BLINDMAN. Well, aren't you cooking lentils?

BOY. Yes; but you can smell them.

BLINDMAN. Well, I see with my nose, too.

BOY. Aw — how can you see with your nose?

BLINDMAN. If you give me some bread I'll show you.

BOY. I can't give you any bread, but I'll give you some raw lentils.

BLINDMAN. All right. Give me lentils.

BOY. . . . I'll put them by the pot. Ready.

BLINDMAN. All right. [*Sniffs. Walks to the pot and gets lentils and puts them in an old pouch.*] Isn't that seeing with my nose?

BOY. H'm! [*In wonder.*] Now see with your ears and I'll give you some more lentils.

BLINDMAN. All right. Speak.

[*The* BOY *gets behind the stool and speaks. The* BLINDMAN *goes toward him. The* BOY *moves around stealthily.*]

BLINDMAN. You're cheating. You've moved.

BOY [*jumping up on the bench*]. Well, where am I?

BLINDMAN. You're standing on something.

BOY. How did you guess it?

BLINDMAN. I didn't guess it. I know it.

BOY. Why can't I do that?

BLINDMAN. You can if you try; but it takes practice.

BOY. Can you see the door now?

BLINDMAN. No, I've turned around too many times. Besides there is more than one door.

BOY. Oh — m-m. . . . You aren't really blind!

BLINDMAN. Blind people learn to use what they have. Once I too could see with my eyes.

BOY. Just like me?

BLINDMAN. Yes. And then I didn't take the trouble to see with my ears and my nose and my fingers — after I became blind I had to learn. . . . Why, I can tell whether a man who passes me at the palace gate is a poor man or a noble or a merchant.

BOY. How can you do that?

BLINDMAN. By the sound of the step.

BOY. Aw — how can you do that?

BLINDMAN. Shut your eyes and try it.

BOY. Well, I know what you are. That would be easy.

BLINDMAN. I'll pretend I'm somebody else. [*Feels with his stick; touches bench. Feels around again.*]

BOY. Why are you doing that?

BLINDMAN. To see how far I can walk without bumping into something.

BOY. Um —

BLINDMAN. Ready.

BOY [*hides face in hands*]. Yes.

BLINDMAN. Don't peep. [*The* BOY *tries hard not to.*]

BOY. I won't.

BLINDMAN. All ready. [*Shuffles like a commoner.*] Who was it?

BOY. A poor man.

BLINDMAN. See how easy?

BOY. I could see him as plain as if I had my eyes open. . . . Now try me again.

BLINDMAN. Ready.

BOY. All right. [*The* BLINDMAN *seems to grow in height. His face is filled with a rare brightness. He steadies himself a moment and then walks magnificently down the room.*]

BOY [*in beautiful wonder*]. A noble! I could see him.

BLINDMAN. All you have to do is try.

BOY. I always thought it was terrible to be blind.

BLINDMAN. Sometimes it is.

BOY. But I thought everything was black.

BLINDMAN. It used to be until I taught myself how to see.

BOY. Why is it terrible sometimes?

BLINDMAN. Because I cannot help the poor who need help. If I had money I could feed the hungry and clothe the poor little beggar children in winter!

BOY. Would a pail of gold and a pair of finger rings help you feed the hungry and clothe the poor little beggar children in winter?

BLINDMAN. A pail of gold! I have dreamed of what I might do with so much wealth!

BOY. I can get a pail of gold if I break a promise.

BLINDMAN. Would *you* break a promise?

BOY. . . . No — but — No!

BLINDMAN. Of course you wouldn't.

BOY. I couldn't break a promise for two pails of gold.

BLINDMAN. Nor twenty-two, little Boy.

BOY. When you walked like a noble I saw a beautiful man behind my eyes with a crown of gold.

BLINDMAN. If you broke a promise for a pail of gold and two finger rings you would never see a beautiful noble with a crown of gold when you closed your eyes. . . .

BOY. Can blindmen see beautiful things even when it's rainy?

BLINDMAN. Blindmen can always see beautiful things if they try. Clouds and rain are beautiful to me — and when I get wet I think of the sunshine. I saw sunshine with my eyes when I was a little boy. Now I see it with my whole body when it warms me. I saw rain with my eyes when I was a little boy. Now I see it with my hands when it falls on them — drop — drop — drop — dropity — dropity — and I love it because it makes the lentils grow.

BOY. I never thought of that. Rain makes me stay in doors and I never like it except in June.

BLINDMAN. You don't have to stay in for long.

BOY. Can blindmen see beautiful things in a beheading?

BLINDMAN. No. But I must be there with the crowd. I shall tell stories to the people and perhaps they will give me food or money.

BOY. Can't you stay and tell me stories?

BLINDMAN. No. I must be on my way. . . . If I do not see the beheading I cannot tell about it when I meet some one who was not there. Oh, I shall make a thrilling tale of it.

BOY. Tell it to me when you come back.

BLINDMAN. If you give me some cooked lentils.

BOY. I'll save you some.

BLINDMAN. Are the lentils nearly done?

BOY. Half.

BLINDMAN. I must be on my way then. . . . Good-bye. [*Starting to go in the wrong direction.*]

BOY. Here's the door.

BLINDMAN. Thank you, little boy. . . . Don't forget to see with your ears and nose and fingers. [*The* BLINDMAN *goes out.*]

BOY. I won't.

BLINDMAN. Good-bye.

BOY. Good-bye. [*The* BOY *covers his eyes and tries*

to see with his ears and his nose.] It's easier with the ears.

[*Singing is heard. Enter the* BALLAD-SINGER.]

Hello!

BOY. Hello!

SINGER. How are you?

BOY. I'm very well.

SINGER. That's good.

BOY. Thank you.

SINGER. Cooking?

BOY. Yes.

SINGER [*coming into the room*]. Something good?

BOY. Lentils.

SINGER. Give me some?

BOY. They aren't done.

SINGER. Nearly. I can smell them.

BOY. Do you like them?

SINGER. When I'm hungry.

BOY. Are you hungry now?

SINGER. I'm always hungry. [*They laugh.*]

BOY. Were you singing?

SINGER. Yes.

BOY. Do you like to sing?

SINGER. When I get something for my ballads.

BOY. Are you a ballad-singer?

SINGER. Yes.

BOY. Sing one for me?

SINGER. Give me some lentils?

BOY. I'll give you some raw lentils.

SINGER. I want some of the cooked ones.

BOY. They aren't done.

SINGER. Are they nearly done?

BOY. More than half.

SINGER. I like them that way.

BOY. All right. Sing me a ballad.

SINGER. Well, give me the lentils first.

BOY. Oh, no, sing the ballad first.

SINGER. No, sir, give me the lentils first.

BOY. That isn't fair.

SINGER. Why not? After I sing to you maybe you won't pay me.

BOY. Yes, I will.

SINGER. Then why not pay me first?

BOY. You might not sing.

SINGER [*laughing*]. Yes, I will.

BOY [*laughing*]. Well, I'll give you some lentils at the end of each verse.

SINGER. That's a bargain.

BOY. Sing.

SINGER [*sings one line*]. Six stalwart sons the miller had — Give me the lentils.

BOY. Finish the verse.

SINGER. I did finish it.

BOY. Now that's not fair. You only sang a line.

SINGER. Well, a line's a verse.

BOY [*with a gesture that indicates how long a verse ought to be*]. I meant a whole verse.

SINGER [*mimicking the gesture*]. A line's a whole verse.

BOY. Oh, now, be fair, I mean a *whole*, whole verse.

SINGER. You mean a *stanza*.

BOY. I always heard it called a verse.

SINGER. Well, keep the bargain. I sang a verse. Give me some lentils.

BOY [*rising and taking a very few lentils on his spoon*]. Next time I mean a stanza. . . . Here are some lentils.

[*The* BALLAD-SINGER *eyes the meager portion, cools it and eats.*]

SINGER.   Stingy.

BOY.   Isn't that *some* lentils?

SINGER [*laughs*].   Well —

BOY.   Now begin again.

SINGER.   At the end of every stanza a spoonful of lentils.

BOY.   I didn't say a spoonful.

SINGER [*starts to go*].   Very well, I won't sing a ballad.

BOY.   All right.   I'll give you a spoonful at the end of each — stanza.   [*He sits on the floor by the pot of lentils.*]

SINGER [*sings*].

The Ballad of the Miller and His Six Sons

Six stalwart sons the miller had
All brave and fair to see —
He taught them each a worthy trade —
And they grew gallantly.
Tara—da—da—da-da-da—da-da-da
Tara—da—da—da-de—da-dee.

Give me some lentils.

BOY.   Here. . . .   Hurry up.

SINGER [*sings*].

The first was John of the dimpled chin
And a fist of iron had he —
He learned to wield the broadsword well
And turned to soldiery.
Tara—da—da, etc.

BOY.   Please!   Please don't stop.

SINGER.   Keep to the bargain.

M

Boy. Here, take two spoonfuls and finish without stopping.

Singer [*sings rest of ballad*].

> The second son was christened Hugh
> And curly locks had he —
> He learned to use the tabor and lute
> And turned to minstrelsy.
> Tara—da—da, etc.

> The third was James of the gentle ways
> And speech of gold had he —
> He learned his psalms and learned his creed
> And turned to simony.
> Tara—da—da, etc.

> The fourth was Dick of the hazel eye,
> And a steady hand had he —
> With a hammer and saw and a chest of tools
> He turned to carpentry.
> Tara—da—da, etc.

> The fifth was Ned of the velvet tread
> And feather fingers had he.
> He used his gifts in a naughty way
> And turned to burglary.
> Tara—da—da, etc.

> The sixth was Robin, surnamed the Rare,
> For always young was he —
> He learned the joy of this sunny world
> And turned to poetry.
> Tara—da—da, etc.

> The miller approached three score and ten
> A happy man was he

His five good sons and the one who was bad,
All turned to gallantry.
Tara—da—da, etc.

BOY. Sing me another.
SINGER. A spoonful at the end of every stanza.
BOY. Don't stop after you begin.
SINGER. Pay me in advance.
BOY. I suppose I'll have to. [*He feeds the* BALLAD-SINGER.]
SINGER [*sings second ballad*].

The Ballad of the Three Little Pigs

Two little pigs were pink — pink — pink —
And one little pig was black — black —
The three little pigs were very good friends,
But one little pig was black — black.

Three little pigs would play — play — play —
But one little pig was black — black —
And three little pigs would have a jolly time,
Though one little pig was black — black.

Three little pigs soon grew — grew — grew —
And one little pig was black — black —
The three little pigs became fat hogs,
And one fat hog was black — black.

The two fat hogs were pink — pink — pink —
And one fat hog was black — black —
The three fat hogs all made good ham,
Though one fat hog was black — black.

BOY. Sing me another.
SINGER. I can't. I'm tired.

Boy. Are you going to sing those at the beheading?

Singer. What beheading?

Boy. At the Queen's beheading.

Singer. Where?

Boy. Over there.

Singer. When?

Boy. To-day.

Singer. I must be going. Certainly I'll sing there and I'll take up a collection.

Boy. It's going to be before the King's four clocks strike twelve.

Singer. It's nearly time now. If I can collect a piece of gold I can buy a vermilion robe and sing at the King's court.

Boy. I could collect a pail of gold and two finger rings and sit at the feet of the King if I'd break a promise.

Singer. Perhaps you will.

Boy. Would you?

Singer. I'd rather sing along the highway all my life. It is better to dream of a vermilion robe than to have one that is not honestly got.

Boy. The Blindman said something like that.

Singer. Who said what?

Boy. The Blindman said if I broke a promise I'd never again see a beautiful noble with a golden crown when I closed my eyes.

Singer. He was right.

Boy. When you get your vermilion robe will you let me see it?

Singer. That I will. Good-bye.

Boy. Good-bye. [Singer *goes out.*]

[Boy *hums a snatch of the ballads.* The Headsman

steps into the door and plants his axe beside him for an impressive picture. The BOY *turns and starts in terror.*]

HEADSMAN. Have you seen the Queen?

BOY. Sir?

HEADSMAN. Have you seen the Queen?

BOY. How should I, sir? I've been cooking the lentils.

HEADSMAN. She is here!

BOY. How — could — she — be — here, sir?

HEADSMAN. Well, if she isn't here, where is she?

BOY [*relieved*]. I don't know where she is if she isn't here, sir.

HEADSMAN. She has too much sense to hide so near the castle and on the short cut to the headsman's block. . . Do you know who I am?

BOY. I think so — sir.

HEADSMAN. Think? Don't you *know?*

BOY. Yes, sir.

HEADSMAN. Who am I, then?

BOY. You're the Dreadful Headsman.

HEADSMAN. I am the winder of the King's four clocks, *and* when I am needed I am the best headsman in three kingdoms. And *this* is my axe.

BOY. Is it sharp?

HEADSMAN. It will split a hair in two. [*Runs finger near blade meaningly.*]

BOY. Oh!

HEADSMAN. A hair in two!

BOY. Would you really cut off the Queen's head?

HEADSMAN. That's my business, to cut off heads; and the nobler the head the better my business.

BOY. She's such a nice Queen.

HEADSMAN. Have you seen her?

Boy.   Y-es, — sir.

Headsman.   When?

Boy.   One day — when I was boiling some lentils.

Headsman.   Did you see her neck?

Boy.   Yes, sir.

Headsman.   Not much bigger than a hair.

Boy [*desperately friendly*].   Have you seen my knife?

Headsman [*sharply*].   *I'm* talking about the Queen and I'm going to talk about myself until I hear the King's trumpeter calling me to the beheading.

Boy.   Yes, sir. [*Edging between the bench and door of the room where the* Queen *is hidden.*]

Headsman.   Sit down.

Boy.   I'd rather stand, sir.

Headsman.   *Sit down!* And I'll tell you how I'm going to behead the Queen.

Boy.   You can't behead her after the King's four clocks have struck twelve.

Headsman.   How did you know that?

Boy [*realizing his blunder*].   Well —

Headsman.   Nobody knows that except the royal family and people of the court.

Boy.   A little — bird told — me.

Headsman.   Where is the little bird that I may cut its head off?

Boy.   Don't hurt the little bird, but tell me how you are going to behead the Queen.

Headsman.   Well — [*At the stool.*] This is the block.   There's the Queen behind the iron gate.   We'll say that door is the gate.   [*The* Boy *starts.*]   And out there is the crowd.   Now, I appear like this and walk up the steps.   The crowd cheers, so I bow and show myself and my axe.   Then I walk over to the gate —

Boy. Don't go in there. That's my mother's room and you might frighten *her*.

Headsman. Who's in your mother's room?

Boy. *She* is.

Headsman. Well, if she's in there, maybe she'd like to hear my story.

Boy. She's in bed.

Headsman. Sick? [*The* Boy *nods vigorously.*] All right. . . . Well, I've bowed to the crowd and I start for the Queen. — If you won't open the door, you pretend you're the Queen.

Boy. I don't want to be the Queen.

Headsman. Come on and pretend. I walk up to the gate — so, and open it and then I say "Your Majesty, I'm going to cut off your head" and she bows — bow — [*The* Boy *bows.*] And then I say "Are you ready?" and she says, "I am ready." Then I blindfold her —

Boy. Now, don't blindfold me, sir!

Headsman. I'm showing you how it's done.

Boy. But if you blindfold me I can't see when you do it.

Headsman [*admitting the point*]. All right. . . . Then I blindfold her and I lead her to the block and I say, "Have you made your peace with Heaven?" and she says, "Yes. . . ."

Boy. If you won't tell me any more I'll give you my knife.

Headsman. Aren't you interested?

Boy. Yes, but your axe is so sharp and it might slip.

Headsman. Sharp? It will cut a hair in two, but I know how to handle it. . . . Come on . . . [*The* Boy *reluctantly falls into the picture again.*] And then. . . [*Raising his axe.*] And then. . . [HEADSMAN *sees the* BUTTERFLY.] And then. . . How-d'ye-do, Butter-fly? [*The* BOY *runs to the pot unnoticed by the* HEADSMAN.]

BOY. Lentils, lentils, boil the time away. That my good Queen may live to-day. [*The* HEADSMAN *and the* BUTTERFLY *are having quite a game. Suddenly the great clock begins to strike and the two next larger follow slowly. The* HEADSMAN *rushes to the back door with his axe.*]

HEADSMAN. Why doesn't the trumpeter blow his call! [*The* BOY *counts the strokes of the clock and as the third clock strikes twelve he rushes to the door of the bedroom.*]

BOY. Queen! Queen! It's mid-day.

HEADSMAN. Queen — Queen — [*He strides to the bedroom and drags the* QUEEN *out.*] The little clock hasn't struck yet! [*He pulls the* QUEEN *toward the rear door and shouts.*] Here! Here! don't let the little clock strike! I've won the pail of gold! [*The* BOY *has set the bench in the doorway so that the* HEADSMAN *stumbles. The* BUTTERFLY *keeps flying against the* HEADSMAN'S *nose, which makes him sneeze.*]

BOY. No one heard you!

QUEEN. Let me go! Let me go!

HEADSMAN [*sneezing as only a headsman can*]. The Queen! The Queen! [*The little clock begins to strike. The* BOY *counts eagerly, one, two, three, etc. Between strokes the* HEADSMAN *sneezes and shouts.*] The Queen! The Queen! [*At the fifth stroke the* HEADSMAN *falls on his knees. The* QUEEN *becomes regal, her foot on his neck. The* BOY *kneels at her side.*]

QUEEN. Base villain! According to the law I am saved! But you are doomed. As winder of the King's four clocks the law commands that you be decapitated because the four clocks did not strike together. Do you know that law?

HEADSMAN. Oh, Lady, I do, but I did but do my duty. I was sharpening my axe this morning and I couldn't wind the clocks. Intercede for me.

QUEEN. It is useless.

BOY. Is there any other headsman?

QUEEN. The law says the Chief Headsman must behead the chief winder of the King's four clocks.

BOY. Can the Dreadful Headsman behead himself?

QUEEN. Aye, there's the difficulty.

HEADSMAN. Oh, your Majesty, pardon me!

BOY. Yes, pardon him.

QUEEN. On one condition: He is to give his axe to the museum and devote all his old age to the care of the King's four clocks. . . . For myself, I shall pass a law requiring the ladies of the court to wear no jewels. So, if the King's aunt can wear no rings, she assuredly cannot have a ring-toe, and hereafter I may step where I please. . . . Sir Headsman, lead the way. . . . And now, my little Boy, to you I grant every Friday afternoon an hour's sport with the Mime, a spotted cow for the little Milkmaid, a cushion and a canopy at the palace gate for the Blindman, a vermilion cloak for the Ballad-Singer, a velvet gown, a silken kerchief and a cloth-of-gold bonnet for your mother, and for yourself a milk-white palfrey, two pails of gold, two finger rings, a castle, and a sword. . . . Arise, Sir Little Boy. . . . Your arm.

BOY. May I take my knife, your Majesty?

QUEEN. That you may. [*He gets the knife and returns to her. She lays her hand on his arm.*] Sir Headsman, announce our coming.

HEADSMAN. Make way — make way — for her Majesty the Queen.

QUEEN [*correcting*]. *And* Sir Little Boy.

HEADSMAN. What's his other name, your Majesty?

BOY [*whispering with the wonder of it all*]. Davie.

QUEEN [*to the* HEADSMAN]. Davie.

HEADSMAN. Make way — make way for her Majesty the Queen and Sir Davie Little Boy. [*They go out. Immediately the* BOY *returns and gets the pot of lentils and runs after the* QUEEN *as*

THE CURTAINS CLOSE

THE SILVER LINING[1]

BY

CONSTANCE D'ARCY MACKAY

[1] From "The Beau of Bath and Other One-Act Plays" by Constance D'Arcy Mackay. Copyright, 1915, by Henry Holt and Company.

Reprinted by arrangement with the publishers.

For permission to perform this play application must be made to the author in care of the publisher.

This delightfully charming little portrait of the eighteenth century was composed to be acted, as are all the plays of Constance D'Arcy Mackay. Their attraction lies in their interesting historical exactness.

The author is a recognized authority on the production of plays in public schools, and the plays bear witness to her very practical instruction and enthusiastic sympathy, together with her interest in all human aspects in literature.

This little play inspires the reader to a further acquaintance with the writer's biographical plays found in "The Beau of Bath." Her folk-plays are especially charming.

THE SILVER LINING

CHARACTERS

FANNY BURNEY
RICHARD BURNEY, *her uncle*
CEPHAS, *an old servant*

PLACE: Chessington.
TIME: 1778.
SCENE: Library in Mr. Crisp's house.

[*A pleasant room, a trifle littered with books and papers. All across the background, windows curtained in palely flowered damask. A hearth at left, with a fire burning rosily. Brass andirons. A bellows. Near the hearth, facing audience, a dark wooden settle with a high back. It is handsomely carved and appears to be quite old. Candles in silver candlesticks are lighted on the hearth shelf, and there are also framed silhouettes standing there.*

[*At right, near background, a door opening into another room of the house. Also at left, towards foreground, a round table with a lighted candelabra, several drawings in striking black and white. A brass inkstand, sand, quills, pens, etc. All along the right wall a dark bookcase full to running over with books. Its top shelf is piled high with them. Their covers are mostly brown and musty. There are also black, dark blue and green ones, but none in bright colors.*

[*At the rise of the curtain* FANNY BURNEY, *rather small,
delicate, with a girlishly pretty face and softly curling unpowdered hair sits writing at the table, a
small work-bag and sampler lying on her lap. She
wears a pale yellow dress, flowered in white, over a
pale yellow petticoat, and a white lace fichu. Black
velvet ribbon at her throat, and about her wrists.
She is deep in her work when there is the sound of
some one opening the door at right. With amazing
swiftness* FANNY *drops her pen, sweeps the drawings over what she is writing, drops her sampler
and bag on top of them, and is crocheting when her
uncle,* RICHARD BURNEY, *enters. He is a tall, portly,
ruddy man, with a most important manner. He
wears a handsome plum-colored traveling suit, and
carries a long churchwarden pipe which he lights
without a "by your leave" at his first opportunity.*]

RICHARD BURNEY

Well, Fanny !

FANNY BURNEY
[*surprised*]
Uncle !

RICHARD BURNEY
Cephas welcomed me.
There's no one else about as I can see.
[FANNY *drops a flurried curtsey.*]
Where's Mrs. Gast ?

FANNY BURNEY
In bed.   And Daddy Crisp
Has gone to London.

RICHARD BURNEY
Cephas, with his lisp,
Has so informed me.   And I also know

Your father left here just three days ago,
So I have missed him.   Lord!   What a to-do!
I'm just from town myself.   Child, how are you?

FANNY BURNEY
[*prettily*]

Quite well, and hope my kinsfolk are the same.

RICHARD BURNEY
[*puffing at his pipe before the fire*]

Um.   Yes.

FANNY BURNEY
What news?

RICHARD BURNEY
The whole town rings with fame
Of a new author, who has writ a book
Called "Evelina."   Everywhere you look
You see it advertised.   Yet no one knows
The author's name and rumor madly goes
Naming first this one, and then that one.

FANNY BURNEY
[*passionately*]

Oh,
If they should ever guess!   [*She grows pale.*]

RICHARD BURNEY
They're sure to know
Sooner or later.   Burke sat up all night
To read it.   Said if he could guess aright
The author's name, that fifty pounds he'd give,
While Dr. Johnson cried out: "As I live
I can't forget the book.   It's my delight!"
Why, Fanny!   How you look!   First red, then white.

FANNY BURNEY
[*trying to speak without a tremor*]

You see, in Chessington, our life is dull,

And everything you say seems wonderful,
And stirs the heart like bells of London town.
And so this — "Katherina" wins renown?

RICHARD BURNEY

Nay, "Evelina," so the novel's named.
The author who has written it is famed
Forever.   'Tis a puzzle.   No one can
Be positive who is the lucky man.
If, when I've read it I have found 'twill do
For you to read, 'twill be permitted you.

FANNY BURNEY
[demurely]

Thank you.

RICHARD BURNEY
How's Charles?

FANNY BURNEY

My father's vastly well,
And busy.

RICHARD BURNEY

Humph.   I think that I could tell
That without asking.   Times are hard.   I saw
A friend of Charles' last night — young Clapperclaw,
Who swears that Clark wrote "Evelina."   Fool!
But when I said 'twas more like Fielding's school
Mrs. Thrale looked at me the oddest way,
Said: "*Did you get the note I sent to-day?*
Go search for 'Evelina' nearer home.
If you would find her you've not far to roam,"
[FANNY *turns and looks at him, aghast; but he continues placidly.*]

I think she means that Anstey's written it.
But, lord, I'm sure that he has not the wit!
Although the strangest people try to write:

Children and fools.   I've not forgot the night
Your father found *you* at it, clipped your wing,
Forbade such nonsense and then burned the thing,
And brought you to your senses.   Pen and ink
Are not for women, but for men who think.
Females are cackling geese.   'Tis only men
Who have the strength of mind to wield a pen.

FANNY BURNEY
[*picking up pen from table*]

And yet this pen is made from a goose feather!

RICHARD BURNEY
[*frowning*]

Well, pens and women do not go together.
A bluestocking is a disguise.   [*Yawns.*]   Heigho!
The hour grows late.   I'll take my candle.
[*He crosses to table, takes candle, and pauses to pick up
    drawings for inspection.   As he lifts one it catches
    on the manuscript beneath, and the latter sweeps to
    the floor, and falls with pages outspread*]

FANNY BURNEY
[*with a stifled exclamation*]

Oh!

RICHARD BURNEY
[*puzzled; then angry*]

What's this?   [*Picks up a few pages.*]   Great heavens!
    Fanny!   Well, I swear
You *have* been writing!   And you've hid it there
Behind your sampler.   Wait till Charles hears this!

FANNY BURNEY
[*imploring him*]

Oh, Uncle Richard, if you'll —

RICHARD BURNEY

Silence, miss!

N

You should be shamed to look me in the face.
Thank God that no one else knows this disgrace.
How far has this thing gone?   Come, answer me.
Who else has seen this rubbish besides me?

FANNY BURNEY
[*terrified*]

Oh, Uncle —

RICHARD BURNEY
[*with mounting rage*]
Wait till Charles and I confer!

Who else?

FANNY BURNEY
[*between sobs*]
I've sent it to a publisher.

RICHARD BURNEY
[*furiously*]

Fanny!   Don't tell me you have been so bold!

FANNY BURNEY
[*sobbing wildly*]

Oh,—worse—than—that! *The—book's—already—*
sold.

RICHARD BURNEY
[*starting violently*]

Sold! Why, God bless me!   Fanny, you don't say
That you got money for it? [*He stares at her, open-*
mouthed.]

FANNY BURNEY
[*with a fresh burst of tears*]
Yes, to-day

A — check — came —

RICHARD BURNEY
[*eagerly*]
For how much?

FANNY BURNEY
[*choked with sobs*]
       Two — hundred — pounds.[1]

RICHARD BURNEY
[*staggered*]

Two hun— Why, Fanny! I am dreaming!
Zounds!
When did you write?

FANNY BURNEY
[*struggling for self-control*]
       A little, every **day.**

I covered it with samplers and crochet.
[*She wipes her eyes.*]

RICHARD BURNEY
[*quite mollified*]

What's the book called?

FANNY BURNEY
[*trembling*]
       'Tis "Evelina."

RICHARD BURNEY
[*stunned*]
            You

Wrote "Evelina"? [FANNY *nods.*] Lord! What
a to-do!
When Burke hears this! That Clapperclaw's a fool!
[*with triumph*]

I knew the book came from some other school!
[*expands as if talking to imaginary people*]
"My niece, the authoress. . . ."

FANNY BURNEY
[*approaching him humbly*]
       Uncle, I know

[1] This is a slight exaggeration for the sake of dramatic effectiveness.

I've been deceitful, but I loved it so —
My book.   Forgive me.   I won't write again.

RICHARD BURNEY

Eh ?   Oh, tut, tut !   I wouldn't cause you pain
For your — er — fault.

FANNY BURNEY
[with emotion]

Uncle, if you could dream
All that it meant to me, the thrill — the gleam —
You'll never guess what dull hours I've beguiled.

RICHARD BURNEY
[patronizingly]

There !   There !   Remember you're my niece, **dear**
child.
One mustn't be too hard on what's one's own.

FANNY BURNEY
[with quick gratitude]

Oh, *Uncle !*

RICHARD BURNEY
[condescendingly]

If you want to be alone
Sometimes, and write, I've no objection — **none.**

FANNY BURNEY
[radiant]

Uncle !

RICHARD BURNEY
[to himself]

And when I think how quick it's done —
Just write a book, and make two hundred pounds !
[CEPHAS *appears at door right, an old man in snuff-
colored livery.   He carries a candle, and an iron ring
with some large keys on it.*]

CEPHAS

Miss Fanny —

FANNY BURNEY
[*to her uncle*]
Cephas wants to make his rounds
And lock the doors.

RICHARD BURNEY
Then, child, good night.

[FANNY *takes a candle from the table. Motions to*
CEPHAS *to go. He exits, right, and* FANNY *drops
a curtsey to her uncle.*]

FANNY BURNEY

Good night.

RICHARD BURNEY
[*intercepting her*]
You think that you might write some more as bright
As "Evelina"?

FANNY BURNEY
[*modestly*]
I can try.

RICHARD BURNEY
Yes, do.

[*Again* FANNY *fetches him a dutiful curtsey. He
smiles at her benignly between puffs of smoke as he
stands with his back to the fire. She exits, right,
with her candle.* RICHARD BURNEY *puffs com-
placently, yet with the air of a man who must speak
aloud in order to give vent to his feelings. His
sentences come between enjoyable whiffs.*]

RICHARD BURNEY
Well, even if the hussy's socks *are* blue
She's my own niece. One shouldn't be repining
To find blue stockings have a silver lining.
The little baggage! Lord! Two hundred pounds!
Well, Charles can spend it fixing up his grounds!

QUICK CURTAIN

BY OURSELVES[1]

BY

LUDWIG FULDA

Translated from the German by Haya Wally

Ludwig Fulda has written many plays, of which "Talisman," "Friends of Youth," and "Twin Sister" are his greatest. He is emphatically an idealist in literature. As will be seen in the social satire, "By Ourselves," Mr. Fulda is an adept at satirical humor. His "Talisman" cost him the emperor's sanction to the Schiller Prize because of its very obvious application to that ruler.

The mastery of the dialogue and the humor of the clever situations serve to show how observant Mr. Fulda is of the follies of modern life.

BY OURSELVES

CHARACTERS

DR. FELIX VOLKART, *physician*
HERMINE, *his wife*
BARON HUBERT VON BERKOW
BAUMANN, *a servant*
LOTTE, *lady's maid*

[*Dining-room in* DR. VOLKART'S *house. Doors at right and left. To the right a window. In the middle of the stage, a long, richly decked table, on which are placed between thirty and forty covers. In the foreground, to the right, a small sofa; to the left several armchairs. In the background, a drawing-room is seen through the portières. Chandeliers in both rooms.*]

SCENE I

HERMINE [*in full evening dress*]. LOTTE. BAUMANN [*busy lighting the chandelier in the drawing-room*]. [*Later*] FELIX.

HERMINE [*to* LOTTE, *who is holding a hand mirror before her, pointing to a rose in her hair*]. Put this rose up a little higher, — still higher. What could that hairdresser have been doing with his eyes! That's right! But be careful; you are mussing up my lace!

LOTTE. You look charming again to-day, dear madam. [*Lays aside the hand mirror.*]

185

HERMINE. Do you think so? I do not feel at all well. Our first party — it is so easy to say; but oh, these cares, this work, this disorder! One must think of a thousand things at once, and there is always the fear that one has forgotten a thousand more. And old BAUMANN is no longer to be depended upon, past sixty as he is. [*Calls.*] Baumann!

BAUMANN [*hurrying forward with a lighted taper in his hand*]. Did you call, madam?

HERMINE. Heavens, it is dripping! Blow it out!

BAUMANN [*blows out the taper*]. Did you call? Everything has been attended to.

HERMINE [*glancing at the table*]. Have the place-cards been properly arranged?

BAUMANN. To be sure! But at the end of the left side —

HERMINE [*impatiently*]. What?

BAUMANN. At the left end three gentlemen are seated together.

HERMINE. There you are! Another confusion! See to it that they are properly arranged.

BAUMANN [*does not move*]. Oh, if only your blessed mother could have lived to see this day! The baroness always used to say —

HERMINE. I know what my mother used to say. Go now, and attend to your work. [BAUMANN *goes to the table.*]

FELIX [*enters at the left in ordinary attire*]. At last I have found you, Hermine! Where is my desk?

HERMINE. In the store-room.

FELIX. A nice place, truly. I must look up something on rheumatism; now, I suppose, I myself shall contract it. [*Hurries away to the right.*]

BAUMANN [*coming forward again*]. The small tables, too, are covered. Shall I not place cards upon them?

HERMINE. Which small tables?

BAUMANN. In the blue drawing-room.

HERMINE. Heavens! Those are the card tables, Baumann. You must remove the covers from them at once.

BAUMANN. Yes, when you were a child in arms, dear madam, I never expected to be so fortunate as to live to see the day of your first party given by yourself —

HERMINE. Terrible! Lotte, kindly see to it —

FELIX [*from the right*]. It's simply awful up there! My desk is there; but not my books. Who has removed them?

LOTTE. They are in the large linen closet in the bathroom.

FELIX. In the bathroom? Fine logic of events! [*Exit to the left.*]

HERMINE. Lotte, kindly go and see whether the carpet has been spread as far as the street. [LOTTE *exit to the right.*] And you, Baumann, go ask the cook whether the lobster has yet been brought; if not, telephone.

BAUMANN. To whom? To the lobster?

HERMINE. No, to the delicatessen dealer. Number seven hundred and forty-six.

BAUMANN. It will all be attended to. Just to think, that twenty years have passed, and that I still have the honor and the pleasure — [*Goes into the drawing-room and busies himself with something.*]

HERMINE [*aside*]. He is incorrigible!

FELIX [*enters at the left, with a lighted cigar*]. I cannot find the key of the linen closet.

HERMINE. It is, doubtless, in your desk.

FELIX. This is a fine wild goose chase! So I must go again to the store-room? No, now I give it up! [*Sits down in an armchair.*]

HERMINE. Felix, you are smoking! Here in the dining-room.

FELIX. No one is here yet.

HERMINE. A smell of stale tobacco at our first party! That would mean our social annihilation.

FELIX. Then I'll stop. [*Puts away his cigar.*]

HERMINE [*calls*]. Baumann!

BAUMANN [*comes from the drawing-room*]. Did you call, madam?

HERMINE. Take this dreadful stump away!

BAUMANN. At once. [*Takes the cigar and smokes it slyly.*] This is the real thing. [*Exit to the right.*]

SCENE II

HERMINE, FELIX

HERMINE. Felix, it is high time that you were dressed.

FELIX. If I can find my dress suit I shall attempt it. Judging by the state of things here, I suppose I shall locate it somewhere in the cellar.

HERMINE. You are in very good humor, indeed.

FELIX. Grim humor, the humor of despair! Besides, we have not yet seen each other to-day. So I thought —

HERMINE. We shall see enough of each other this evening.

FELIX. Just in passing by, among all the people.

HERMINE. Have you no feeling whatsoever of the duties of a host?

FELIX. Certainly! But also of other duties. It is just about this very thing that I should like to chat with you for a moment or two.

HERMINE. Chat, now? This is no time for chatting. To-morrow.

FELIX. But to-morrow you are going to the races.

HERMINE. Well, then, the day after to-morrow.

FELIX. In the morning you are going to the matinée for the benefit of the water sufferers, and in the evening to the living pictures for the benefit of the fire sufferers. What do you call the picture in which you are taking part?

HERMINE. Home life.

FELIX. Is that so? Home life. A very promising name. So you see, my dear, that for the present we shall have no time to chat, just as we have had no time until now. It is almost four months since we were married; but we always have time only for others, never for ourselves.

HERMINE. Felix, I still have a hundred things to attend to; please get dressed at once. What if people should come —

FELIX [*looking at his watch*]. Nobody ever comes during the first half hour, and you know with what marvellous rapidity I can slip on my dress suit.

HERMINE. Well, for goodness' sake, tell me in as few words as you can, what is on your mind. Otherwise, I see, I shall not get rid of you.

FELIX. Will things continue on in this way, Hermine?

HERMINE. What are you talking about?

FELIX. Well, that we associate with each other only at a distance, that the only privileges of my dignity as your husband consist in this: to accompany you to parties and then to bring you home again; to sit behind you in your box at the theater; at races to follow you about holding your field glass; at dances to hold your bouquet or fan; and everywhere, when any one pays homage to you, to stand near by with face expressing the utmost satisfaction and indifference. I am like a subordinate figure in a show, that only spoils the effect when it interferes with the action of the play. And people regard me as a perfect model of the wholly noiseless husband. For, since you consider it most improper that I should ever sit near you at a supper, or dance with you at a party —

HERMINE. To be sure it is improper. Married people are together enough at home; in society, on the contrary —

FELIX. At home? But when are we at home, dear child? At home — that is, so to speak, merely a geographical idea for us; that is only the base of operations from which we undertake our expeditions out into the world at large.

HERMINE. How you exaggerate! Do we not have the whole morning for ourselves?

FELIX. The morning? You are in bed the whole morning.

HERMINE. But when I get up —

FELIX. I have my consultation hour and am busy.

HERMINE. And as soon as you are through —

FELIX. You are already gone on a round of visits, or you receive company — the very best society, I must admit. They are all people of merit, were it only the merit of being nobly born, of having ribbons in their buttonholes, and of being able to speak on every subject under the sun, particularly on such as they do not understand. At lunch we either have guests or are invited elsewhere.

HERMINE. Did you not find it charming at the Chinese ambassador's, the other day?

FELIX. Very interesting. Even the spirit of the lady who sat next to me at table was completely surrounded by a Chinese wall. When you are in Rome, do as the Romans do. I made spasmodic efforts to entertain her, but the only answer she made was, "How funny!" In my despair, I finally read her a lecture on hydrophobia. How funny!

HERMINE. That was your own fault! I enjoyed myself ever so much better.

FELIX. With Herr von Walheim?

HERMINE. An extremely amiable companion.

FELIX. What did you talk about?

HERMINE [*trying to recall*]. Well, about — about —

FELIX. Yes, that is what one always talks about with people of that kind.

HERMINE. Why, you do not even know what we were talking about.

FELIX. Nor do you know, — and still less does Herr von Walheim know.

HERMINE. But we do have the afternoon for ourselves.

FELIX. In the afternoon you go out riding, or shopping, or you have guests for tea. And in the evening —

HERMINE. You exaggerate!

FELIX. And in the evening, — we usually do not get home until next morning.

SCENE III

HERMINE.   FELIX.   BAUMANN [*entering from the right*].

BAUMANN.   The lobster is here.

HERMINE.   That is good.

BAUMANN.   A splendid animal! It is still alive.

FELIX.   Very good, Baumann.

BAUMANN.   Shall I kill it?

HERMINE.   Just give it to the cook.

BAUMANN.   Ah, could your mother only have seen this.   [*Exit to the right.*]

SCENE IV

FELIX.   HERMINE

FELIX [*after a short pause*].   Remarkable, that your family doctor should have started on his journey on the very day that your mother got a headache. I still recall quite clearly how I was called in his stead to attend to Madam von Forstner.

HERMINE [*earnestly*].   I also recall it.

FELIX.   The case stamped itself upon my memory, because it was the third I had had in all my medical practice to that day, and the first two can hardly be counted. The first was a servant girl who had sprained her hand, and the second, a young man who confidentially asked for a prescription to prevent his hair from falling out. But a baroness, who had a headache, that was a decisive turning point, decisive also for another reason; for that was the beginning of our acquaintance.

HERMINE. Felix, I really believe you are becoming sentimental.

FELIX. Well, why not for once? It is only for the sake of variety. Yes, it was the beginning of our acquaintance. Your mother was perfectly well then; I, however, left your house a sick man. Even the arrow of love, in the light of modern science, proves to be a sort of microbe. I was head over heels in love with you. And after a few more visits, in order to prescribe the purest raspberry juice for your mother, a tablespoonful every hour, I knew it was all over with me; I was passionately in love with you.

HERMINE. Had you not better put on your dress suit, before you repeat your declaration of love to me?

FELIX. I shall soon finish. I knew perfectly well that you were a true worldling, reared in a whirl of pleasures; that you regarded the art of sewing on a button as a sort of higher magic, and that for you, a cook book was a book closed with seven seals. But I also knew from experience that girls who are trained for a domestic life become more eager for pleasure after marriage. From this I inferred that the opposite would occur with you; and as I said before, I love you, and if you have no objections, I love you still.

HERMINE. Well, that is just as it should be.

FELIX. Naturally.

HERMINE. On the other hand, you have not yet told me how you like my new dress.

FELIX. I do not know the value of such works of art, until I see the — dressmaker's bill. You had better ask the experts that will be here this evening. I like you in any dress, even in a simple one.

o

HERMINE. You have no taste.

FELIX. At least none that keeps pace with the current number of the fashion journal. I read this paper too irregularly. In such things I cannot at all compete with our friend Hubert. He is coming this evening, is he not?

HERMINE. We have asked him.

FELIX. Have we?

HERMINE. It would be a thousand pities if he did not come. He dances divinely.

FELIX. It would be horrible! [*Suddenly steps up to her.*] Hermine, either you do not understand me or you do not wish to understand me. Can you not see that this life is a torture for me, that it brings me to despair? Can you not feel that it is my most earnest desire to have my wife for myself and to be able to feel at home in my own house? And if you do not feel it, so much the worse. I am neither a toy nor a dummy to be exhibited for a show; I shall make an end to these doings.

HERMINE. I understand you perfectly; but since the moralizer has developed into a stern tyrant, I must tell you that the time is very ill chosen. I have no desire to continue such a scene ten minutes before the arrival of our guests. I have never given you occasion to doubt my love; you know that I preferred your hand to the most brilliant offers.

FELIX. I suppose I should regard it a great favor!

HERMINE. It was no favor; I have already told you that it was love. If, however, you demand that I shall mope away my youth in a chimney corner; that I shall rave over you all day like a mawkish boarding-house spinster; if you demand that I die of ennui because of my love, then I shall never yield, never! It is my right, my inalienable right, to enjoy my youth, and instead of its being a torture, it should please you when people find your wife charming and do homage to her. I need these attentions; they give wings to my soul, they fill my existence with a thousand delights, for which your humdrum chimney corner can offer me no compensation. The great world at which you sneer animates, charms, intoxicates me. Are not all of you ambitious, you men? You are, every one of you, and why should not we women be likewise? I am ambitious; I want to be the queen of the feast; I want all to envy you your possession of me. Time enough to bury myself within my own four walls, when I am old. But now I am young, I am young; I want to dance, laugh, jest, be vivacious, and this you should not prevent.

FELIX. I find that there is nothing more sad than this everlasting mirth, and nothing more tedious than to amuse oneself so systematically. Do as you please; but, henceforth, I shall no longer play the part of your satellite.

HERMINE. I am of age, and if you think you will be able to justify such conduct to the world, then I release you.

FELIX. I am responsible for my conduct to my own conscience, not to the so-called world, which I despise.

HERMINE. Because you never took the trouble to make its acquaintance without prejudice.

FELIX. It is not worth the trouble.

HERMINE. Perhaps more than your everlasting studies and staying-at-home.

FELIX. Hermine, you are reproaching me for taking my professional duties seriously!

HERMINE. It was not I who began with reproaches, but you.

FELIX. Under such circumstances it will perhaps be better that we be alone together as little as possible; for you — [*blurting it out*] you are a coquette!

HERMINE. And you are a prig!

FELIX [*excitedly walking up and down*]. A very pleasant evening, truly!

HERMINE [*in an injured tone*]. The evening of our first party, too!

FELIX. Yes, now I shall put on my dress suit. [*En exint.*] And I shall take as much time as possible in doing so, as much as possible. [*Exit hurriedly to the right.*]

SCENE V

HERMINE. [*Later*] BAUMANN *and* HUBERT

HERMINE [*alone*]. Such a scene at this time! Oh, it is unpardonable! [*Looks into a hand mirror.*] How do I look? All flushed and agitated. And thus I must receive my guests! [*Calls.*] Baumann!

BAUMANN [*from the drawing-room*]. Everything has been attended to.

HERMINE. Bring me a Seidlitz powder, quickly!

BAUMANN. At once. [*Looking out of the window.*] A carriage has just driven up to the door. Oh, what joy! [*The doorbell is heard ringing.*]

HERMINE. Quickly, take the ladies and gentlemen into the drawing-room!

BAUMANN. At once! [*Exit to the right.*]

HERMINE [*calls after him*]. And do not bring the Seidlitz powder. [*Aside.*] This mood! Heavens, I must smile, I must be amiable! Now all my pleasure is spoiled. [*Goes to the rear.*]

HUBERT [*for whom* BAUMANN *opens the door, enters from the right. He is in traveling dress*]. Dear friend, first of all grant me your pardon for appearing before you at so late an hour and in such questionable attire. But when one has been forced to live for a whole week far from you, there can be no more urgent business, on one's return home, than kissing your hand. I am come directly from the station, and since I had to pass here on my way home, I thought I would stop my carriage in order to — but what do I see? You are in full dress, and this table, these formal preparations. — Do you await guests?

HERMINE [*very much surprised*]. Did you not receive our invitations?

HUBERT. I am thunderstruck, my word of honor! I have been out of town for a week on affairs connected with my estate. Your invitation has probably been lying all this time unopened at my house.

HERMINE. At all events, we hope that —

HUBERT. You may be sure that I shall appear as soon as I have made myself presentable. 'Twas my good angel brought me back. May I ask, who is coming?

HERMINE. Only our best friends. Fortunately, no one has declined.

HUBERT. Charming!

HERMINE. The wife of Government-Counselor Heuer with her four daughters —

HUBERT. So much learning en masse, each one separately is a walking encyclopedia.

HERMINE. Malicious, but true. Then your friend, the painter, Woronzow.

HUBERT. That is to say, he does not paint; he only lives here in order to get inspiration. He has lived here twenty years. He must, by this time, have gathered a marvellous amount of inspiration.

HERMINE [*smiling*]. Slanderous tongue! And what fault have you to find with Graf Walheim?

HUBERT. None, save that he pays too much attention to you.

HERMINE. Further, Baron Marling and his wife.

HUBERT. A beautiful woman.

HERMINE. Ah, she pleases you. She is to sit at your left.

HUBERT. And at my right?

HERMINE. I.

HUBERT. Then no more. You shall be as ever, the most beautiful and the most elegant.

HERMINE. You will say the same thing to your neighbor at the left.

HUBERT. Cruel! You misjudge me. Lady von Marling is a cold beauty, a statue. She speaks as little as if every word cost her six pfennig — doubtless because her husband is the director of telegraphs. You, on the contrary — however, I must not disturb you any longer. I shall fly home and return a transformed man. Permit me —

BAUMANN [*at right, with a Seidlitz powder and a glass half filled with water*]. Here is the Seidlitz powder.

HERMINE [*softly to* BAUMANN]. Did I not tell you not to bring it? How stupid!

BAUMANN [*loudly*]. I thought because Madam was so excited. May it do you good. [*Exit to the right.*]

HUBERT [*aside*]. Something is amiss here. [*Aloud.*]
You are not ill, I hope.

HERMINE. It is nothing, nothing at all! Merely an
error.

HUBERT. No, you cannot deceive me. You are
excited, out of sorts. Do, please, drink the Seidlitz
powder.

HERMINE. But, Baron!

HUBERT [*while he prepares the powder*]. You must
allow me this small service.

HERMINE [*laughing*]. If you compel me —

HUBERT [*after throwing in the second powder*]. It
effervesces! Drink it quickly! [HERMINE *drinks.*] At
one draught! That will make you feel better. That
is right! [*Puts away the glass.*] Do you feel better?

HERMINE [*gayly*]. Certainly! How worried you
are about me.

HUBERT. More than about my own life! Oh, I
see it all. This Seidlitz powder has played the traitor;
it tells me everything clearly and distinctly, everything! Hermine, you are not happy!

HERMINE [*with a forced laugh*]. What a tragic
tone! It does not become you, really.

HUBERT. No matter, when it is a question of your
happiness. I have known Felix since we went to school
together. He is a thoroughly good man, a thoroughly
honorable man, in short, a character, and I am his
friend. But —

HERMINE. No more, sir! I am his wife and demand —

HUBERT. No, I must speak! Your happiness is
so dear to me that I must risk your displeasure. He is
a character; therefore he is also narrow, and because

he is narrow, he is unjust. He does not understand you, he will never understand you; for you —

HERMINE. I forbid you —

HUBERT [*continuing eagerly*]. You — you are also a character, but not like him. You are high-spirited, gifted, intended for a fashionable life. You are born to rule, to command. The man who loves you must needs be at your feet, must needs regard it a favor if you raise him to yourself, fortunate man. Fatal error! How comes this Provence rose in the vegetable garden! No, do not deny it. He offered you but the well-tempered warmth of his study, where you had expected the glowing, flaming rays of passion.

HERMINE. Please go, sir; I must not hear another word from you. My husband may come at any moment. Be silent, or I shall tell him everything.

HUBERT. If you feel that I have not spoken the truth, do so. But you do feel that I have, you know it. It is in vain that you take refuge behind a pride which cannot disarm me, because it is powerless against the strength of my conviction —

HERMINE. That which you call pride is only my anger at your presumption, which I —

HUBERT. Which you must forgive me.

HERMINE. Never — !

HUBERT. Just one more word, Hermine, and then you may condemn me. You knew that I loved you long before Felix entered your house. I had decided to ask for your hand; I wanted to lay my whole self at your feet, for good or evil. Just then a mortal illness confined me to my bed for weeks. My first thought, when I recovered consciousness, was of you; my first glance, when I was able to rise, fell upon the card announcing your engagement. And if I cannot, even now, stifle my feelings, and overcome my grief, do I deserve your anger? Will you not now forgive me?

HERMINE. Perhaps —

HUBERT [*with a rapid change of tone*]. And may I ask you for the first waltz this evening?

HERMINE. For aught I care, if you will only go now.

SCENE VI

HERMINE. HUBERT. FELIX [*in full dress, enters at the left*]. [*Later*] BAUMANN

FELIX. Good evening, Hubert.

HUBERT. I am merely here for the time being, Felix. I came directly from the station and have only this moment heard from your wife that I have been invited for this evening.

BAUMANN [*from the right*]. Madam, the cook wishes to ask you something. It is something about the goose liver.

HUBERT. Capital old fellow, this Baumann.

HERMINE. He is not of much use any longer. You will excuse me, Baron. We shall expect you later.

HUBERT. My dear madam! [*Exeunt* HERMINE *and* BAUMANN *to the right.*]

SCENE VII

FELIX. HUBERT

HUBERT [*aside*]. If I work things cleverly now, all is won. [*Aloud.*] Felix, I suppose you have had a small scene here, somewhat of a diplomatic understanding?

FELIX. How do you know about it?

HUBERT. I guessed it from some allusions made by old Baumann. — Poor friend!

FELIX. Your sympathy is in rather bad taste, I must say.

HUBERT. Because it is candid. Your wife is the best woman in the world, beautiful, amiable, clever, and, believe me, she is a character.

FELIX. At any rate, you know her better than I do. It is true, we are married; but we see each other so seldom.

HUBERT. She seeks pleasure, too much so, let us say. Why are you so weak as to let her have things her own way? Women like to be impressed. My great experience —

FELIX. Does not suit this case.

HUBERT. It does, I assure you. Women are puzzles; but he who has thoroughly solved one, knows all. I have been in this school long enough —

FELIX. And have paid dearly enough for the lesson.

HUBERT. Very dearly. The principal thing, however, is the method. Show yourself for once in all your dignity; be harsh, tyrannical, and if that has no effect, be intolerable. At first she will cry, then sulk, and then she will throw herself into your arms, [*aside*] or in mine.

FELIX. Perhaps you are right. But in order to do so, we must be alone, by ourselves, and for that there is, at present, not the least prospect.

HUBERT. This evening.

FELIX. At our first party? We shall be able to say very little to each other this evening. At such times, our whole conversation consists in her whispering to me to take away her lemonade glass, or to engage one of the wall-flowers for the quadrille. Under such circumstances, it is impossible for me to be tyrannical.

HUBERT. Certainly; but follow my advice as soon as possible. You will excuse me if I come somewhat late. My dress requires arrangement. Auf wiedersehen, — poor friend!

FELIX. The deuce. Spare me your sympathy!

HUBERT [*aside, in exit*]. He does not suspect how I pity him. [*Exit to the right.*]

SCENE VIII

FELIX. [*A moment later*] HERMINE.
[*Then*] BAUMANN

FELIX [*alone*]. Shall I try Hubert's recipe? Or shall I find another for myself? This, however, is not the time for it; we may be interrupted by our guests at any moment. I must play the host, however inhospitable I may feel. It were best to pretend illness and go to bed; but my bed has been taken down, and goodness knows where it is to be found. Perhaps I could decamp and take a room at a hotel for the night. No, that would be cowardly! I shall remain. [HERMINE *appears in the drawing-room.*] Here she is. I believe she is really angry at me. [*Sits down on the sofa to the right.*]

HERMINE [*entering, aside*]. It is already half-past eight. They are very late, in all probability, because no one wants to be the first to arrive. [*Seats herself in an armchair to the left. Aside.*] He is angry at me.

I cannot help it.   Hubert is right; he does not understand me.   I am a Provence rose in a vegetable garden. [*Short pause, during which they look at each other.*]

FELIX.   Hermine!

HERMINE.   What?

FELIX.   Should we not go into the drawing-room?

HERMINE.   As soon as any one comes.

FELIX.   Very well.   [*Short pause.*]

HERMINE.   This waiting is tedious.

FELIX.   Yes, indeed.

HERMINE.   I am freezing.

FELIX.   Have the heat turned on.

HERMINE.   Impossible; the heat would become unbearable later.   Please hand me my ermine wrap.

FELIX.   With pleasure.   [*Both arise; he helps her on with her wrap.*]

HERMINE.   Thanks.   [*They sit down again in their former places.   After a short pause, the doorbell rings. They jump up.*]

FELIX.   Some one is coming.

HERMINE.   At last!

FELIX.   Shall we not go to meet them?

HERMINE.   It's surely the Marlings.   They are always punctual.   [*They go to the rear.*]

BAUMANN [*coming towards them from the drawing-room*].   Dear madam, they are — here.

HERMINE.   Who, the Marlings?

BAUMANN.   No, the goose livers.   They were just brought.

HERMINE [*disappointed*].   Oh!

FELIX.   Go back to your post, Baumann.

BAUMANN.   At once.   [*As he starts to go to the right, he glances through the window.*]   A carriage!

HERMINE. Hurry! Open the carriage door!

BAUMANN. It has passed. Oh, how I wish they would come! [*Exit to the right.*]

SCENE IX

FELIX. HERMINE

HERMINE [*sits down again*]. How tiresome!

FELIX. Terrible! [*Also sits down.*] Hubert will come rather late.

HERMINE. Is that so?

FELIX. It has been a fine day, somewhat raw, to be sure.

HERMINE. What are you leading up to?

FELIX. I am making an effort to begin a conversation.

HERMINE. A very weak effort.

FELIX. You should have helped me.

HERMINE. What can we talk about now?

FELIX. Really, I have no idea.

HERMINE [*rises and goes to the table*]. I wonder are the place-cards properly arranged. [*Pretends to be busy at the right side of the table.*]

FELIX [*goes to the left side of the table*]. Where do I sit, anyhow?

HERMINE. Just where you are standing now.

FELIX. As far as possible from you.

HERMINE. It could not be arranged otherwise.

FELIX. I am convinced of that. [*Looks at several cards.*] At my right old mother Heuer, at my left, the aunt of Graf Walheim — charming, what provision you have made for me!

HERMINE. I had to provide for my guests, first of all.

FELIX. Undoubtedly. [*Sits down at the table and pretends to be speaking to some one beside him.*] Dear madam, you go to many parties, I suppose? Will you have white or red?

HERMINE. What are you doing?

FELIX. I am arranging a rehearsal of our conversation at table this evening. It is only in order that I may be sure I know how to act. [*Continues rapidly.*] Do you often go to the theater, dear madam? No? Naturally! I see you frequently in the lobby; I had the pleasure at the last concert, too. You say the pleasure was all yours; no, indeed, it was all mine! Do you like the new tenor? His high C is more than high; it is inspired. He is said to come from a very good family. He has a brother in Manchester, who is a rich silk merchant; there is a rumor that he is the possessor of millions. His sister is married to a building contractor, whom I met in Baden-Baden. Do you like Baden-Baden?

HERMINE [*laughing*]. You are ludicrous!

FELIX. Do not interrupt. Yes, dear madam, away, over there, in the distant horizon, sits my wife. I would much rather be conversing with her at this moment than with you; but fate has decreed otherwise. Shall I put another piece of calf's head on your plate?

HERMINE. Your rehearsal was not at all bad. I never thought you could be so delightfully malicious.

FELIX [*rising*]. And now you perceive it for the first time, after we have been married four months, and one moment before the arrival of our guests!

And this time, too, I am but the makeshift, who, at most, is useful only to help you pass a few tedious moments.

HERMINE. Did you ever take the trouble to entertain me?

FELIX. I only took the trouble to try and make you happy.

HERMINE. I am happy when I am merry.

FELIX. I am harder to please; I demand much more in order to be happy. I could not find it in me to trifle with you, once I had decided to live with you.

HERMINE. Listen! Did you not hear anything?

FELIX. No.

HERMINE. I thought some one was ringing.

FELIX. You were mistaken. [*The bell rings.*]

HERMINE. But now! [*She takes off the ermine wrap, and goes towards the rear.*]

FELIX [*aside*]. What a pity!

SCENE X

The former. LOTTE [*from the right*]

HERMINE. What is it? Who has come?

LOTTE. The hairdresser. He forgot his curling irons when he was here.

HERMINE. Take them to him. [*Aside.*] How annoying, to wait so long! [*Exit* LOTTE *to the right.*]

SCENE XI

FELIX. HERMINE

HERMINE [*goes to the window and softly drums on the pane*].

FELIX [*seats himself again at the table and pours himself a glass of wine*].

HERMINE [*turns and sees it*]. Felix, what are you doing!

FELIX. I am thirsty. [*He drinks.*]

HERMINE. Inexcusable!

FELIX. A charming state of affairs. I am in my own house and should like to make myself comfortable in the evening; but instead of that, I must sit here in my dress suit and be bored. I have cigars and must not smoke them; I have wine and must not drink it; I have a wife and must not be alone with her. My study is cleared out and serves as a wardrobe. My desk is in the store-room; my books are in the linen closet; where my comfortable easy chair has gotten to, the gods alone can tell. I am furious and must play the amiable man. And all this for whom? For people, not one of whom interests me in the least; for whom, in fact, I do not care. Why, I am not the family physician of even one of them. Yes, our most gracious Madam Government-Counselor at my right, and our most charming lady-aunt at my left, you are of the utmost indifference to me. [*Rises as if to make a toast.*] And you, my worthy guests, make yourselves at home; for I should be very glad were you indeed at home. With this sentiment, I raise my glass and say, fare ye well!

HERMINE [*laughing*]. Your malice is irresistible!

FELIX. But in vain. They are coming, all of them; they will eat their fill, they will gossip, they will dance, and I must smile to them. But my smile will be nothing but a sugar-coated dynamite bomb. Hermine, how different things might be! How comfortably we could sit here together — by ourselves, and chat —

HERMINE. And yawn. A whole evening by ourselves! I have no idea what we could do to pass the time.

FELIX. We should not try to pass the time; we should be glad if the moments linger.

HERMINE. But we must find some diversion.

FELIX. On the contrary, we should spend the time calmly. We should give audiences to our good spirits, the shy house spirits who are frightened away by noise, and are summoned forth by quietness. They dare not appear at parties; but when two people are alone, by themselves, two people who love — hush, here they come! Do you not hear?

HERMINE. No, not yet.

FELIX. But you will hear them. There is still too much dance music ringing in your ears. They are already here and they are whispering of the charm and blessing of home life. And suddenly this apparition of the invitations, the ball-room, and the long tables disappears. We are in my study, naturally not in the one that is cleared out; let us imagine it in its normal condition.

HERMINE. I imagine it.

FELIX. I am sitting in my comfortable easy chair [*sits down in armchair*] and am smoking a cigar. May I light one?

HERMINE. No, indeed!

FELIX. Then let's imagine it. You are sitting at some little distance from me, on a low chair. Will you be so kind?

HERMINE [*sits down in an armchair*]. Well, I am sitting here.

P

FELIX. I sharply close a heavy book which I have been reading till now; you lay aside your needle-work which is, naturally, to be a surprise for my birthday.

HERMINE. What next?

FELIX. Now we are glad that we are in our cosy room, during this blinding snowstorm.

HERMINE [*looking out*]. It is not snowing at all.

FELIX. That's nothing. We are pretending that it is; it will put us in the right frame of mind. My lamp throws its pleasant glow upon your dear face, and I find you charming in your simple house dress. The snowstorm becomes more and more violent; you are apprehensive and move nearer to me. [HERMINE *moves her chair*.] The wind whistles and howls, and we hear a broken window-pane go clattering down from the second floor on to the pavement. You become more apprehensive and move still nearer.

HERMINE. Still nearer? [*She moves very close to him.*]

FELIX. I dispel your apprehension with a kiss.

HERMINE. Can we not imagine that too?

FELIX. Impossible. That I must give you [*kisses her*].

HERMINE. So far, I like the thing very well.

FELIX. You place your hand in mine. [HERMINE *does so*.] We let the events of the past go in procession before our mind's eye, and dream of the future, where we —

HERMINE [*quickly*]. Let us rather remain at the past.

FELIX. As you wish. We confess all sorts of small secrets of the days when our love was beginning, of the time when you were still my unattainable ideal, about whom I raved at a distance.

HERMINE. Yes, you were dreadfully timid, and I used to laugh at you.

FELIX. There you are. And I bribed old Baumann to spy on you. Thus I discovered —

HERMINE. What?

FELIX. That you had confided to your mother that I danced quite miserably.

HERMINE. But I secretly painted your portrait. At first, you see, I persuaded myself that it was only your interesting head that had captivated the artist within me.

FELIX. Fortunately, however, you were no artist.

HERMINE. And your head was not all interesting. I soon discovered that the thing that really interested me was your heart.

FELIX. And since then you have given up painting altogether.

HERMINE. Oh, I can still paint. I'll wager I can make a good likeness of you in a few strokes.

FELIX. I don't believe you can.

HERMINE. You shall see.

FELIX [*pulling out his memorandum book*]. Here is my notebook. You may draw me in it.

HERMINE. But you will have to sit very quietly.

FELIX. Like a pillar of salt.

HERMINE [*begins to draw*]. Head more to the left; now a little more to the right. [*She raises his head.*] Now, look happy.

FELIX. If you wish, I shall even look happy.

HERMINE [*drawing*]. No, — no, it is not a likeness.

FELIX [*takes the book and looks at it*]. Can this be I? It looks like Samuel in "Der Freischütz."

HERMINE [*sighing*]. I have forgotten a great deal. Why do I never have time?

FELIX. Because you have too much time.

HERMINE. It is really sad that I should never have time.

FELIX. You must pretend to be sick again, as at that time.

HERMINE. Yes, I only did that in order that I might be able to speak to you.

FELIX. I know. "You must come at once to Mademoiselle," said old Baumann. "Mademoiselle has a cold." I did not wait to hear another word, but instead of declaring my love, I only felt your pulse six times, although it was entirely unnecessary, and read you a lecture on colds and their deeper significance.

HERMINE. Then you wrote a prescription, which I took up as though it were a love letter.

FELIX. At home, however, I wrote something far different. Let me confess — but do not be frightened — it was an awful mixture.

HERMINE. Surely, not poison!

FELIX. Oh, no, verses.

HERMINE [*laughing*]. Why did you not show them to me?

FELIX. Thank goodness, I never sank so low! But it was touching, heartrending:

> "My bleeding heart
> Suffers great smart,
> And in my breast
> There is no rest.
> My thoughts are of you,
> And I always feel blue,
> And this indescribable care
> Haunts me like a nightmare."

HERMINE. Poor fellow!

FELIX. And then, my modes of address. At first I called you simply, "Lovely creature," later "Sweet child," or "Goddess of my songs," and once, when you did not give me a favor in the cotillion —

HERMINE [*frankly*]. There were no more.

FELIX. Then I felt out of tune with the whole world, and I called you: "Serpent deceiving." This I rhymed with, "Oh, how I am grieving!" It was simply awful!

HERMINE. "Serpent deceiving," — that is the language of real jealousy. I must give you a kiss for that.

FELIX. Gratefully accepted. [*They kiss. The door-bell rings; they jump up.*]

HERMINE. Oh, these everlasting disturbances!

FELIX. It is really inconsiderate of our guests not to leave us alone.

HERMINE. Why are they so late! Now they might have stayed at home altogether.

FELIX. You cannot expect that, after you have yourself invited them.

SCENE XII

The former. BAUMANN [*from the right*]

FELIX [*to* BAUMANN]. Well, who is here?

BAUMANN. Nobody.

HERMINE. Who rang then?

BAUMANN. I hardly dare to say it.

FELIX. Who was it? Out with it!

BAUMANN. Myself. I went out into the street to see whether any of the carriages were coming;

just then the door clapped to behind me and locked me out.

HERMINE. How provoking! See to it that we are not again needlessly disturbed.

FELIX. Yes, allow no one to enter. Guard the way with your life. Barricade the door! Pull up the drawbridge! I shall defend myself against our guests to the last drop of blood!

BAUMANN. You are surely jesting; we have delighted so long in the thought —

HERMINE. Yes, we have been awfully delighted! Go, now, Baumann.

BAUMANN. At once. [*Exit to the right.*]

SCENE XIII

FELIX. HERMINE

HERMINE. Felix!

FELIX. What do you wish?

HERMINE. Do you really think that the people who will come to-night are false friends?

FELIX. At least not true ones.

HERMINE. But Hubert, surely, is your friend?

FELIX. Perhaps. He has good cause to be thankful to me.

HERMINE. Thankful to you? Why?

FELIX. I once saved his life.

HERMINE. Did you? You never told me about it.

FELIX. Why should I have told you?

HERMINE. Tell me, please!

FELIX. Well, it was shortly before our engagement; Baron Hubert had a small affair of honor. It had long been whispered in society that he was assiduously devoted to a lady. But the lady, as it happened, was already married.

HERMINE. Married? [*Aside.*] Oh, the hypocrite!

FELIX. One day, the insulted husband found out about this gallantry; they fought a duel, and Baron Hubert was badly wounded.

HERMINE. Go on, go on.

FELIX. The physicians had already given him up. I was his schoolmate, and made every effort to save him. I was successful; that is all.

HERMINE [*aside*]. And he — oh, fie! How could I be so blind! And are these the people we seek to please! [*Aloud.*] Felix, perhaps the terrible snowstorm is preventing the people from coming?

FELIX [*gayly*]. But it is not snowing at all.

HERMINE. I wish it were.

FELIX. Are you in earnest?

HERMINE. I still have so much to tell you; and what do we really care about these strangers?

FELIX. I agree with you.

HERMINE. Let them come; we shall act as though they were not here.

FELIX. If you think —

HERMINE [*passionately*]. Felix, I deserved this lesson; I — I —

FELIX. What is the matter?

HERMINE [*throws herself into his arms*]. I love you, Felix!

FELIX [*earnestly*]. Hermine, my wife!

HERMINE. You fool, why did you not open my eyes sooner! Could I believe in the joys of a world that I had never seen? In this small world, which is yet greater than the large one? Let me be your pupil; teach me the magic of that deep, quiet happiness that is a thousand times better than loud, tumultuous joys. Let us fly far, far from the world!

FELIX. Need we fly any further than into our own house, Hermine? Do these four walls not give us shelter enough? Let us live for each other here, we and our true friends. That self-seeking and empty society, those people who are agreeable only out of calculation, who do one homage out of vanity, who know merely friendliness, not friendship, amiableness instead of love, — those people shall cross our threshold to-night for the first and last time!

HERMINE. For the first and last time! Just look here! [*She hurries to the table and changes several cards.*]

FELIX [*in front, aside*]. Who said there are no miracles! We are alone for the first time in four months on the evening of our first great party. [*Observes* HERMINE *and goes to the table.*] What are you doing?

HERMINE. Look here!

FELIX. I no longer sit near the two relics of the good old days! Where then?

HERMINE [*triumphantly*]. Here!

FELIX [*following her motion*]. Near you? What will people say?

HERMINE. Whatever they please. We two should be together.

FELIX. That is what I say.

HERMINE [*drawing out a card*]. Here is my dance card. Have the goodness to engage me at once.

FELIX. For which dances?

HERMINE. For as many as possible.

Felix [*writing on the card*].   Just as you wish.

Hermine.   And you must court me; that is my only condition.   How vexed they will all be!

Felix.   That shall be attended to promptly.   Yes, how bored they will be!

Hermine.   And we shall move the hands of the clocks two hours forward, so that they will leave early.

Felix.   Yes, we could also get up a conflagration; such a general panic —

Hermine.   I agree; I hate them all!

Felix.   I have never been so happy since our engagement.   I must again write poetry:

> Oh, my dear wife
> You were very ill;
> Your cure is now rife.
> Praise God, we will!

Hermine.   Magnificent!   Yes, I am cured forever.

Felix [*looking at his watch*].   And do you know what time it is?

Hermine.   No.

Felix.   Five minutes of ten.

Hermine.   Impossible!   And our guests —

Felix.   I can't understand it!   Has heaven performed a miracle in favor of a poor husband?   Experience is against it.

Hermine.   This is absolutely uncanny.   Why, I wrote all the invitations myself.

Felix.   And did you mail them yourself?

Hermine.   No, I gave them to Lotte.   She surely can't have — [*rings*].

SCENE XIV

Felix. Hermine. Lotte. [*Later*] Baumann

Lotte [*comes from the drawing-room*]. Did madam ring?

Hermine. The other day I gave you some invitations; did you mail them?

Lotte. I gave them to Baumann, because he was just going out.

Felix [*opens the door at right and calls*]. Baumann!

Baumann [*from the right*]. Did you call? Everything has been attended to.

Felix. And the invitations?

Baumann [*taken aback*]. The invitations? I do not know —

Lotte. But I gave them to you last Wednesday morning.

Baumann [*repeating mechanically*]. Last Wednesday morning. Did you? I must have attended to them; I must — [*reflecting*]. Of course I have attended to them! I wore this very coat that day. I stuck them into this pocket, and —

Felix [*catching hold of* Baumann's *pocket*]. And here they are still.

Baumann. Oh, unhappy mortal that I am! [*Sinks down upon the sofa.*]

Felix [*pulling a large number of small envelopes of the same size out of* Baumann's *pocket*]. This is charming! No wonder not one of them declined. Our whole party is to be found in the pocket of old Baumann. [*He breaks open one of the invitations and reads.*] "Dr. and Mrs. Volkart have the honor" — etc., etc. The other invitations, probably, contain the same words. Victory, we are saved!

HERMINE.   And I have been running about like mad, for the last three days! And look at all the fine food!

FELIX.   We shall eat it all by ourselves.

HERMINE.   Lotte, run to the kitchen, quickly! Save as much as possible! [*Exit* LOTTE *to the right.*]

FELIX [*to* BAUMANN, *who is still lying upon the sofa as if stunned*].   Brace up, old brick! It isn't a matter of life and death.

BAUMANN [*contritely*].   Oh, madam, sir, send me away; I do not deserve any better.   It is true, I had the honor and the pleasure of carrying madam in my arms; but I am no longer fit for anything. The thought that our dear little baroness had become a woman, a woman who gives parties. This thought gave me happiness beyond measure, and in my joy, in my happiness, I must have forgotten —

HERMINE.   You are already forgiven, Baumann.

FELIX.   Forgiven? No, on the contrary, were I a prince, Baumann, I should confer upon you, at least, a patent of nobility. You have given me the most agreeable disappointment of my whole life. Give me your hand.

HERMINE.   And give me the other. [*The bell rings.*]

BAUMANN [*starting up*].   Now some one is coming. [*Hurries off to the right.*]

FELIX.   Credulous soul! He still has hopes.

HERMINE.   But what if guests did come —

FELIX.   Without being invited! Oh, no. To-morrow, however, I shall have it published broadcast that Dr. and Mrs. Volkart will be at home this winter only in the morning, from five to six.   And now —

HERMINE. Now we shall celebrate our party — by ourselves. The table is covered, the rooms are brilliantly illuminated, we are in full evening dress, and we shall be riotously merry.

FELIX. And have a capital supper. Do you hear now what the house-spirits whisper?

HERMINE. Very clearly.

BAUMANN [*returning*]. The pianist has come.

FELIX. Then tell him to sit down at once at the grand piano in the ball-room and play a waltz. [*Exit* BAUMANN *through the drawing-room, with a deep bow.*] Madam, may I ask you for the first waltz?

HERMINE [*pulling out her dance card*]. Sir, you have already engaged me for it some time ago. [*From behind the scene come the strains of a waltz.*]

FELIX. Your arm, madam!

HERMINE. Forever! [*Exeunt both through drawing-room. The music continues. The stage remains empty for a second. The bell rings.*]

BAUMANN [*comes from the drawing-room and goes to the window*]. Who is ringing again? [*Opens the window and looks out.*] It is Herr von Berkow; I recognize his carriage. But it is my master's wish to remain alone. [*The bell rings again, more loudly. He closes the window.*] Yes, yes, ring as long as you please. I wouldn't dream of opening. [*Sits down on the sofa, crossing his arms upon his breast.*]

[FELIX *and* HERMINE *become visible dancing in the drawing-room. While the waltz continues and the bell is again violently rung, the curtain slowly falls.*]

THE RIDER OF DREAMS [1]

BY

RIDGELY TORRENCE

[1] Reprinted by permission of the author and by special arrangement with The Macmillan Company, Publishers.

For permission to perform this play application must be made to the author in care of the publisher.

Ridgely Torrence was born a native of Ohio, in 1875, was graduated from Princeton, and is known as a writer principally through his volume of verse called "The House of a Hundred Lights." But in April, 1918, came a production of three plays — folk-plays for a folk theater — performed by a company of negro players in the Old Garden Theatre of New York. In these is found vivid drama selected from a vast storehouse of material which may lead, perhaps, to the establishment of a folk theater. In the three plays, "Granny Maume," an impressive tragedy; "Simon of Cyrene," a very suggestive allegory; "The Rider of Dreams," a comedy resembling the Irish drama in its mysticism, are introduced the author's ability to show not only the imagination, piety, superstition, humor, and simplicity of the negro, but the dissembling relations between the two races. The author has painted with sympathy, power, and delicate art. In "The Rider of Dreams" there is a burst of poetry, and a display of the writer's sensitiveness to psychological effects.

THE RIDER OF DREAMS

SCENE: *Night in a room used for kitchen, dining-room, and laundry by a colored family. A lamp is set upon a central table laid with a spotless table cloth. Baskets of clothes stand on several chairs. At the back is a cook-stove and to the left of this a door. There are also doorways at the right and left of the room. LUCY SPARROW, a worn, sweet-faced woman of forty, is sprinkling clothes at an ironing-board at left with her back turned to the table beside which, on a high stool, is perched a small boy, BOOKER SPARROW. Both the boy and the woman as well as the room show a painstaking neatness despite the disorder necessary in the process of a professional " wash."*

LUCY. Who make you?

BOOKER. God. Ain't the mush done now?

LUCY. It's done but I ain't done wif you. You got to learn good befo' you can eat good. Who redeem you?

BOOKER. Christ. I'll stop being hungry for it if I don't get it now.

LUCY. Bettah lose youah wishes an' youah ahms an' laigs an' everything youah body's fix wif an' keep youah immortal soul. Who sanctify you?

BOOKER. The Holy Ghost. I don't want nothing but mush.

LUCY.   Well, you ain' goin' to git hit twell you luhns de questions.   What de chief en' of man?

BOOKER.   Chief end of man is to glorify God and enjoy himself for ever.

LUCY [*coming swiftly forward and confronting him with a threatening look*].   Enjoy *hisself!*   I ain' neveh teach you dat.   You know betteh'n dat.   Man got no right to enjoy hisself.   He got to enjoy Gawd.   You knows dat as well as you knows eatin'.   An' you got to say it an' what's mo' you got to live it.   Now what de chief en' of man?

BOOKER.   Enjoy God forever.

LUCY.   Dat's mo' like it.   [*She turns her back and going to the ironing-board resumes her labors, still talking.*]   I'm raisin' you fo' de Kingdom an' you'ah goin' in de Kingdom ef pushin' 'll lan' you dere.   Because dis time anutheh yeah you may be in some lonesome graveyard.   [*Singing.*]

> In some lonesome graveyard
> Oh, Lawd, no time to pray.

[*As she sings* BOOKER *stealthily slips off his stool and going around to the opposite side of the table takes a spoon with which he approaches a dish set upon a warming-shelf fixed to the stove.   He furtively dips his spoon in the dish and begins to eat.* LUCY *continuing her singing.*]

> Play on youah harp, little David,
> Little Davy, how ole are you?
> "I'm only twelve yeahs ole."

[*She turns and discovers* BOOKER.]   What!   You stealin'!   I'll show you!   [*She gives him a cuff and a shake, depositing him again upon his stool.*]   You shorely is on de way to de fieh but I'm goin' pluck you out ef it skins you alive. Steal, will you? What de sevenf commandment?

BOOKER [*sniveling*]. Thou shalt not steal.

LUCY. See dat. You knows it but you des won't live hit. Well, I'm goin' live it into you. I'm goin' slap sin out of you. [*She gives him another shake.*] An' de grace into you. Now you say dat commandment sevumty times sevun. Begin. Say hit.

BOOKER. Thou shalt not steal. Thou shalt not steal — [*The door at back opens and* MADISON SPARROW *stands in the doorway looking on the scene within the room. He is a tall, loose-jointed, lazy-looking man. In one hand he carries a long green bag.*]

MADISON [*after a survey of the situation*]. What de boy do?

LUCY. He steal, dat what he do.

MADISON. Um. What he steal?

LUCY. Mush. I tole him not to tech it.

MADISON. Well, he was hongry, weren't he?

LUCY. Dat ain' de p'int. 'Tweren't his till I give it to him.

MADISON [*places the bag carefully by the doorway, throws his hat upon it, then seats himself at the table*]. Bring on dat mush. I'm tia'hd of dese fool doin's. Dey ain't no git ahead wif um. Ef de boy wants mush let him git mush.

LUCY [*placing food before him on the table*]. Yes, but not rob it.

MADISON. Who talkin' 'bout robbin'?

LUCY. Madison, dat's de wrong kin' of trash fo' dis baby to heah. Go lay down, honey. Tek de bowl wif you. [BOOKER *whines but takes a dish and goes to doorway at left.*]

Q

MADISON. No, hit's de right kin' of preachin'. I'm tia'hd of all dat ol' fashion way of doin'. Ef I wuz to wuk my ahms off dat ol' fashion way I couldn't git no furder.

LUCY. What you bin wukin' at dis yeah, Madison?

MADISON. Dat's it. You know dat I'm bin lookin' fo' it and couldn't find hit.

LUCY. What you wuk at last yeah?

MADISON. You knows I wuk in the strippin' factory.

LUCY. Jes' two weeks.

MADISON. You knows I wuk till I strain my back. But neveh min' about all dat. I done tuhn oveh a new leaf. I goin' to be a business man. I goin' to let de otheh man wuk.

LUCY. S'posin' everybody was to do dat way.

MADISON. Let 'em do hit. I don' ask nothin' of nobody. I goin' to have every toof in my haid covehed wif gol'. I'll get youah'n an Book's fix dat way too. I goin' to have plenty society grub in me all de time. I ain' goin' to let my fam'ly suffeh. I got too sweet a disposishun fo' dat. I'll git 'em whateveh I want.

BOOKER [*lingering in doorway*]. When you get rich will you get me the guitar, Daddy?

[LUCY *waves* BOOKER *through doorway. He vanishes.*]

MADISON. I'll git it an' I got it. Watch me now. [*He goes over to the bag by the door and reaching in it produces a handsome guitar.*] Dat's de beginnin' er good times, boy.

LUCY [*with sickening apprehension*]. Madison, where you git dat insterment?

MADISON. Dat's de Lawd's insterment, Lucy. He done pervide it.

LUCY. Oh, Madison, dat ain' youah'n.

MADISON. 'Tis now, honey.

LUCY. No, youah las' dime you spent Sunday an'
I ain' give you no money since. You got it wifout
payin' for it. You charged it.

MADISON. Yassah, I got it wifout paying for it an'
I going to keep on a-gettin' it wifout payin' for hit as
long as de gittin's good.

LUCY. How you like to be treat dat way?

MADISON. What way?

LUCY. If you was keepin' a store, to have folks
charge things when dey didn' know how dey could pay.

MADISON. I'm willin' fo' to be treat dat way ef dey
can do hit. Let 'em come an' git my things if dey finds
any.

LUCY [*breaking down*]. Oh, I cain' stan' hit. Youah
sinkin' fas' down to de fiery lake an' you's pullin' my
Baby down too.

MADISON. No, I's raisin' him up an' I goin' to lan'
us all in a sof' place on dat Easy Street I heah em singin'
'bout so long wifout seein'.

LUCY [*suddenly examining the guitar*]. Wheah you
git dis guitar?

MADISON. What guitar?

LUCY. Dis. Oh, Madison, dis is 'Zek'l Williams'
own guitar dat he wouldn' sell. Dis is de guitar dat
nobody couldn' buy. How you come by it?

MADISON. Look heah, woman. You ack like I
stole de guitar. You don't think I'm a thief, do you?

LUCY. How you come by hit?

MADISON. I got it off Wilson Byrd.

LUCY. Dat sneakin' w'ite man. How'd he git it?

MADISON. I didn' ask him.

LUCY. What you give him fo' hit?

MADISON. Oh, dat's anotheh story. Him an' me's goin' in business togetheh.

LUCY. Oh, Madison, dat w'ite man stole dis guitar. Oh, take it back dis minute an' snatch youah soul from de bu'nin'.

MADISON. Who, me? What you tak me fo', gal? Take back a guitar to de rich man, de man what own de very house we live in!

LUCY. Well, we soon will buy it.

MADISON. Dat's right. We will. But dat ain' de question. I didn' git dis guitar fo' to return it, I git it fo' to play it. I boun' to play it cause I'm goin' to be er rich man soon an' I got to have a plenty music in me.

LUCY. You goin' to git rich playin' guitar?

MADISON [*laughing comfortably*]. Eh, yah, yah. Whoopee! No, indeedy. I flies higher dan music flies. I'm one er dese heah kine er 'lectioneerin' mens which make dere money work fo' um. Dey sen's one dollah out in de heat an' sweats her twell she rolls home wif anutheh.

LUCY. How you goin' to put money out, Madison, lessen you wuks an' gits de money?

MADISON [*cunningly*]. Oh, don' yo' botheh youah haid long er dat. I bin down low and folks trample me des same as a wu'm but now I'm goin' spread my wings an' sting 'em like a king bee. Whaffo' I lay dere an' let'm trample me? 'Twere because I lack conference. I puts my 'pen'ance on dis promis', I puts my 'pen'ance on dat, an' dey all fails me.

LUCY. You ain't neveh put youah trus' in Gawd.

MADISON. Yassuh, I did, an' Gawd He up an' gimme de go-by too. What He bin doin' fo' me? Nuthin'. Now I goin' spit on my han's an' whu'll in an' trus' myse'f. An' I feels lots betteh. I can feel conferdence wukin' all oveh me. I casts 'em all off. I'm lookin' out fo' myse'f. M-m-m — It took me long time to git heah but now I'm heah let 'em look out for me. [*His voice rises to a chant.*]

M-m-m — Midnight on de sea. All de lights out. I'm carryin' hod on Jacob' laddeh to build me a new house an' I'm buildin' it high, man. Don' tech me. I'm a flame of fieh an' I'll singe you sho'. If dey asks fo' me tell 'em say, "I saw somethin' sailin' up but he was headin' fo' a high hill on de sun an' my eyes failed me." Tell 'em say, "He had de fo' win's runnin' like stallions to fetch up wif him but dey carried 'em out, an' buried 'em in the valley. He bus' dere hea'ts!" Tell 'em say, "He was herdin' lightnin's like sheep an' dey wuz too slow an' he picked 'em up an' sheared 'em an' sent 'em home."

Dat's me, I'm de one you'll be talkin' 'bout. Fer why? 'Cause I cas' off ever'thing an' I puts my trus' in myself an' nuthin' can't hole me. De mo' I says it de mo' I feels conferdence. I feels it a-wukin'.

LUCY. You goin' to wuk, Madison?

MADISON. Yes, indeedy. I got to wuk an' wuk ha'd. I can't shirk none.

LUCY. What wuk you goin' to do?

MADISON. I'm a stock brokin' man. I goin' into de stock brokin' business tomorrer.

LUCY. How?

MADISON. Buyin' an' sellin', dat's how an' which too.

LUCY. De Devil's wrastlin' wif you, Madison, an' you's perishin' fas'. Ef you keeps on in dis paf you'll lan' mongs' de rocks er mournin'. You's let somebody tu'n you roun'.

MADISON. Not me. Nobody can't tu'n me roun'.
I dreamed it an' I dreamed it right, face fo'mos' an' on
de run.

LUCY. How dream?

MADISON. Las' night an' day befo' yistiddy night
an' night befo' dat. I wuz layin' groanin', "O Lawd,
how long," an' I heah a voice say, "Git up an' come
a-runnin'." Looks up an' sees a fine w'ite saddle hoss.
Hoss say,

> "Ride me right an' I'll guide you right."

On I gits an' off he goes, slick as a rancid transom
car. Comes to high hill lookin' down on de sun an'
moon. Hoss stop an' say,

> "Brung you heah to give you noos
> De worl' is youahn to pick an' choose."

I ax him "How dat?" Hoss say:

> "How is how an' why is why,
> Buy low an' sell high."

I say to him, "I got no money to buy. Wheah I
goin' git de fun's to buy low?" Hoss respon':

> "Trus' yo'se'f an' take youah own,
> Git de meat an' leave de bone,
> Bus' de nut an' fling em de shell,
> Ride an' let em walk a spell,
> Findeh's keepeh's, loseh's weepeh's,
> I hope dese few lines find you well."

I ax him who tole him all dis an' hoss say:

> "Ole hoss *Grab* will nevah balk,
> All dis heah is w'ite man talk."

Dat what de hoss say to me in my true dream ev'y night dis week an' I'm a-goin' to bide by hit twell de las' er pea time. 'Cause I'm er true dreameh an' my mammy she wuz befo' me.

LUCY. What come of de hoss in de dream, Madison?

MADISON. Dat's all. Hoss went up in smoke an' I come down in bed.

LUCY. Hoss went up in smoke! No, hit went down in smoke an' fiah.

MADISON. Now look-a heah, woman. I'm goin' to make you a good livin' f'um now on. I'm goin' into business termorrer. I'm goin' in de specalatin' wu'k. I'm goin' to buy low an' sell high.

LUCY. What kin you buy wif? You got no money.

MADISON [*hesitating but collecting his forces gradually*]. Oh, ain't I tell you 'bout dat? I got it in de dream.

LUCY. In de dream?

MADISON. Um hmmm. You know dat hoss I tole you 'bout. Well'm, jes' fo' we pa'ted he prance up th'ough a starry fiel' an' come to a gyarden fence. Oveh dat fence he lep an', man, she was a fine gyarden. "Whose patch dish yer?" I say to him. Hoss say: "If you asks me grab what you see."

Den he reaches down an' pulls up a tu'nip wif his teef an' gives it to me an' say,

"Dis gyarden truck will fetch you luck."

[*He watches* LUCY *furtively*.] An' I takes an' sta'ts to peel dis tu'nip an' what does I find? I find she's a fine fat roll er bills, dem tu'nip tops is greenbacks.

LUCY. So youah money is dream money?

MADISON. Well, no, not ezackly. De hoss whispeh sumpin' in my eah an' told me how to make dat dream money real money. An' I took de hint an' done it today. An' on dat money I'll buy low an' gouge 'em all good.

LUCY. How much you got?

MADISON. Well'm — [*He hesitates.*] I got a little an' den some. I got erbout — fifty er so.

LUCY. Wheah you git it? [*She catches hold of him.*]

MADISON. Tu'n me loose, woman. I goin' to baid. I got to make early sta't. [*He pulls off his coat.*]

LUCY [*wildly*]. I ain' goin' to let you stay in sin. [*She snatches the coat from him.*] I goin' take dis money an' make you say wheah you got it.

[*She begins hastily searching through the pockets of the coat.*]

MADISON [*calmly regarding her with great good humor and breaking into a laugh as she fails in her search*]. Eh, yah, yah, sea'ch an' look, sea'ch an' look.

LUCY. Oh, Madison, ain' you' got no honin' ter be hones' at all?

MADISON. Hones'! What kin' er fool talk is dat? I done got my ear-string bus' now an' dem preachah wu'ds can't fool me no mo'. You'll neveh fin' it, honey. 'Cause why? 'Cause I'm got it in my pants an' I goin' to keep it f'um a foolish woman.

LUCY [*running to him desperately*]. You got to give it to me.

MADISON. Gal, if you don' tu'n me loose I'll git ugly. Now, look heah. I wants to heah de las' er dis. I got new ideahs. I got big plots en plans. I done give you de plankses in my platfo'm an' I'm a-goin' to stan' on hit. When I makes a lot mo' money in de broker business I'm a-goin' to give you all de gold youah ap'un'll hold, ev'y day er youah life, an' you won' have to wait long. But till dat day an' to dat time I'm de treasu'eh er dis lodge an' I'm de stake holdeh er dis race an' dat money stays in de pu'se in de hip er my ol' jeanses. [*He says this last slowly and with growing emphasis and as he ends, gives himself a resounding whack on the hip over his pocket. There is a moment's pause. He puts his hand hurriedly in the pocket and then dazedly into one on the other hip.*] What dis? Wheah dat roll?

LUCY [*fearfully*]. I ain' tech it. You know I ain' ben neah you.

MADISON [*rushing to her*]. Gimme de coat.

[*He snatches the coat and begins going through the pockets, from time to time searching and slapping the garments he is wearing.*] Didn't you git it? You mus' er tuk it.

LUCY. No, Madison, I ain' see nor tech it. You watched me.

MADISON. Oh, Lawd, he'p me look.

[*He begins to run around the room, looking on the table, picking up articles and letting them fall, dropping on his knees and hunting under the table and chairs. As he searches he grows more frantic.*]

Oh, my Lawd, oh, wheah is it? I got to have it. Oh, I couldn' lose it, hit ain' mine ter lose. Stay by me, Lucy, an' he'p me fin' it; git down on youah knees, Lucy. Oh, wheah did I drop it? I'm gittin' old an' needs it. Ef I lose dis I lose all my push. I was jes' goin' into business an' we all wuz goin' to fly high. I got to fin' it. I ain' give up. Lemme think. Oh, I hopes some hones' puson foun' it. Lemme come on down — Know I put it on dat side 'cause dat de side Mistah Long he wuz on — Oh, I'll go crazy — [*He strikes his forehead, groaning.*]

LUCY [*starting*]. Mistah Long! He's cashiah in de Dime Savin's! How he give you money?

MADISON. Oh, lemme see — he gimme de money an' put it right in yere. [*He fumbles again distractedly in his pocket.*]

LUCY [*pursuing him desperately*]. Onliest money at de Dime Savin's is *de* money. You couldn't draw *hit* out. You didn' do dat, — you couldn' — Tell me if you did fo' I'll fin' it out tomorrer — Oh, tell me true — you couldn' when it's in my name — tell me now fo' I'll find it out.

MADISON. Oh, I can't stand it.

LUCY. Ef you wan' me to he'p you den be free wif me. How you draw money from de Bank? I give you no papeh. You *couldn'* draw *de* money.

MADISON. Wilson Byrd, he gimme de papeh.

LUCY. I give him no papeh.

MADISON. He write it fo' you.

LUCY. Oh, Gawd, dat w'ite man write my name. You drawed de money — I see it now. You had dealin's wif a fo'geh, Wilson Byrd.

MADISON. Spar' me an' he'p me. He tol' me ef I draw de money he'd take me into business wif him an' gimme de guitar besides.

LUCY. Did you spar' me? Fifty dollahs! You said fifty, didn' you? How could you do hit? More'n six months' ha'd slavin'. Six months mo' befo' I can resto' it back. I could a bought de house tomorrer mo'nin' an' now hit's six months off to pay in dat fifty. It *was* fifty, didn' you say? Maybe 'twuzzn' dat much. Tell me right. I'll fin' it out tomorrer.

MADISON. Dis yere'll kill me ef I can't think.

LUCY. How much you draw? Tell me right. Look

at me. Were hit fifty? [*She holds his eye.*] Less? Mo'? How much? [*She continues to hold his lustreless eyes, reading them.*] A hunde'd? Two hunde'd? Eight hunde'd? [*A pause ensues as she reads the truth in his face.*] All of hit. [*She sinks in a chair.*] Twelve yeahs' labor sence I married you an' termorrer I wuz goin' to mek de payment an' we'd a bin undeh owah own roof. I'm done. I could a paid off pa't, mebbe fifty, but I won' las' twelve yeahs mo' at de same thing. But I thank Thee, Lawd, dat it wuz stole f'um us all ef hit had to be stole.

MADISON. Ef I could on'y think. Had hit in de bank — felt hit an' had it on Thu'd Street — slapped hit an' had it at Joe's house — slapped hit an' had it coming up de alley — jes' fo' I clum de hill — lemme see — clum de hill — went in th'oo Wilson Byrd's hedge fence — he gimme de guitar — scrape my back comin' out — [*His face shows gradual recollection, and suddenly brightens.*] I knows now! Dat's hit! In dat white man's yard wheah he gimme de guitar! I wuz jes' goin' to give him de money when somebody grabbed him f'um behin'. He give a squawk an' skeered me. I run out th'oo his hedge fence an' scrape my back. I scrape de pocketbook out. She's dere! In dat Wilson Byrd's yard. I'll git it yit. Watch me. [*He grabs his hat and runs excitedly toward the door.*]

LUCY [*rushing toward him*]. No, sumpin' might happen. You might git mix up wif him ergin. Lemme go, but I mus' resto' dis guitar at Uncle Williams' as I go by his house. I'll slip it on his porch. Maybe he'll neveh know it wuz gone. Oh, if somebody had seen it heah! How could I have stood it?

[*She puts on a shawl and takes up the bag, but as she*

*lays her hand on the door-knob a loud knock is heard on
the door. Both start back and wait. The knock is repeated. She throws off the shawl, places the bag in a
corner, and returning to the door, opens it. She greets
the visitor in a strained voice, almost with a shriek.*]

Uncle Williams! Step in, please.

[*A man enters. The newcomer is old, with white hair
and beard. He is probably of Moorish descent. He is
so small and weazened as to be almost a dwarf, but his whole
demeanor indicates great latent power. A strong person-
ality, dominating the two others from the first instant.*]

WILLIAMS. Good evenin', Lucy.

[*He seems to be unaware of the presence of* MADISON.
*He comes forward with little mincing steps and an old
man's gesture, then takes off his hat and sees about him.
The others stand watching him transfixed.*]

Ain' you goin' shut de do', Lucy? I feels draf's.
I'm gittin' old an' catches cold easy. Ain' you goin'
take my hat? [*She reaches for it mechanically, watching him apprehensively.*] No, de hat — not de stick —
ol' pu'son like me always need good stout stick er club
case er havin' faintin' spell — sumpin' to lean on.
Now, wheah a cheer, better fetch me er cheer fo' feah
I might set on sumpin' you wouldn't choose fo' me.
[*She obeys dumbly and brings a chair to him.*] Set it
neareh. Dat's right. Now gimme youah shouldeh
an' ease me down. Ah — [*He leans heavily on her and
sinks totteringly into the chair with a great show of feeble-
ness.*] Now take a cheer yo'se'f. I 'sprize to see a
lady standin' an' me takin' my res', old ez I is. [*She
obeys, watching him with doubt and dread.*] Set it dah,
wheah I can see you good. [MADISON *is standing up
by the wall, right, gazing at him as though paralyzed with*

fear.] Dah now. We kin be ca'm and have a nice talk. Does you know what business I come yere fo' tonight? [*He pauses.*] You does, doesn't you?

LUCY [*almost beside herself with nervous tension*]. You — come to see — ef — [*Recovering herself with a mighty effort.*] Oh, yes, you come to look oveh de stove an' see ef you like to buy hit.

WILLIAMS [*musingly*]. M-m. Well, I reckon — dat's hit. Yes, dey tells me y'all has a wahmin' stove to sell an' now katydid cease, fros' ain' fur off, an' I needs hit. Is dish yere de one?

LUCY [*rising and rushing toward door at side*]. No, not dat. Hit's outside — ef you please to step out.

WILLIAMS. Well'm, I'll take'n look her oveh. [*She hastily lights a candle as he rises and totters in the wrong direction.*]

LUCY. Th'oo heah, th'oo heah. De stove's out in de woodshed. [*She grasps and guides him.*]

WILLIAMS. Ah — well'm. Um hm. I always gives things er good lookin' oveh befo' takin' stock in 'm. You needn' come erlong. I lived so long in dis house befo' you wuz bawn dat I knows my way. Is de stove an easy wood eateh?

LUCY. Yes, yes. [*She gives him the candle and almost pushes him through doorway at side as she follows him out.* MADISON, *who has watched fearfully from a dark corner, darts forward and looks after them, listening. He then runs toward the door at back but hesitates before it and turns as* LUCY *comes swiftly in from outer room, closing the door softly.*]

MADISON. What he say? Do he know?

LUCY [*desperately seizing the bag and pressing it into his hands as she turns him again toward doorway at back*]. Oh, I cain' tell. On'y resto' dis in case he don' know er case he do. Now's de one chance to be hones'.

MADISON. Huh. What erbout dat eight hunderd dollah?

LUCY. I don' know. Trus' Gawd an' be hones'.

MADISON. Huh uh. One of us has got to go look fo' dat money.

LUCY. One of us has got to take back de guitar.

MADISON. I'm goin' fo' de money.

LUCY. Den I'll take dis. [*She takes up the guitar and she and* MADISON *go toward door at back. Then she halts.*] Oh, Madison, you can do bofe. One of us has got to stay wif Uncle Williams. But take back de guitar first.

MADISON. All right. I'll go. An' I ain't played on dis heah but twice. [*He takes the guitar from her.*]

LUCY. Go now. Can you fin'. youah way to his porch in de dahk?

MADISON. Will we find de money? Dat's de p'oblem I wants de answeh fo'.

[LUCY *opens door at back to go out.* MADISON *is at her side. Both start back.* WILLIAMS *stands before them in the open doorway.*]

LUCY [*haltingly, after a pause*]. How — you like — de stove?

WILLIAMS [*entering more vigorously than before*]. Well'm befo' we goes any furder we betteh come neareh de real p'int and question. I didn't come fo' no stove dis night. [MADISON *shrinks back into the shadows.*]

LUCY [*slowly*]. Yo' — don' — wan' —

WILLIAMS. No'm. To be sho', I might tek de stove one er dese days, but dat ain' my erran' now.

Hit's dis; does you know when we mek de bargum about you buying dis heah house?

Lucy. Twelve yeah ago.

Williams. Gal, you dreamin'! 'Tweren't but las' year. 'Twere de fus' er Octobah las' year an' I say I gives you de refusals fer one yeah. 'Membeh dat?

Lucy. Yassuh.

Williams. So fui so good. Now does you know what day de month dis is?

Lucy. Fus' er Octobah.

Williams. Dat's true as preachin'. Well'm, time's up.

Lucy. What you mean?

Williams. I'm er man er my wuhd. Pay me de money an' tek de house.

Lucy. Termorrer —

Williams. No. Termorrer won' do.

Lucy. Why you push me so? Oh, please spar' me an' wait — wait anutheh day.

Williams. No, I'm er business man. I kin sell de house fer mo' money termorrer but I hold's to my wuhd ter sell it to you. I holds to it an' loses money, but it falls due dis day an' night an' I won' stretch it one jump er my hea't.

Lucy. You know — de bank — ain't open —

Williams. Sign de check fer hit. You kin do dat, cain't you?

Lucy. I — s'pose — I — kin.

Williams. Den up an' do hit. Heah's er check, all wrote out but de signin'. [*She takes the check he produces.*] An' heah's one er dese fountum pins. [*She takes the pen.*] Octobeh fus' — pay to Zek'l Williams — eight hunderd dollahs. Des write "Lucy Sparrow."

[*She mechanically turns to do so.*] Looks easy, sho'. But de law allows hit; dis writin' out money. [*He pauses, then adds impressively.*] Dat is, *ef* you got de money in de bank. Co'se ef de money ain' dah an' you writes de check fer hit de law puts you in State prism. [*She stops and stares at him. The pen falls from her hand and the check flutters to the floor.*] What de matteh? You wants de house, don' you? [Lucy's *head sinks.*] An' you got de money, ain' you?

MADISON. Dat's de question. [*He comes forward out of the shadow.*]

WILLIAMS [*seemingly observing* MADISON *for the first time during the evening*]. Why, heighyo, Madison. I bin lookin' fer you dis very evenin'. Whah you bin?

MADISON. Bin home.

WILLIAMS. Sho'ly not, Madison, sho'ly not all evenin'? Has you?

MADISON. Yes.

WILLIAMS. Well, ain' dat de whu'lygig? I wuz lookin' fer you at Pratt's sto' at eight o'clock an' day say you jes' lef' dah. You wuz dah, weren't you?

MADISON. No, suh.

WILLIAMS. Well, dere I am fool agin. An' who you think done fool me?

MADISON. Dunno.

WILLIAMS. Well suh, 'tweren't no one but — [*He pauses a moment.*] Wilson Byrd.

LUCY. Byrd! [*Springing to her feet with the shock.*]

WILLIAMS [*after watching the two a moment*]. So you ain' got de money no mo', is you? [*They are speechless before him.*] I knows you ain' ca'se I knows who *has* got hit.

MADISON [*involuntarily*]. Who?

WILLIAMS. I has. [*He observes them and then chuckles softly.*] I has de money an' de bargum's closed, fer de goods is bin delivered an' dey're right in dis room in dat corner. One guitar at eight hunderd dollahs. Insterments comes higher'n what dey did once but you would have it an' now you got it an' everybody's fixed.

MADISON [*groaning and bending over the table*]. Oh!

WILLIAMS. Yassuh, de man what buys guitars at dat price su'tinly plays on de golden strings. Eight hunderd fer one guitar makes 'm mighty near twenty thousand dollehs er dozen. De cos' er livin' is shore gone up but ef you mus' you mus'.

MADISON. Oh!

WILLIAMS. Well, I cain' stay heah, I got er be amblin' on. I much erblige ter you to mek youah plans to move out er heah fo' I got ter sell de house befo' sundown. Well, so long, an' I hopes you gits all de good er youah high price music. [*He turns again with his feeble old man's step toward the doorway, putting on his hat.*] I wish y'all good evenin'.

MADISON [*moving toward him with the threatening determination of despair*]. Say, I've got to have dat money. I sees red. I'm gone bad an' I'll kill befo' I'll lose hit.

[WILLIAMS *suddenly turns with a swiftness and agility astounding in so old a man. Starting forward he confronts* MADISON *with such dominance and fire that he seems suddenly to tower.*]

WILLIAMS. *You* kill *me*! *You* tek money away from *me*! Why, you po' grain er chaff, you don' know me. I'm a king in my own right. I got ways an' means er pertecktin' myse'f dat you don' even dream

on an' I don' need to lay a fingeh on you to do hit
Furdermo' I could brain you wif dis stick but ef you
cross me I won' be dat easy on you. Ef you don' wan'
wuss'n dat don' cross me no furder er youah troubles'll
begin fer fa'r.

Lucy. Oh, please don' lay nothin' on him.

Williams. You po' sufferin' gal, I won' lay nothin'
onto 'im but I'm to tek sumpin' off'n you. I'm goin'
tek de burding er dish yere pack er laziness off'n you.
An' fus' I wants ter show you dish yere piece er papeh.
[*He produces a folded document and opens it.*] Does you
know who wrote it ? Answeh me. [*He shoves the paper
under* Madison's *eye.*]

Madison. It looks like dat Wilson Byrd's writin'.

Williams. Yassuh, an' what's mo' it is dat man's
writin'. It's his confession dat he fo'ge Lucy Sparrow's
name. I saw dat man steal my guitar an' follered him
home. Dah I grabbed him, dah I foun' de purse wif
Lucy's name inside an' dah I made dat thief write out
his confession. Knowed so much of his meanness already dat he had to do hit. An' now I owns you. Does
you undehstan' dat ? Answeh me.

Madison. Yas suh, no suh.

Williams. Well, I'll take'n cl'ar up de myst'ry fer
you. I got dis confession outer Byrd an' got other
things ter prove hit an' I kin bring him an' you too, bofe
befo' de gran' jury.

Lucy. Oh, my sweet Jesus, save him. [*The old
man stands watching the two before him for some time in
silence.* Lucy *falls on her knees before him.*] Oh, don't
sen' Madison to de lawyers.

Williams. No, Lucy, I ain't wishful ter.

Lucy. You won't ?

WILLIAMS. Mebbe not. But fus', les' put all dis talk aside dat I bin talkin' up to now. I bin puttin' on an' pretendin' in ordeh ter try you bofe an' sif' de chaff from grain in you. I des bin playin' wif you ter see how good you is an' how ornry dish yere man er youahn is. Yit I'll take an' give him er chance even so, an' I'll pluck him f'um de bu'nin' ef he follers de paf I p'ints out ter him. But we all got ter have cl'ar unde'stan'in' 'bout dat. Fus' an' fo' mos' youah money is all safe wif me. De house is youah'n.

LUCY. You means you sell it fer de money.

WILLIAMS. In co'se. You didn't speck I'd steal, too, like a w'ite man, did you? I'll fetch you de deeds fo' hit fus' thing in de mo'nin'.

LUCY. Oh, fu'give me, I was all mix up. But you won' sen' Madison to de gran' jury neitheh?

WILLIAMS. I say I ain' honin' ter.

LUCY. Oh, my Makeh, I thank Thee fo' Thy mercy.

WILLIAMS. But I shorely goin' to put dis man er youah'n th'oo er tes' ter see whetheh he's fitten ter keep out er jail. Madison, will tek er tes'?

MADISON [*humbly*]. Yassuh. What is it?

WILLIAMS. A guitar.

MADISON. A guitar!

WILLIAMS. Yassuh, dat's hit, no mo' ner no less. I'm goin' give you dat guitar — but — dere's suhtinly goin' to be a string tied to it. You kin take dat guitar, but you got to make somethin' outer yourself wif her or back she'll come to me. You kin give lessons an' learn folks music or you kin write down de music you make, but you got to do somethin' wif it fer Lucy. You got to wake up or I'll take de guitar. Which'll it be? Make youah choice.

MADISON [*crushed*]. I'll — keep de guitar.

WILLIAMS. An' dat ain' all. You got ter quit runnin' wif Byrd an' Byrd wif you, you got ter be a better husban' an' you got to min' everything Lucy tells you. Will you do hit?

MADISON. Yassuh.

WILLIAMS. An' you ain' much of er temp'unce man neitheh, is you, Madison?

MADISON. I's a temp'unce man but I ain' no frantic.

WILLIAMS. Well, suh, you got ter jine de frantics now. No dram drinking at all. Will you quit hit er go ter jail?

MADISON. I'll quit.

WILLIAMS. Well, dat's on'y a promise but I'll shore hol' you to hit er put you behin' de bahs. Why, look heah, man, does you know how you stan' pon top er dis yu'th? Does you know how you liken to er tree? S'posin' sumpin' wif er cool eye like er tree could see you an talk. I cain' jedge you ca'm but er tree could. Tree would look at you and say, "Does dat 'ere man wu'k?" Win' 'ud whispeh, "No." "Do he eat?" "Yas'n git fat," respon' de win'. "Who shines on him?" "His wife," win' say. "Do he put fo'th flower an' bless de wife?" say de tree. "No." "Do he give shade an' shelteh ter de wife?" say de tree. "No." "Well, chop'm down an' bu'n him befo' he rots," say de tree. "Dat's all." But mebby I kin mek mo' of him dan dat an' so I'll try prunin' him an' graftin' some good labeh onto him. An' I kin' er think hit'll sabe him yit. Well'm, I must be er goin' now. Hit's late an' I mus' git my res' fer I got to do a lot er bossin' termorrer an' dat's allers ha'd fer me. Lucy, I'll fetch you de deeds ter de house befo' nine termorrer an'

Madison, you kin repo't to me at eight o'clock sha'p an' give my little boy a lesson on de guitar. You'll be dah, won't you?

MADISON [*meekly*]. Yassuh.

WILLIAMS. Ready to whu'l in an' scratch.

MADISON. Yassuh.

WILLIAMS. Well, den, les' all shek han's on de noo nes' an' de noo aig. [*They shake hands. He puts on his hat and turns to the door.*]

An' dat remin's me, Lucy, you better tell Madison to play on dat guitar a plenty tonight because he'll need music fer to stan' up undeh all de lessons I'm goin' to lay onto him. Well, I wish you good night. I'm er gittin' kin'er ole an' I cain' stay up late no mo' without bein' crosser in de mornin'. Good night den an' far' you well bofe. Eight o'clock, Madison. Good night. [*He goes, closing the door after him. The pair stand silent for a moment,* MADISON *with hanging head and in deep dejection.*]

LUCY [*throwing her arms around him*]. Oh, my husban', I'll pray fer you. Don' sorrer now. Git youah res' tonight. We kin be hones' now. We've got de house at las' an' heah's de guitar.

MADISON. Yassuh, heah's de guitar. [*He plays it and fondles it. Then his face assumes again its melancholy look.*]

LUCY. What's de trouble?

MADISON. I don' undehstan' dis worl'. If I wants to make music why cain't folks lemme alone to make music? If I dream a fine dream why is it I always wake up? Looks to me like somebody's always tryin' to crowd me out an' git me in a tight place.

LUCY. You wuz doin' all right till you got mix up

wif dat white man an' his tricks. De trouble wuz dat dis dream of youahs wuzn't a good dream.

MADISON. Yes, but not all of my dreams is bad ones. All I wants is room to dream my good dreams an' make my own music.

CURTAIN

SPREADING THE NEWS[1]

BY

AUGUSTA GREGORY

In this play is found Irish idiom that should stand the criticism of George Moore. If, as he says, Lady Gregory has written plays in which the language is merely sprinkled with rural speech, surely "Spreading the News" is not one of them. This play has the living speech which Yeats attributes to this Irish dramatist, and which Moore says is lost to modern English through the decadent educated classes.

The value of the play lies in the intimate study of the characters. They live on the printed page or on the stage. In "Seven Short Plays," from which volume this play is taken, and "New Comedies," the characters show a primitive strength together with what Edward Storer has called the talk of "intoxicated poets." Their speech is racy in expression and quaint in metaphor, abounding in charming images of fun and fancy.

SPREADING THE NEWS

Persons

Bartley Fallon	James Ryan
Mrs. Fallon	Mrs. Tarpey
Jack Smith	Mrs. Tully
Shawn Early	Jo Muldoon, *a policeman*
Tim Casey	A Removable Magistrate

Scene: The outskirts of a fair. An apple stall, Mrs. Tarpey sitting at it. Magistrate and Policeman enter.

Magistrate. So that is the fair green. Cattle and sheep and mud. No system. What a repulsive sight!

Policeman. That is so, indeed.

Magistrate. I suppose there is a good deal of disorder in this place?

Policeman. There is.

Magistrate. Common assault?

Policeman. It's common enough.

Magistrate. Agrarian crime, no doubt?

Policeman. That is so.

Magistrate. Boycotting? Maiming of cattle? Firing into houses?

Policeman. There was one time, and there might be again.

MAGISTRATE. That is bad. Does it go any farther than that?

POLICEMAN. Far enough, indeed.

MAGISTRATE. Homicide, then! This district has been shamefully neglected! I will change all that. When I was in the Andaman Islands my system never failed. Yes, yes, I will change all that. What has that woman on her stall?

POLICEMAN. Apples mostly — and sweets.

MAGISTRATE. Just see if there are any unlicensed goods underneath — spirits or the like. We had evasions of the salt tax in the Andaman Islands.

POLICEMAN [*sniffing cautiously and upsetting a heap of apples*]. I see no spirits here — or salt.

MAGISTRATE [*to* MRS. TARPEY]. Do you know this town well, my good woman?

MRS. TARPEY [*holding out some apples*]. A penny the half-dozen, your honor?

POLICEMAN [*shouting*]. The gentleman is asking do you know the town! He's the new magistrate!

MRS. TARPEY [*rising and ducking*]. Do I know the town? I do, to be sure.

MAGISTRATE [*shouting*]. What is its chief business?

MRS. TARPEY. Business, is it? What business would the people here have but to be minding one another's business?

MAGISTRATE. I mean what trade have they?

MRS. TARPEY. Not a trade at all but to be talking.

MAGISTRATE. I shall learn nothing here.

[JAMES RYAN *comes in, pipe in mouth. Seeing* MAGISTRATE *he retreats quickly, taking pipe from mouth.*]

MAGISTRATE. The smoke from that man's pipe had a greenish look; he may be growing unlicensed tobacco at home. I wish I had brought my telescope to this district. Come to the post-office; I will telegraph for it. I found it very useful in the Andaman Islands.

[MAGISTRATE *and* POLICEMAN *go out left.*]

MRS. TARPEY. Bad luck to Jo Muldoon, knocking my apples this way and that way. [*Begins arranging them.*] Showing off he was to the new magistrate.

[*Enter* BARTLEY FALLON *and* MRS. FALLON.]

BARTLEY. Indeed it's a poor country and a scarce country to be living in. But I'm thinking if I went to America it's long ago the day I'd be dead!

MRS. FALLON. So you might, indeed.

[*She puts her basket on a barrel and begins putting parcels in it, taking them from under her cloak.*]

BARTLEY. And it's a great expense for a poor man to be buried in America.

MRS. FALLON. Never fear, Bartley Fallon, but I'll give you a good burying the day you'll die.

BARTLEY. Maybe it's yourself will be buried in the graveyard of Cloonmara before me, Mary Fallon, and I myself that will be dying unbeknownst some night, and no one a-near me. And the cat itself may be gone straying through the country, and the mice squealing over the quilt.

MRS. FALLON. Leave off talking of dying. It might be twenty years you'll be living yet.

BARTLEY [*with a deep sigh*]. I'm thinking if I'll be living at the end of twenty years, it's a very old man I'll be then!

MRS. TARPEY [*turns and sees them*].   Good morrow, Bartley Fallon; good morrow, Mrs. Fallon. Well, Bartley, you'll find no cause for complaining to-day; they are all saying it was a good fair.

BARTLEY [*raising his voice*].   It was not a good fair, Mrs. Tarpey. It was a scattered sort of a fair. If we didn't expect more, we got less. That's the way with me always; whatever I have to sell goes down and whatever I have to buy goes up. If there's ever any misfortune coming to this world, it's on myself it pitches, like a flock of crows on seed potatoes.

MRS. FALLON.   Leave off talking of misfortunes and listen to Jack Smith that is coming the way, and he singing.

[*Voice of* JACK SMITH *heard singing*.]

I thought, my first love,
    There'd be but one house between you and me,
And I thought I would find
    Yourself coaxing my child on your knee.
Over the tide
    I would leap with the leap of a swan,
Till I came to the side
    Of the wife of the Red-haired man!

[JACK SMITH *comes in; he is a red-haired man, and is carrying a hayfork*.]

MRS. TARPEY.   That should be a good song if I had my hearing.

MRS. FALLON [*shouting*].   It's "The Red-haired Man's Wife."

MRS. TARPEY.   I know it well. That's the song that has a skin on it!

[*She turns her back to them and goes on arranging her apples*.]

MRS. FALLON. Where's herself, Jack Smith?

JACK SMITH. She was delayed with her washing; bleaching the clothes on the hedge she is, and she daren't leave them, with all the tinkers that do be passing to the fair. It isn't to the fair I came myself, but up to the Five Acre Meadow I'm going, where I have a contract for the hay. We'll get a share of it into tramps to-day. [*He lays down hayfork and lights his pipe.*]

BARTLEY. You will not get it into tramps to-day. The rain will be down on it by evening, and on myself too. It's seldom I ever started on a journey but the rain would come down on me before I'd find any place of shelter.

JACK SMITH. If it didn't itself, Bartley, it is my belief you would carry a leaky pail on your head in place of a hat, the way you'd not be without some cause of complaining.

[*A voice heard, "Go on, go on out o' that. Go on, I say."*]

JACK SMITH. Look at that young mare of Pat Ryan's that is backing into Shaughnessy's bullocks with the dint of the crowd! Don't be daunted, Pat, I'll give you a hand with her. [*He goes out, leaving his hayfork.*]

MRS. FALLON. It's time for ourselves to be going home. I have all I bought put in the basket. Look at there, Jack Smith's hayfork he left after him! He'll be wanting it. [*Calls.*] Jack Smith! Jack Smith!— He's gone through the crowd — hurry after him, Bartley, he'll be wanting it.

BARTLEY. I'll do that. This is no safe place to be leaving it. [*He takes up fork awkwardly and upsets the basket.*] Look at that now! If there is any basket in the fair upset, it must be our own basket! [*He goes out to right.*]

MRS. FALLON. Get out of that! It is your own fault, it is. Talk of misfortunes and misfortunes will come. Glory be! Look at my new egg-cups rolling in every part — and my two pound of sugar with the paper broke —

MRS. TARPEY [*turning from stall*]. God help us, Mrs. Fallon, what happened your basket?

MRS. FALLON. It's himself that knocked it down, bad manners to him [*putting things up*]. My grand sugar that's destroyed, and he'll not drink his tea without it. I had best go back to the shop for more, much good may it do him!

[*Enter* TIM CASEY.]

TIM CASEY. Where is Bartley Fallon, Mrs. Fallon? I want a word with him before he'll leave the fair. I was afraid he might have gone home by this, for he's a temperate man.

MRS. FALLON. I wish he did go home! It'd be best for me if he went home straight from the fair green, or if he never came with me at all! Where is he, is it? He's gone up the road [*jerks elbow*] following Jack Smith with a hayfork. [*She goes out to left.*]

TIM CASEY. Following Jack Smith with a hayfork! Did ever any one hear the like of that? [*Shouts.*] Did you hear that news, Mrs. Tarpey?

MRS. TARPEY. I heard no news at all.

TIM CASEY. Some dispute I suppose it was that rose between Jack Smith and Bartley Fallon, and it seems Jack made off, and Bartley is following him with a hayfork!

Mrs. Tarpey. Is he now? Well, that was quick work! It's not ten minutes since the two of them were here, Bartley going home and Jack going to the Five Acre Meadow; and I had my apples to settle up, that Jo Muldoon of the police had scattered, and when I looked round again Jack Smith was gone, and Bartley Fallon was gone, and Mrs. Fallon's basket upset, and all in it strewed upon the ground — the tea here the two pound of sugar there — the egg-cups there — Look, now, what a great hardship the deafness puts upon me, that I didn't hear the commencement of the fight! Wait till I tell James Ryan that I see below; he is a neighbor of Bartley's, it would be a pity if he wouldn't hear the news!

[*She goes out. Enter* SHAWN EARLY *and* MRS. TULLY.]

Tim Casey. Listen, Shawn Early! Listen, Mrs. Tully, to the news! Jack Smith and Bartley Fallon had a falling out, and Jack knocked Mrs. Fallon's basket into the road, and Bartley made an attack on him with a hayfork, and away with Jack, and Bartley after him. Look at the sugar here yet on the road!

Shawn Early. Do you tell me so? Well, that's a queer thing, and Bartley Fallon so quiet a man!

Mrs. Tully. I wouldn't wonder at all. I would never think well of a man that would have that sort of a moldering look. It's likely he has overtaken Jack by this.

[*Enter* JAMES RYAN *and* MRS. TARPEY.]

James Ryan. That is great news Mrs. Tarpey was telling me! I suppose that's what brought the police and the magistrate up this way. I was wondering to see them in it awhile ago.

Shawn Early. The police after them? Bartley

Fallon must have injured Jack so. They wouldn't meddle in a fight that was only for show!

MRS. TULLY. Why wouldn't he injure him? There was many a man killed with no more of a weapon than a hayfork.

JAMES RYAN. Wait till I run north as far as Kelly's bar to spread the news! [*He goes out.*]

TIM CASEY. I'll go tell Jack Smith's first cousin that is standing there south of the church after selling his lambs. [*Goes out.*]

MRS. TULLY. I'll go telling a few of the neighbors I see beyond to the west. [*Goes out.*]

SHAWN EARLY. I'll give word of it beyond at the east of the green. [*Is going out when* MRS. TARPEY *seizes hold of him.*]

MRS. TARPEY. Stop a minute, Shawn Early, and tell me did you see red Jack Smith's wife, Kitty Keary, in any place?

SHAWN EARLY. I did. At her own house she was, drying clothes on the hedge as I passed.

MRS. TARPEY. What did you say she was doing?

SHAWN EARLY [*breaking away*]. Laying out a sheet on the hedge. [*He goes.*]

MRS. TARPEY. Laying out a sheet for the dead! The Lord have mercy on us! Jack Smith dead, and his wife laying out a sheet for his burying! [*Calls out.*] Why didn't you tell me that before, Shawn Early? Isn't the deafness the great hardship? Half the world might be dead without me knowing of it or getting word of it at all! [*She sits down and rocks herself.*] O my poor Jack Smith! To be going to his work so nice and so hearty, and to be left stretched on the ground in the full light of the day!

[*Enter* TIM CASEY.]

TIM CASEY. What is it, Mrs. Tarpey? What happened since?

MRS. TARPEY. O my poor Jack Smith!

TIM CASEY. Did Bartley overtake him?

MRS. TARPEY. O the poor man!

TIM CASEY. Is it killed he is?

MRS. TARPEY. Stretched in the Five Acre Meadow!

TIM CASEY. Mercy on us! Is that a fact?

MRS. TARPEY. Without the rites of the Church or a ha'porth!

TIM CASEY. Who was telling you?

MRS. TARPEY. And the wife laying out a sheet for his corpse. [*Sits up and wipes her eyes.*] I suppose they'll wake him the same as another?

[*Enter* MRS. TULLY, SHAWN EARLY, *and* JAMES RYAN.]

MRS. TULLY. There is great talk about this work in every quarter of the fair.

MRS. TARPEY. Ochone! Cold and dead. And myself maybe the last he was speaking to!

JAMES RYAN. The Lord save us! Is it dead he is?

TIM CASEY. Dead surely, and the wife getting provision for the wake.

SHAWN EARLY. Well, now, hadn't Bartley Fallon great venom in him?

MRS. TULLY. You may be sure he had some cause. Why would he have made an end of him if he had not? [*To* MRS. TARPEY, *raising her voice.*] What was it rose the dispute at all, Mrs. Tarpey?

MRS. TARPEY. Not a one of me knows. The last I saw of them, Jack Smith was standing there, and

s

Bartley Fallon was standing there, quiet and easy, and he listening to "The Red-haired Man's Wife."

MRS. TULLY. Do you hear that, Tim Casey? Do you hear that, Shawn Early and James Ryan? Bartley Fallon was here this morning listening to red Jack Smith's wife, Kitty Keary that was! Listening to her and whispering with her! It was she started the fight so!

SHAWN EARLY. She must have followed him from her own house. It is likely some person roused him.

TIM CASEY. I never knew, before, Bartley Fallon was great with Jack Smith's wife.

MRS. TULLY. How would you know it? Sure it's not in the streets they would be calling it. If Mrs. Fallon didn't know of it, and if I that have the next house to them didn't know of it, and if Jack Smith didn't himself know of it, it is not likely you would know of it, Tim Casey.

SHAWN EARLY. Let Bartley Fallon take charge of her from this out so, and let him provide for her. It is little pity she will get from any person in this parish.

TIM CASEY. How can he take charge of her? Sure he has a wife of his own. Sure you don't think he'd turn souper and marry her in a Protestant church?

JAMES RYAN. It would be easy for him to marry her if he brought her to America.

SHAWN EARLY. With or without Kitty Keary, believe me it is for America he's making at this minute. I saw the new magistrate and Jo Muldoon of the police going into the post-office as I came up — there was hurry on them — you may be sure it was to telegraph they went, the way he'll be stopped in the docks at Queenstown!

Mrs. Tully. It's likely Kitty Keary is gone with him, and not minding a sheet or a wake at all. The poor man, to be deserted by his own wife, and the breath hardly gone out yet from his body that is lying bloody in the field! [*Enter* Mrs. Fallon.]

Mrs. Fallon. What is it the whole of the town is talking about? And what is it you yourselves are talking about? Is it about my man Bartley Fallon you are talking? Is it lies about him you are telling, saying that he went killing Jack Smith? My grief that ever he came into this place at all!

James Ryan. Be easy now, Mrs. Fallon. Sure there is no one at all in the whole fair but is sorry for you!

Mrs. Fallon. Sorry for me, is it? Why would any one be sorry for me? Let you be sorry for yourselves, and that there may be shame on you for ever and at the day of judgment, for the words you are saying and the lies you are telling to take away the character of my poor man, and to take the good name off of him, and to drive him to destruction! That is what you are doing!

Shawn Early. Take comfort now, Mrs. Fallon. The police are not so smart as they think. Sure he might give them the slip yet, the same as Lynchehaun.

Mrs. Tully. If they do get him, and if they do put a rope around his neck, there is no one can say he does not deserve it!

Mrs. Fallon. Is that what you are saying, Bridget Tully, and is that what you think? I tell you it's too much talk you have, making yourself out to be such a great one, and to be running down every respectable person! A rope, is it? It isn't much of a rope was needed to tie up your own furniture the day you came into Martin Tully's house, and you never bringing as much as a blanket, or a penny, or a suit of clothes with you, and I myself bringing seventy pounds and two feather beds. And now you are stiffer than a woman would have a hundred pounds! It is too much talk the whole of you have. A rope, is it? I tell you the whole of this town is full of liars and schemers that would hang you up for half a glass of whiskey. [*Turning to go.*] People they are you wouldn't believe as much as daylight from without you'd get up to have a look at it yourself. Killing Jack Smith indeed! Where are you at all, Bartley, till I bring you out of this? My nice, quiet little man! My decent comrade! He that is as kind and as harmless as an innocent beast of the field! He'll be doing no harm at all if he'll shed the blood of some of you after this day's work! That much would be no harm at all. [*Calls out.*] Bartley! Bartley Fallon! Where are you? Bartley Fallon! [*Going out.*] Did any one see Bartley Fallon? [*All turn to look after her.*]

JAMES RYAN. It is hard for her to believe any such a thing, God help her!

[*Enter* BARTLEY FALLON *from right, carrying hayfork.*]

BARTLEY. It is what I often said to myself, if there is ever any misfortune coming to this world, it is on myself it is sure to come!

[*All turn round and face him.*]

BARTLEY. To be going about with this fork, and to find no one to take it, and no place to leave it down, and I wanting to be gone out of this. — Is that you, Shawn Early? [*Holds out fork.*] It's well I met you. You have no call to be leaving the fair for a while the way I have, and how can I go till I'm rid of this fork? Will you take it and keep it until such time as Jack Smith —

SHAWN EARLY [*backing*]. I will not take it, Bartley Fallon, I'm very thankful to you!

BARTLEY [*turning to apple stall*]. Look at it now, Mrs. Tarpey, it was here I got it; let me thrust it in under the stall. It will lie there safe enough and no one will take notice of it until such time as Jack Smith —

MRS. TARPEY. Take your fork out of that! Is it to put trouble on me and to destroy me you want? Putting it there for the police to be rooting it out maybe. [*Thrusts him back.*]

BARTLEY. That is a very unneighborly thing for you to do, Mrs. Tarpey. Hadn't I enough care on me with that fork before this, running up and down with it like the swinging of a clock, and afeared to lay it down in any place! I wish I never touched it or meddled with it at all!

JAMES RYAN. It is a pity, indeed, you ever did.

BARTLEY. Will you yourself take it, James Ryan? You were always a neighborly man.

JAMES RYAN [*backing*]. There is many a thing I would do for you, Bartley Fallon, but I won't do that!

SHAWN EARLY. I tell you there is no man will give you any help or any encouragement for this day's work. If it was something agrarian now —

BARTLEY. If no one at all will take it, maybe it's best to give it up to the police.

TIM CASEY. There'd be a welcome for it with them, surely! [*Laughter.*]

MRS. TULLY. And it is to the police Kitty Keary herself will be brought.

Mrs. Tarpey [*rocking to and fro*]. I wonder now who will take the expense of the wake for poor Jack Smith?

Bartley. The wake for Jack Smith!

Tim Casey. Why wouldn't he get a wake as well as another? Would you begrudge him that much?

Bartley. Red Jack Smith dead! Who was telling you?

Shawn Early. The whole town knows of it by this.

Bartley. Do they say what way did he die?

James Ryan. You don't know that yourself, I suppose, Bartley Fallon? You don't know he was followed and that he was laid dead with the stab of a hayfork?

Bartley. The stab of a hayfork!

Shawn Early. You don't know, I suppose, that the body was found in the Five Acre Meadow?

Bartley. The Five Acre Meadow!

Tim Casey. It is likely you don't know that the police are after the man that did it!

Bartley. The man that did it!

Mrs. Tully. You don't know, maybe, that he was made away with for the sake of Kitty Keary, his wife?

Bartley. Kitty Keary, his wife!

Mrs. Tully. And what have you to say now, Bartley Fallon?

Bartley [*crossing himself*]. I to bring that fork here, and to find that news before me! It is much if I can ever stir from this place at all, or reach as far as the road!

Tim Casey. Look, boys, at the new magistrate,

and Jo Muldoon along with him! It's best for us to quit this.

SHAWN EARLY. That is so. It is best not to be mixed in this business at all.

JAMES RYAN. Bad as he is, I wouldn't like to be an informer against any man.

[*All hurry away except* MRS. TARPEY, *who remains behind her stall. Enter* MAGISTRATE *and* POLICEMAN.]

MAGISTRATE. I knew the district was in a bad state, but I did not expect to be confronted with a murder at the first fair I came to.

POLICEMAN. I am sure you did not, indeed.

MAGISTRATE. You heard the same story from every one you asked?

POLICEMAN. The same story — or if it was not altogether the same, anyway it was no less than the first story.

MAGISTRATE. What is that man doing? He is sitting alone with a hayfork. He has a guilty look. The murder was done with a hayfork!

POLICEMAN [*in a whisper*]. That's the very man they say did the act; Bartley Fallon himself!

MAGISTRATE. He must have found escape difficult — he is trying to brazen it out. A convict in the Andaman Islands tried the same game, but he could not escape my system! Stand aside — don't go far — have the handcuffs ready. [*He walks up to* BARTLEY, *folds his arms, and stands before him.*] Here, my man, do you know anything of John Smith?

BARTLEY. Of John Smith! Who is he, now?

POLICEMAN. Jack Smith, sir — Red Jack Smith!

MAGISTRATE [*coming a step nearer and tapping him on the shoulder*]. Where is Jack Smith?

BARTLEY [*with a deep sigh, and shaking his head slowly*]. Where is he, indeed?

MAGISTRATE. What have you to tell?

BARTLEY. It is where he was this morning, standing in this spot, singing his share of songs — no, but lighting his pipe — scraping a match on the sole of his shoe —

MAGISTRATE. I ask you, for the third time, where is he?

BARTLEY. I wouldn't like to say that. It is a great mystery, and it is hard to say of any man, did he earn hatred or love.

MAGISTRATE. Tell me all you know.

BARTLEY. All that I know — Well, there are the three estates; there is Limbo, and there is Purgatory, and there is —

MAGISTRATE. Nonsense! This is trifling! Get to the point.

BARTLEY. Maybe you don't hold with the clergy so? That is the teaching of the clergy. Maybe you hold with the old people. It is what they do be saying, that the shadow goes wandering, and the soul is tired, and the body is taking a rest — The shadow! [*Starts up.*] I was nearly sure I saw Jack Smith not ten minutes ago at the corner of the forge, and I lost him again — Was it his ghost I saw, do you think?

MAGISTRATE [*to* POLICEMAN]. Conscience-struck! He will confess all now!

BARTLEY. His ghost to come before me! It is likely it was on account of the fork! I to have it and he to have no way to defend himself the time he met with his death!

MAGISTRATE [*to* POLICEMAN]. I must note down his

words. [*Takes out notebook. To* BARTLEY.] I warn you that your words are being noted.

BARTLEY. If I had ha' run faster in the beginning, this terror would not be on me at the latter end! Maybe he will cast it up against me at the day of judgment — I wouldn't wonder at all at that.

MAGISTRATE [*writing*]. At the day of judgment —

BARTLEY. It was soon for his ghost to appear to me — is it coming after me always by day it will be, and stripping the clothes off in the night time? — I wouldn't wonder at all at that, being as I am an unfortunate man!

MAGISTRATE [*sternly*]. Tell me truly. What was the motive of this crime?

BARTLEY. The motive, is it?

MAGISTRATE. Yes, the motive; the cause.

BARTLEY. I'd sooner not say that.

MAGISTRATE. You had better tell me truly. Was it money?

BARTLEY. Not at all! What did poor Jack Smith ever have in his pockets unless it might be his hands that would be in them?

MAGISTRATE. Any dispute about land?

BARTLEY [*indignantly*]. Not at all! He never was a grabber or grabbed from any one!

MAGISTRATE. You will find it better for you if you tell at once.

BARTLEY. I tell you I wouldn't for the whole world wish to say what it was — it is a thing I would not like to be talking about.

MAGISTRATE. There is no use in hiding it. It will be discovered in the end.

BARTLEY. Well, I suppose it will, seeing that

mostly everybody knows it before. Whisper here now. I will tell no lie; where would be the use? [*Puts his hand to his mouth, and* MAGISTRATE *stoops.*] Don't be putting the blame on the parish, for such a thing was never done in the parish before — it was done for the sake of Kitty Keary, Jack Smith's wife.

MAGISTRATE [*to* POLICEMAN]. Put on the handcuffs. We have been saved some trouble. I knew he would confess if taken in the right way.

[POLICEMAN *puts on handcuffs.*]

BARTLEY. Handcuffs now! Glory be! I always said, if there was ever any misfortune coming to this place it was on myself it would fall. I to be in handcuffs! There's no wonder at all in that.

[*Enter* MRS. FALLON, *followed by the rest. She is looking back at them as she speaks.*]

MRS. FALLON. Telling lies the whole of the people of this town are; telling lies, telling lies as fast as a dog will trot! Speaking against my poor respectable man! Saying he made an end of Jack Smith! My decent comrade! There is no better man and no kinder man in the whole of the five parishes! It's little annoyance he ever gave to any one! [*Turns and sees him.*] What in the earthly world do I see before me? Bartley Fallon in charge of the police! Handcuffs on him! O Bartley, what did you do at all at all?

BARTLEY. O Mary, there has a great misfortune come upon me! It is what I always said, that if there is ever any misfortune —

MRS. FALLON. What did he do at all, or is it bewitched I am?

MAGISTRATE. This man has been arrested on a charge of murder.

MRS. FALLON. Whose charge is that? Don't believe them! They are all liars in this place! Give me back my man!

MAGISTRATE. It is natural you should take his part, but you have no cause of complaint against your neighbors. He has been arrested for the murder of John Smith, on his own confession.

MRS. FALLON. The saints of heaven protect us! And what did he want killing Jack Smith?

MAGISTRATE. It is best you should know all. He did it on account of a love affair with the murdered man's wife.

MRS. FALLON [*sitting down*]. With Jack Smith's wife! With Kitty Keary! — Ochone, the traitor!

THE CROWD. A great shame, indeed. He is a traitor, indeed.

MRS. TULLY. To America he was bringing her, Mrs. Fallon.

BARTLEY. What are you saying, Mary? I tell you —

MRS. FALLON. Don't say a word. I won't listen to any word you'll say! [*Stops her ears.*] O, isn't he the treacherous villain? Ohone go deo!

BARTLEY. Be quiet till I speak! Listen to what I say!

MRS. FALLON. Sitting beside me on the ass car coming to the town, so quiet and so respectable, and treachery like that in his heart!

BARTLEY. Is it your wits you have lost or is it I myself that have lost my wits?

MRS. FALLON. And it's hard I earned you, slaving, slaving — and you grumbling, and sighing, and coughing, and discontented, and the priest wore out anointing you, with all the times you threatened to die!

BARTLEY. Let you be quiet till I tell you!

MRS. FALLON. You to bring such a disgrace into the parish! A thing that was never heard of before!

BARTLEY. Will you shut your mouth and hear me speaking?

MRS. FALLON. And if it was for any sort of a fine handsome woman, but for a little fistful of a woman like Kitty Keary, that's not four feet high hardly, and not three teeth in her head unless she got new ones! May God reward you, Bartley Fallon, for the black treachery in your heart and the wickedness in your mind, and the red blood of poor Jack Smith that is wet upon your hand!

[*Voice of* JACK SMITH *heard singing.*]

The sea shall be dry,
The earth under mourning and ban!
Then loud shall he cry
For the wife of the red-haired man!

BARTLEY. It's Jack Smith's voice — I never knew a ghost to sing before — It is after myself and the fork he is coming! [*Goes back. Enter* JACK SMITH.] Let one of you give him the fork and I will be clear of him now and for eternity!

MRS. TARPEY. The Lord have mercy on us, Red Jack Smith! The man that was going to be waked!

JAMES RYAN. Is it back from the grave you are come?

SHAWN EARLY. Is it alive you are, or is it dead you are?

TIM CASEY. Is it yourself at all that's in it?

Mrs. Tully. Is it letting on you were to be dead?

Mrs. Fallon. Dead or alive, let you stop Kitty Keary, your wife, from bringing my man away with her to America!

Jack Smith. It is what I think, the wits are gone astray on the whole of you. What would my wife want bringing Bartley Fallon to America?

Mrs. Fallon. To leave yourself, and to get quit of you she wants, Jack Smith, and to bring him away from myself. That's what the two of them had settled together.

Jack Smith. I'll break the head of any man that says that! Who is it says it? [*To* Tim Casey.] Was it you said it? [*To* Shawn Early.] Was it you?

All Together [*backing and shaking their heads*]. It wasn't I said it!

Jack Smith. Tell me the name of any man that said it!

All Together [*pointing to* Bartley]. It was *him* that said it!

Jack Smith. Let me at him till I break his head!

[Bartley *backs in terror. Neighbors hold* Jack Smith *back.*]

Jack Smith [*trying to free himself*]. Let me at him! Isn't he the pleasant sort of a scarecrow for any woman to be crossing the ocean with! It's back from the docks of New York he'd be turned [*trying to rush at him again*], with a lie in his mouth and treachery in his heart, and another man's wife by his side, and he passing her off as his own! Let me at him, can't you? [*Makes another rush but is held back.*]

MAGISTRATE [*pointing to* JACK SMITH]. Policeman, put the handcuffs on this man. I see it all now. A case of false impersonation, a conspiracy to defeat the ends of justice. There was a case in the Andaman Islands, a murderer of the Mopsa tribe, a religious enthusiast —

POLICEMAN. So he might be, too.

MAGISTRATE. We must take both these men to the scene of the murder. We must confront them with the body of the real Jack Smith.

JACK SMITH. I'll break the head of any man that will find my dead body!

MAGISTRATE. I'll call more help from the barracks. [*Blows* POLICEMAN'S *whistle.*]

BARTLEY. It is what I am thinking, if myself and Jack Smith are put together in the one cell for the night, the handcuffs will be taken off him, and his hands will be free, and murder will be done that time surely!

MAGISTRATE. Come on! [*They turn to the right.*]

THE SWAN SONG [1]

BY

ANTON TCHEKHOFF

TRANSLATED BY

MARIAN FELL

[1] Reprinted from the volume "Plays" by permission of the publishers, Charles Scribner's Sons.

For permission to perform this play application must be made to the author in care of the publisher.

Of all modern writers perhaps Tchekhoff is the dearest to the Russian people. Though he was the grandchild of a serf, he was graduated in medicine from the University of Moscow in 1884, and afterwards worked strenuously at both medicine and literature. He died in 1904 in a little village of the Black Forest, Germany.

Unlike most of the great Russian writers, Tchekhoff couples his sadness with the smiles of a great humorist; but his sympathy with suffering brings all of his laughter near to tears. The "Sea Gull" tells of his own experience as a young author. "The Cherry Orchard," his last play, redolent of country life and Russian character in general, caused him to be fêted as one of Russia's greatest dramatists. "The Swan Song," heavy with the author's power of analysis, is one of his innumerable glimpses into the lives of Russian characters.

THE SWAN SONG

CHARACTERS

VASILI SVIETLOVIDOFF, *a comedian, 68 years old.*
NIKITA IVANITCH, *a prompter, an old man.*

The scene is laid on the stage of a country theatre, at night, after the play. To the right a row of rough, unpainted doors leading into the dressing-rooms. To the left and in the background the stage is encumbered with all sorts of rubbish. In the middle of the stage is an overturned stool.

SVIETLOVIDOFF [*with a candle in his hand, comes out of a dressing-room and laughs*]. Well, well, this is funny! Here's a good joke! I fell asleep in my dressing-room when the play was over, and there I was calmly snoring after everybody else had left the theatre. Ah! I'm a foolish old man, a poor old dodderer! I have been drinking again, and so I fell asleep in there, sitting up. That was clever! Good for you, old boy! [*Calls.*] Yegorka! Petrushka! Where the devil are you? Petrushka! The scoundrels must be asleep, and an earthquake wouldn't wake them now! Yegorka! [*Picks up the stool, sits down, and puts the candle on the floor.*] Not a sound! Only echoes answer me. I gave Yegorka and Petrushka each a tip to-day, and now they have disappeared without leaving a trace behind them. The rascals have gone off and have probably locked up the theatre. [*Turns his head about.*]

I'm drunk! Ugh! The play to-night was for my benefit, and it is disgusting to think how much beer and wine I have poured down my throat in honor of the occasion. Gracious! My body is burning all over, and I feel as if I had twenty tongues in my mouth. It is horrid! Idiotic! This poor old sinner is drunk again, and doesn't even know what he has been celebrating! Ugh! My head is splitting. I am shivering all over, and I feel as dark and cold inside as a cellar! Even if I don't mind ruining my health, I ought at least to remember my age, old idiot that I am! Yes, my old age! It's no use! I can play the fool, and brag, and pretend to be young, but my life is really over now, I kiss my hand to the sixty-eight years that have gone by; I'll never see them again! I have drained the bottle, only a few little drops are left at the bottom, nothing but the dregs. Yes, yes, that's the case, Vasili, old boy. The time has come for you to rehearse the part of a mummy, whether you like it or not. Death is on its way to you. [*Stares ahead of him.*] It is strange, though, that I have been on the stage now for forty-five years, and this is the first time I have seen a theatre at night, after the lights have been put out. The first time. [*Walks up to the footlights.*] How dark it is! I can't see a thing. Oh, yes, I can just make out the prompter's box, and his desk; the rest is in pitch darkness, a black, bottomless pit, like a grave, in which death itself might be hiding. . . . Brr . . . How cold it is! The wind blows out of the empty theatre as though out of a stone flue. What a place for ghosts! The shivers are running up and down my back. [*Calls.*] Yegorka! Petrushka! Where are you both? What on earth makes me think of such gruesome things here? I must give up drinking; I'm an old man, I shan't live much longer. At sixty-eight people go to church and prepare for death, but here I am — heavens! A profane old drunkard in this fool's dress — I'm simply not fit to look at. I must go and change it at once. . . This is a dreadful place, I should die of fright sitting here all night. [*Goes toward his dressing-room; at the same time* NIKITA IVANITCH *in a long white coat comes out of the dressing-room at the farthest end of the stage.* SVIETLOVIDOFF *sees* IVANITCH — *shrieks with terror and steps back.*] Who are you? What? What do you want? [*Stamps his foot.*] Who are you?

IVANITCH. It is I, sir.

SVIETLOVIDOFF. Who are you?

IVANITCH. [*Comes slowly toward him.*] It is I, sir, the prompter, Nikita Ivanitch. It is I, master, it is I!

SVIETLOVIDOFF. [*Sinks helplessly on to the stool, breathes heavily and trembles violently.*] Heavens! Who are you? It is you . . . you Nikitushka? What . . . what are you doing here?

IVANITCH. I spend my nights here in the dressing-rooms. Only please be good enough not to tell Alexi Fomitch, sir. I have nowhere else to spend the night; indeed, I haven't.

SVIETLOVIDOFF. Ah! It is you, Nikitushka, is it? Just think, the audience called me out sixteen times; they brought me three wreaths and lots of other things, too; they were all wild with enthusiasm, and yet not a soul came when it was all over to wake the poor, drunken old man and take him home. And I am an old man, Nikitushka! I am sixty-eight years old, and I am ill. I haven't the heart left to go on. [*Falls on* IVAN-

ITCH's *neck and weeps.*] Don't go away, Nikitushka; I am old and helpless, and I feel it is time for me to die. Oh, it is dreadful, dreadful!

IVANITCH [*tenderly and respectfully*]. Dear master! It is time for you to go home, sir!

SVIETLOVIDOFF. I won't go home; I have no home — none! none! — none!

IVANITCH. Oh, dear! Have you forgotten where you live?

SVIETLOVIDOFF. I won't go there. I won't! I am all alone there. I have nobody, Nikitushka! No wife — no children. I am like the wind blowing across the lonely fields. I shall die, and no one will remember me. It is awful to be alone — no one to cheer me, no one to caress me, no one to help me to bed when I am drunk. Whom do I belong to? Who needs me? Who loves me? Not a soul, Nikitushka.

IVANITCH [*weeping*]. Your audience loves you, master.

SVIETLOVIDOFF. My audience has gone home. They are all asleep, and have forgotten their old clown. No, nobody needs me, nobody loves me; I have no wife, no children.

IVANITCH. Oh, dear, oh, dear! Don't be so unhappy about it.

SVIETLOVIDOFF. But I am a man, I am still alive. Warm, red blood is tingling in my veins, the blood of noble ancestors. I am an aristocrat, Nikitushka; I served in the army, in the artillery, before I fell as low as this, and what a fine young chap I was! Handsome, daring, eager! Where has it all gone? What has become of those old days? There's the pit that has swallowed them all! I remember it all now. Forty-five years of my life lie buried there, and what a life, Nikitushka! I can see it as clearly as I see your face: the ecstasy of youth, faith, passion, the love of women — women, Nikitushka!

IVANITCH. It is time you went to sleep, sir.

SVIETLOVIDOFF. When I first went on the stage, in the first glow of passionate youth, I remember a woman loved me for acting. She was beautiful, graceful as a poplar, young, innocent, pure, and radiant as a summer dawn. Her smile could charm away the darkest night. I remember, I stood before her once, as I am now standing before you. She had never seemed so lovely to me as she did then, and she spoke to me so with her eyes — such a look! I shall never forget it, no, not even in the grave; so tender, so soft, so deep, so bright and young! Enraptured, intoxicated, I fell on my knees before her, I begged for my happiness, and she said: "Give up the stage!" Give up the stage! Do you understand? She could love an actor, but marry him — never! I was acting that day, I remember — I had a foolish, clown's part, and as I acted, I felt my eyes being opened; I saw that the worship of the art I had held so sacred was a delusion and an empty dream; that I was a slave, a fool, the plaything of the idleness of strangers. I understood my audience at last, and since that day I have not believed in their applause, or in their wreaths, or in their enthusiasm. Yes, Nikitushka! The people applaud me, they buy my photograph, but I am a stranger to them. They don't know me, I am as the dirt beneath their feet. They are willing enough to meet me . . . but allow a daughter or a sister to marry me, an outcast, never! I have no faith in them, [*Sinks on to the stool.*] no faith in them.

IVANITCH. Oh, sir! you look dreadfully pale, you frighten me to death! Come, go home, have mercy on me!

SVIETLOVIDOFF. I saw through it all that day, and the knowledge was dearly bought. Nikitushka! After that . . . when that girl . . . well, I began to wander aimlessly about, living from day to day without looking ahead. I took the parts of buffoons and low comedians, letting my mind go to wreck. Ah! but I was a great artist once, till little by little I threw away my talents, played the motley fool, lost my looks, lost the power of expressing myself, and became in the end a Merry Andrew instead of a man. I have been swallowed up in that great black pit. I never felt it before, but to-night, when I woke up, I looked back, and there behind me lay sixty-eight years. I have just found out what it is to be old! It is all over . . . [*sobs*] . . . all over.

IVANITCH. There, there, dear master! Be quiet . . . gracious! [*Calls.*] Petrushka! Yegorka!

SVIETLOVIDOFF. But what a genius I was! You cannot imagine what power I had, what eloquence; how graceful I was, how tender; how many strings [*beats his breast*] quivered in this breast! It chokes me to think of it! Listen now, wait, let me catch my breath, there; now listen to this:

"The shade of bloody Ivan now returning
Fans through my lips rebellion to a flame,
I am the dead Dimitri! In the burning
Boris shall perish on the throne I claim.
Enough! The heir of Czars shall not be seen
Kneeling to yonder haughty Polish Queen!" [1]

[1] From "Boris Godunoff," by Pushkin.

Is that bad, eh? [*Quickly.*] Wait, now, here's something from King Lear. The sky is black, see? Rain is pouring down, thunder roars, lightning — zzz-zzz-zzz — splits the whole sky, and then, listen:

"Blow, winds, and crack your cheeks! rage! blow!
You cataracts and hurricanoes spout
Till you have drench'd our steeples, drown'd the cocks!
You sulphurous thought-executing fires,
Vaunt-couriers of oak-cleaving thunderbolts,
Singe my white head! And thou, all shaking thunder,
Strike flat the thick rotundity o' the world!
Crack nature's moulds, all germens spill at once
That make ungrateful man!"

[*Impatiently.*] Now, the part of the fool. [*Stamps his foot.*] Come, take the fool's part! Be quick, I can't wait!

IVANITCH. [*Takes the part of the fool.*] "O, Nuncle, court holy-water in a dry house is better than this rainwater out o' door. Good Nuncle, in; ask thy daughter's blessing: here's a night pities neither wise men nor fools."

SVIETLOVIDOFF.

"Rumble thy bellyful! spit, fire! spout, rain!
Nor rain, wind, thunder, fire, are my daughters;
I tax not you, you elements, with unkindness;
I never gave you kingdom, call'd you children."

Ah! there is strength, there is talent for you! I'm a great artist! Now, then, here's something else of the same kind, to bring back my youth to me. For instance, take this, from Hamlet, I'll begin . . . let me see, how does it go? Oh, yes, this is it. [*Takes the part of Hamlet.*]

"O! the recorders, let me see one. — To withdraw with you. Why do you go about to recover the wind of me, as if you would drive me into a toil?"

IVANITCH. "O, my lord, if my duty be too bold, my love is too unmannerly."

SVIETLOVIDOFF. "I do not well understand that. Will you play upon this pipe?"

IVANITCH. "My lord, I cannot."

SVIETLOVIDOFF. "I pray you."

IVANITCH. "Believe me, I cannot."

SVIETLOVIDOFF. "I do beseech you."

IVANITCH. "I know no touch of it, my lord."

SVIETLOVIDOFF. "'Tis as easy as lying: govern these ventages with your finger and thumb, give it breath with your mouth, and it will discourse most eloquent music. Look you, these are the stops."

IVANITCH. "But these I cannot command to any utterance of harmony: I have not the skill."

SVIETLOVIDOFF. "Why, look you, how unworthy a thing you make of me. You would play upon me; you would seem to know my stops; you would pluck out the heart of my mystery; you would sound me from my lowest note to the top of my compass; and there is much music, excellent voice, in this little organ, yet cannot you make it speak. S'blood! Do you think I am easier to be played on than a pipe? Call me what instrument you will, though you can fret me, you cannot play upon me!" [*Laughs and clasps.*] Bravo! Encore! Bravo! Where the devil is there any old age in that? I'm not old, that is all nonsense, a torrent of strength rushes over me; this is life, freshness, youth! Old age and genius can't exist together. You seem to be struck dumb, Nikitushka. Wait a second, let me come to my senses again. Oh! Good Lord! Now then, listen! Did you ever hear such tenderness, such music? Sh! Softly;

"The moon had set. There was not any light,
Save of the lonely legion'd watch-stars pale
In outer air, and what by fits make bright
Hot oleanders in a rosy vale
Searched by the lamping fly, whose little spark
Went in and out, like passion's bashful hope."

[*The noise of opening doors is heard.*] What's that?

IVANITCH. There are Petrushka and Yegorka coming back. Yes, you have genius, genius, my master.

SVIETLOVIDOFF. [*Calls, turning toward the noise.*] Come here to me, boys! [*To* IVANITCH.] Let us go and get dressed. I'm not old! All that is foolishness, nonsense! [*Laughs gayly.*] What are you crying for? You poor old granny, you, what's the matter now? This won't do! There, there, this won't do at all! Come, come, old man, don't stare so! What makes you stare like that? There, there! [*Embraces him in tears.*] Don't cry! Where there is art and genius there can never be such things as old age or loneliness or sickness . . . and death itself is half. . . [*Weeps.*] No, no, Nikitushka! It is all over for us now! What sort of a genius am I? I'm like a squeezed lemon, a cracked bottle, and you — you are the old rat of the theatre . . . a prompter! Come on! [*They go.*] I'm no genius, I'm only fit to be in the suite of Fortinbras, and even for that I am too old. . . . Yes. . . . Do you remember those lines from Othello, Nikitushka?

"Farewell the tranquil mind! Farewell content!
Farewell the plumed troops and the big wars

That make ambition virtue! O farewell!
Farewell the neighing steed and the shrill trump,
The spirit-stirring drum, the ear-piercing fife,
The royal banner, and all quality,
Pride, pomp and circumstance of glorious war!"

    IVANITCH. Oh! You're a genius, a genius!
    SVIETLOVIDOFF. And again this:

"Away! the moor is dark beneath the moon,
Rapid clouds have drunk the last pale beam of even:
Away! the gathering winds will call the darkness soon,
And profoundest midnight shroud the serene lights of
    heaven."

    [*They go out together, the curtain falls slowly.*]

THE MAN ON THE KERB [1]

A DUOLOGUE

BY

ALFRED SUTRO

[1] Reprinted from the volume "Five Little Plays" by permission of the author.   For permission to perform this play application must be made to the author in care of the publisher, Brentano.

It was well that Alfred Sutro, the son of an English country physician, once a commission merchant and then a manufacturer, retired at thirty to write high comedy, and gave us "The Walls of Jericho" and "The Builders of Bridges." In story and presentation he is strong, as becomes the writer of comedy of manners, giving in ordinary speech of ordinary people incidents cleverly contrived.

In the pathetic, one-act play, "The Man on the Kerb," there is no imaginative language, no splendid phrases, but it is very close to life.

THE MAN ON THE KERB

THE PERSONS OF THE PLAY

JOSEPH MATTHEWS
MARY [*his wife*]

TIME: The present.
SCENE: Their home in the West End.

SCENE: *An underground room, bare of any furniture except two or three broken chairs, a tattered mattress on the stone floor, and an old trunk. On a packing chest are a few pots and pans and a kettle. A few sacks are spread over the floor, close to the empty grate; the walls are discolored, with plentiful signs of damp oozing through. Close to the door, at back, is a window, looking on to the areas; two of the panes are broken and stuffed with paper.*

On the mattress a child is sleeping, covered with a tattered old mantle; MARY *is bending over her, crooning a song. The woman is still quite young, and must have been very pretty; but her cheeks are hollow and there are great circles round her eyes; her face is very pale and bloodless. Her dress is painfully worn and shabby, but displays pathetic attempts at neatness. The only light in the room comes from the street lamp on the pavement above.*

JOE *comes down the area steps, and enters. His clothes are of the familiar colorless, shapeless kind one sees*

*at street corners; he would be a pleasant looking
young fellow enough were it not that his face is ab-
normally lined, and pinched, and weather-beaten.
He shambles in, with the intense weariness of a man
who has for hours been forcing benumbed limbs to
move; he shakes himself, on the threshold, dog-fashion,
to get rid of the rain.* MARY *first makes sure that
the child is asleep, then rises eagerly and goes to him.
Her face falls as she notes his air of dejection.*

MARY [*wistfully*]. Nothing, Joe?

JOE. Nothing. Not a farthing. Nothing.

[MARY *turns away and checks a moan.*]

JOE. Nothing at all. Same as yesterday — worse
than yesterday — I *did* bring home a few coppers —
And you?

MARY. A lady gave Minnie some food —

JOE [*heartily*]. Bless her for that!

MARY. Took her into the pastrycook's, Joe —

JOE. And the kiddie had a tuck-out? Thank God!
And you?

MARY. Minnie managed to hide a great big bun
for me.

JOE. The lady didn't give you anything?

MARY. Only a lecture, Joe, for bringing the child
out on so bitter a day.

JOE [*with a sour laugh, as he sits on a chair*]. Ho, ho!
Always so ready with their lectures, aren't they?
"Shouldn't beg, my man! Never give to beggars in the
street!" — Look at me, I said to one of them.   Feel my
arm. Tap my chest. I tell you I'm starving, and
they're starving at home. — "Never give to beggars
in the street."

MARY [*laying a hand on his arm*]. Oh, Joe, you're wet!

JOE. It's been raining hard the last three hours—pouring. My stars, it's cold. Couldn't we raise a bit of fire, Mary?

MARY. With what, Joe?

JOE [*after a look round, suddenly getting up, seizing a rickety chair by the wall, breaking off the legs*]. With this! Wonderful fine furniture they give you on the Hire System — so solid and substantial — as advertised. [*He breaks the flimsy thing up, as he speaks.*] And to think we paid for this muck, in the days we were human beings — paid about three times its value! And to think of the poor devils, poor devils like us, who sweated their life-blood out to make it — and of the blood-sucking devils who sold it and got fat on it — and now back it goes to the devil it came from, and we can at least get warm for a minute. [*He crams the wood into the grate.*] Got any paper, Mary?

MARY [*taking an old newspaper from the trunk*]. Here, Joe.

JOE. That will help to build up a fire. [*He glances at it, then lays it carefully underneath the wood.* MARY *gets lamp from table.*] The Daily Something or other — that tells the world what a happy people we are — how proud of belonging to an Empire on which the sun never sets. And I'd sell Gibraltar to-night for a sausage with mashed potatoes; and let Russia take India if some one would give me a clerkship at a pound a week. — There, in you go! A match, Mary?

MARY [*standing above* JOE, *handing him one*]. Oh, Joe, be careful — we've only two left!

JOE. I'll be careful. Wait, though — I'll see whether there's a bit of tobacco still in my pipe. [*He fishes the pipe out of his pocket.*] A policeman who warned me away from the kerb gave me some tobacco. "Mustn't beg," he said. "Got a pipe? Well, here's some tobacco." I believe he'd have given me money. But it was the first kind word I had heard all day, and it choked me. — There's just a bit left at the bottom. [*He bustles.*] Now, first the fire. [*He puts the match to the paper — it kindles.*] And then my pipe. [*The fire burns up; he throws himself in front of it.*] Boo-o-oh, I'm sizzling . . . I got so wet that I felt the water running into my lungs — my feet didn't seem to belong to me — and as for my head and nose! [*Yawns.*] Well, smoke's good — by the powers, I'm getting warm — come closer to it, Mary. It's a little after midnight now — and I left home, this fine, luxurious British home, just as soon as it was light. And I've tramped the streets all day. Net result, a policeman gave me a pipeful of tobacco, I lunched off a bit of bread that I saw floating down the gutter — and I dined off the kitchen smell of the Café Royal. That's my day.

MARY [*stroking his hand*]. Poor boy, poor boy!

JOE. I stood for an hour in Leicester Square when the theatres emptied, thinking I might earn a copper, calling a cab, or something. There they were, all streaming out, happy and clean and warm — broughams and motor-cars — supper at the Savoy and the Carlton — and a hundred or two of us others in the gutter, hungry — looking at them. They went off to their supper — it was pouring, and I got soaked — and there I stood, dodging the policemen, dodging the horses' heads and the motors — and it was always — get away, you loafer, get away — get away — get away —

MARY. We've done nothing to deserve it, Joe —

JOE [*with sudden fury*]. Deserve it! What have I ever done wrong! Wasn't *my* fault the firm went bankrupt and I couldn't get another job. I've a first-rate character — I'm respectable — what's the use? I want to work — they won't let me!

MARY. That illness of mine ate up all our savings. O Joe, I wish I had died!

JOE. And left me alone? That's not kind of you, Mary. How about Mrs. Willis? Is she worrying about the rent?

MARY. Well, she'd like to have it, of course — they're so dreadfully poor themselves — but she says she won't turn us out. And I'm going to-morrow to her daughter's upstairs — she makes match-boxes, you know — and I don't see why I shouldn't try — I could earn a shilling a day.

JOE. A shilling a day! Princely! [*His pipe goes out. He takes a last puff at it, squints into it to make sure all the tobacco is gone, then lays it down with a sigh.*] I reckon *I'll* try making 'em too. I went to the Vestry again, this morning, to see whether they'd take me as sweeper — but they've thirty names down, ahead of me. I've tried chopping wood, but I can't — I begin to cough the third stroke — there's something wrong with me inside, somewhere. I've tried every Institution on God's earth — and there are others before me, and there is no vacancy, and I mustn't beg, and I mustn't worry the gentlemen. A shilling a day — can one earn as much as that! Why, Mary, that will be fourteen shillings a week — an income! We'll do it!

MARY. It's not quite a shilling, Joe — you have to find your own paste and odds and ends. And of course it takes a few weeks to learn, before you begin to make any money.

JOE [*crestfallen*]. Does it though? And what are we going to do, those few weeks? I thought there was a catch in it somewhere. [*He gets up and stretches himself.*] Well, here's a free-born Englishman, able to conduct correspondence in three languages, book-keeping by double entry, twelve years' experience — and all he's allowed to do is to starve. [*He stretches himself again.*]

> But in spite of all temptations
> To belong to other nations —

[*With sudden passion.*] God! I wish I were a Zulu!

MARY [*edging to him*]. Joe —

JOE [*turning*]. Well?

MARY. Joe, Joe, we've tried very hard, haven't we?

JOE. Tried! Is there a job in this world we'd refuse? Is there anything we'd turn up our nose at? Is there any chance we've neglected?

MARY [*stealing nervously to him and laying a hand on his arm*]. Joe —

JOE [*raising his head and looking at her*]. Yes — what is it? [*She stands timidly with downcast eyes.*] Well? Out with it, Mary!

MARY [*suddenly*]. It's this, Joe.

[*She goes feverishly to the mattress, and from underneath it she pulls out a big, fat purse which she hands him.*]

JOE [*staring*]. A purse!

MARY [*nodding*]. Yes.

JOE. You —

MARY. Found it.

JOE [*looking at her*]. Found?

MARY [*awkwardly*]. In a way I did — yes.

JOE. How?

MARY. It came on to rain, Joe — and I went into a Tube Station — and was standing by a bookstall, showing Minnie the illustrated papers — and an old lady bought one — and she took out her purse — this purse — and paid for it — and laid the purse on the board while she fumbled to pick up her skirts — and then some one spoke to her — a friend, I suppose — and — there were lots of people standing about — I don't know how it was — I was out in the street, with Minnie —

JOE. You had the purse?

MARY. Yes —

JOE. No one followed you?

MARY. No one. I couldn't run, as I had to carry Minnie.

JOE. What made you do it?

MARY. I don't know — something in me did it — She put the purse down just by the side of my hand — my fingers clutched it before I knew — and I was out in the street.

JOE. How much is there in it?

MARY. I haven't looked, Joe.

JOE [*wonderingly*]. You haven't looked?

MARY. No; I didn't dare.

JOE [*sorrowfully*]. I didn't think we'd come to this, Mary.

MARY [*desperately*]. We've got to do something. Before we can earn any money at making matchboxes we'll have to spend some weeks learning. And you've not had a decent meal for a month — nor have I. If there's money inside this purse you can get some clothes — and for me too — I need them! It's not

as though the old lady would miss it — she's rich enough
— her cloak was real sable — and no one can find us
out — they can't tell one piece of money from the other.
It's heavy, Joe — I think there's a lot inside.

JOE [*weighing it mechanically*]. Yes — it's heavy —

MARY [*eagerly*]. Open it, Joe.

JOE [*turning to her again*]. Why didn't you?

MARY. I just thought I'd wait — I'd an idea something might have happened; that some one might have
stopped you in the street, some one with a heart —
and that he'd have come in with you to-night — and
seen us — seen Minnie — and said — "Well, here's
money — I'll put you on your legs again" — And then
we'd have given the purse back, Joe.

JOE [*as he still mechanically balances it in his hand*].
Yes.

MARY. Can't go on like this, can we? You'll
cough all night again, as you did yesterday — and the
stuff they gave you at the Dispensary's no good. If
you had clothes, you might get some sort of a job perhaps — you know you had to give up trying because
you were so shabby.

JOE. They laugh at me.

MARY [*with a glance at herself*]. And I'm really
ashamed to walk through the streets —

JOE. I know — though I'm getting used to it.
Besides, there's the kiddie. Let's have a look at her.

MARY. Be careful you don't wake her, Joe!

JOE. There's a fire.

MARY. She'll be hungry.

JOE. You said that she had some food?

MARY. That was at three o'clock. And little
things aren't like us — they want their regular meals.

Night after night she has been hungry, and I've had nothing to give her. That's why I took the purse.

JOE [*still holding it mechanically and staring at it*]. Yes. And, after all, why not?

MARY. We can get the poor little thing some warm clothes, some good food —

JOE [*under his breath*]. A thief's daughter.
[*Covers his face with his hands.*]

MARY. Joe!

JOE. Not nice, is it? Can't be helped, of course. And who cares? For three months this game has gone on — we getting shabbier, wretcheder, hungrier, — no one bothers — all *they* say is "keep off the pavement." Let's see what's in the purse.

MARY [*eagerly*]. Yes, yes!

JOE [*lifting his head as he is on the point of opening the purse*]. That's the policeman passing.

MARY [*impatiently*]. Never mind that —

JOE [*turning to the purse again*]. First time in my life I've been afraid when I heard the policeman.

[*He has his finger on the catch of the purse when he pauses for a moment — then acting on a sudden impulse, makes a dart for the door, opens it, and is out, and up the area steps.*]

MARY [*with a despairing cry*]. Joe!

[*She flings herself on the mattress, and sobs silently, so as not to awaken the child.* JOE *returns, hanging his head, dragging one foot before the other.*]

MARY [*still sobbing, but trying to control herself*]. Why did you do that?

JOE [*humbly*]. I don't know —

MARY. You gave it to the policeman?

JOE. Yes.

MARY. What did you tell him?

JOE. That you had found it.

MARY. Where?

JOE. In a Tube Station. Picked it up because we were starving. That we hadn't opened it. And that we lived here, in this cellar.

MARY [*with a little shake*]. I expect he'll keep it himself!

JOE [*miserably*]. Perhaps.

[*There is silence for a moment; she has ceased to cry; suddenly she raises herself violently on her elbow.*]

MARY. You fool! You fool!

JOE [*pleading*]. Mary!

MARY. With your stupid ideas of honesty! What have they done for you, or me?

JOE [*dropping his head again*]. It's the kiddie, you know — her being a thief's daughter —

MARY. Is that worse than being the daughter of a pair of miserable beggars?

JOE [*under his breath*]. I suppose it is, somehow —

MARY. You'd rather she went hungry?

JOE [*despairingly*]. I don't know how it was — hearing his tramp up there —

MARY. You were afraid?

JOE. I don't want you taken to prison.

MARY [*with a wail*]. I'll be taken to the graveyard soon, in a pauper's coffin!

JOE [*starts suddenly*]. Suppose we did that?

MARY [*staring*]. The workhouse?

JOE. Why not, after all? That's what it will come to, sooner or later.

MARY. They'd separate us.

JOE. At least you and the kiddie'd have food.

MARY. They'd separate us. And I love you, Joe. My poor, poor Joe! I love you.

[*She nestles up to him and takes his hand.*]

JOE [*holding her hand in his, and bending over her*]. You forgive me for returning the purse?

MARY [*dropping her head on his shoulder*]. Forgive you! You were right. It was the cold and the hunger maddened me. You were right!

JOE [*springing to his feet, with sudden passion.* MARY *staggers back*]. I *wasn't* right — I was a coward, a criminal — a vile and wicked fool.

MARY [*startled*]. Joe!

JOE. I had money there — money in my hand — money that you need so badly, you, the woman I love with all my ragged soul — money that would have put food into the body of my little girl — money that was mine, that belonged to me — and I've given it back, because of my rotten honesty! What right have I to be honest? They've made a dog of me — what business had I to remember I was a man?

MARY [*following him and laying a hand on his arm*]. Hush, Joe — You'll wake Minnie.

JOE [*turning and staring haggardly at her*]. I could have got clothes — a job, perhaps — we might have left this cellar. We could have gone out to-morrow and bought things — gone into shops — we might have had food, coal —

MARY. Don't, Joe — what's the use? And who knows — it may prove a blessing to us. You told the policeman where we lived?

JOE. A blessing! I'll get up to-morrow, after having coughed out my lungs all night — and I'll go into the streets and walk there from left to right and from right to left, standing at this corner and at that, peering into men's faces, watching people go to their shops and their offices, people who are warm and comfortable — and so it will go on, till the end comes.

MARY [*standing very close to him, almost in a whisper*]. Why not now, Joe?

JOE [*with a startled glance at her*]. The end?

MARY. There's no room for us in this world —

JOE. If I'd taken that money —

MARY. It's too late for that now. And I'm glad you didn't — yes, I am — I'm glad. We'll go before God clean-handed. And we'll say to Him we didn't steal, or do anything He didn't want us to. And we'll tell Him we've died because people wouldn't allow us to live.

JOE [*with a shudder*]. No. Not that — we'll wait, Mary. Don't speak of that.

MARY [*wistfully*]. You've thought of it too?

JOE. Thought of it! Don't, Mary, don't! It's bad enough, in the night, when I lie there and think of to-morrow! Something will happen — it must.

MARY. What? We haven't a friend in the world.

JOE. I may meet some one I used to know.

MARY. You've met them before — they always refuse —

JOE [*passionately*]. I've done nothing wrong — I haven't drunk or gambled — I can't help being only a clerk, and unable to do heavy work! I can't help my lungs being weak! I've a wife and a child, like other people — and all we ask is to be allowed to live!

MARY [*pleading*]. Let's give it up, Joe. Go away together, you'd sleep without coughing. Sleep, that's all. And God will be kinder than men.

JOE [*groaning*]. Don't, Mary — don't!

MARY. Joe, I can't stand it any longer — I can't. Not only myself — but Minnie — Joe, it's too much for me! I can't stand Minnie crying, and asking me for her breakfast, as she will in the morning. Joe, dear Joe, let there be no morning!

JOE [*completely overcome*]. Oh, Mary, Mary!

MARY. It's not *your* fault, dear — you've done what you could. Not *your* fault they won't let you work — you've tried hard enough. And no woman ever had a better husband than you've been to me. I love you, dear Joe. And let's do it — let's make an end. And take Minnie with us.

JOE [*springing up*]. Mary, I'll steal something to-morrow.

MARY. And they'd send you to prison. Besides, then God would be angry. Now we can go to Him and need not be ashamed. Let us, dear Joe — oh, do let us! I'm so tired!

JOE. No.

MARY [*sorrowfully*]. You won't?

JOE [*doggedly*]. No. We'll go to the workhouse.

MARY. You've seen them in there, haven't you?

JOE. Yes.

MARY. You've seen them standing at the window, staring at the world? And they'd take you away from me.

JOE. That's better than —

MARY [*firmly*]. I won't do it, Joe. I've been a good wife to you — I've been a good mother: and I love you, though I'm ragged and have pawned all my clothes; and I'll strangle myself rather than go to the workhouse and be shut away from you.

JOE [*with a loud cry*]. No! I'll make them give me something; and if I have to kill, it shan't be my wife and child! To-morrow I'll come home with food and money — to-morrow —

[*There is a sudden wail from the child;* JOE *stops and stares at her;* MARY *goes quickly to the mattress and soothes the little girl.*]

MARY. Hush, dear, hush — no, it's not morning yet, not time for breakfast. Go to sleep again, dear. Yes, daddy's come back, and things are going to be all right now — No, dear, you can't be hungry, really — remember those beautiful cakes. Go to sleep, Minnie, dear. You're cold? [*She takes off her ragged shawl and wraps it round the child.*] There, dear, you won't be cold now. Go to sleep, Minnie —

[*The child's wail dies away, as* MARY *soothes her back to sleep.*]

JOE [*staggering forward with a sudden cry*]. God, O God, give us bread!

THE CURTAIN SLOWLY FALLS

THE SHADOWED STAR [1]

BY

MARY MacMILLAN

In her preface to the volume called "Short Plays," from which this play is taken, the author says, "Some are born dramatists, — like Shakespeare; some achieve dramatic construction, — like Ibsen; and some have drama thrust upon them — like me." She explains that she was commanded by some clubwomen to write a drama that could be acted by five or six persons in forty-five minutes. Certainly Mary Mac-Millan's dialogue is most pleasing and real, and from the point of view of technique the construction is most apt.

The following play was published separately by the Consumers' League for reasons perfectly obvious from the reading. Miss MacMillan's big heart and complete understanding of human longings are here made so concrete in the words of the Old Woman, that one wishes a more intimate knowledge of her through the reading of her other dramas in the above volume.

THE SHADOWED STAR

CAST

A WOMAN, *the mother*
AN OLD WOMAN, *the grandmother*
TWO GIRLS, *the daughters*
A MESSENGER BOY
A NEIGHBOR
ANOTHER NEIGHBOR

[*A very bare room in a tenement house, uncarpeted, the
boards being much worn, and from the walls the
bluish whitewash has scaled away; in the front
on one side is a cooking-stove, and farther back
on the same side a window; on the opposite side is
a door opening into a hallway; in the middle of the
room there is a round, worn dining-table, on which
stands a stunted, scraggly bit of an evergreen-tree;
at the back of the room, near the window, stands
an old-fashioned safe with perforated tin front;
next it a door opening into an inner room, and next
it in the corner a bed, on which lies a pallid woman;
another woman, very old, sits in a rocking-chair
in front of the stove and rocks. There is silence
for a long space, the old woman rocking and the
woman on the bed giving an occasional low sigh or
groan. At last the old woman speaks.*]

THE OLD WOMAN. David an' Michael might be
kapin' the Christmas wid us to-morrow night if we

hadn't left the ould counthry. They'd never be crossin' the sea — all the many weary miles o' wetness an' fog an' cold to be kapin' it wid us here in this great house o' brick walls in a place full o' strange souls. They would never be for crossin' all that weary, cold, green wather, groanin' an' tossin' like it was the grave o' sivin thousan' divils. Ah, but it would be a black night at sea! [*She remains silent for a few minutes, staring at the stove and rocking slowly.*] If they hadn't to cross that wet, cold sea they'd maybe come. But wouldn't they be afeard o' this great city, an' would they iver find us here? Six floors up, an' they niver off the ground in their lives. What would ye be thinkin'? [*The other woman does not answer her. She then speaks petulantly.*] What would ye be thinkin', Mary, have ye gone clane to slape? [*Turns her chair and peers around the back of it at the pallid woman on the bed, who sighs and answers.*]

THE WOMAN. No, I on'y wisht I could. Maybe they'll come — I don't know, but father an' Michael wasn't much for thravel. [*After a pause and very wearily.*] Maybe they'll not come, yet [*slowly*] maybe I'll be kapin' the Christmas wid them there. [*The* OLD WOMAN *seems not to notice this, wandering from her question back to her memories.*]

THE OLD WOMAN. No, they'll niver be lavin' the ould land, the green land, the home land. I'm wishing I was there wid thim. [*Another pause, while she stares at the stove.*] Maybe we'd have a duck an' potatoes, an' maybe something to drink to kape us warm against the cold. An' the boys would all be dancin' an' the girls have rosy cheeks. [*There is another pause, and then a knock at the door. "Come in," the two women call, in reedy, weak voices, and a thin, slatternly Irish woman enters.*]

THE NEIGHBOR. Good evenin' to ye; I came in to ask if I might borrow the loan o' a bit o' tay, not havin' a leaf of it left.

THE WOMAN. We have a little left, just enough we was savin' for ourselves to-night, but you're welcome to it — maybe the girls will bring some. Will ye get it for her, mother? Or she can help herself — it's in the safe. It's on the lower shelf among the cups an' saucers an' plates. [THE OLD WOMAN *and* NEIGHBOR *go to the safe and hunt for the tea, and do not find it readily. The safe has little in it but a few cracked and broken dishes.*]

THE NEIGHBOR [*holding up a tiny paper bag with an ounce perhaps of tea in it*]. It's just a scrap!

THE OLD WOMAN. To be sure! We use so much tay! We're that exthravagant!

THE NEIGHBOR. It hurts me to take it from ye — maybe I'd better not.

THE OLD WOMAN. The girls will bring more. We always have a cupboard full o' things. We're always able to lend to our neighbors.

THE NEIGHBOR. It's in great luck, ye are. For some of us be so poor we don't know where the next bite's comin' from. An' this winter whin iverything's so high an' wages not raised, a woman can't find enough to cook for her man's dinner. It isn't that ye don't see things — oh, they're in the markets an' the shops, an' it makes yer mouth wather as ye walk along the sthrates this day before Christmas to see the turkeys an' the ducks ye'll niver ate, an' the little pigs an' the or'nges an' bananies an' cranberries an' the cakes an' nuts an' — it's worse, I'm thinkin', to see thim whin there's no money to buy than it was in the ould counthry, where there was nothing to buy wid the money ye didn't have.

THE WOMAN. It's all one to us poor folk whether there be things to buy or not. [*She speaks gaspingly, as one who is short of breath.*] I'm on'y thinkin' o' the clane air at home — if I could have a mornin' o' fresh sunshine — these fogs an' smoke choke me so. The girls would take me out to the counthry if they had time an' I'd get well. But they haven't time. [*She falls into a fit of coughing.*]

THE OLD WOMAN. But it's like to be bright on Christmas Day. It wouldn't iver be cloudy on Christmas Day, an' maybe even now the stars would be crapin' out an' the air all clear an' cold an' the moon a-shinin' an' iverything so sthill an' quiet an' gleamin' an' breathless [*her voice falls almost to a whisper*], awaitin' on the Blessed Virgin. [*She goes to the window, lifts the blind, and peers out, then throws up the sash and leans far out. After a moment she pulls the sash down again and the blind and turns to those in the room with the look of pathetic disappointment in little things of the aged.*] No, there's not a sthar, not one little twinklin' sthar, an' how'll the shepherds find their way? Iverything's dull an' black an' the clouds are hangin' down heavy an' sthill. How'll the shepherds find their way without the sthar to guide thim? [*Then almost whimpering.*] An' David an' Michael will niver be crossin' that wet, black sea! An' the girls — how'll they find their way home? They'll get lost somewhere along by the hedges. Ohone, ohone!

THE NEIGHBOR. Now, grannie, whay would ye be

sayin'? There's niver a hedge anywhere but granite blocks an' electric light poles an' plenty o' light in the city for thim to see all their way home. [*Then to* THE WOMAN.] Ain't they late?

THE WOMAN. They're always late, an' they kape gettin' lather an' lather.

THE NEIGHBOR. Yis, av coorse, the sthores is all open in the avnin's before Christmas.

THE WOMAN. They go so early in the mornin' an' get home so late at night, an' they're so tired.

THE NEIGHBOR [*whiningly*]. They're lucky to be young enough to work an' not be married. I've got to go home to the childer an' give thim their tay. Pat's gone to the saloon again, an' to-morrow bein' Christmas I misdoubt he'll be terrible dhrunk again, an' me on'y jist well from the blow in the shoulder the last time. [*She wipes her eyes and moves towards the door.*]

THE OLD WOMAN. Sthay an' kape Christmas wid us. We're goin' to have our celebratin' to-night on Christmas Eve, the way folks do here. I like it best on Christmas Day, the way 'tis in the ould counthry, but here 'tis Christmas Eve they kape. We're waitin' for the girls to come home to start things — they knowin' how — Mary an' me on'y know how to kape Christmas Day as 'tis at home. But the girls'll soon be here, an' they'll have the tree an' do the cookin' an' all, an' we'll kape up the jollity way into the night.

THE NEIGHBOR [*looks questioningly and surprised at* THE WOMAN, *whose eyes are on the mother*]. Nay, if Pat came home dhrunk an' didn't find me, he'd kill me. We have all to be movin' on to our own throubles. [*She goes out, and* THE OLD WOMAN *leaves the*

x

Christmas tree which she had been fingering and admiring and sits down in the rocking-chair again. After a while she croons to herself in a high, broken voice. This lasts some time, when there is the noise of a slamming door and then of footsteps approaching.]

THE WOMAN. If I could on'y be in the counthry!

THE OLD WOMAN. Maybe that would be the girls! [*She starts tremblingly to her feet, but the steps come up to the door and go by.*] If David and Michael was to come now an' go by — there bein' no sthar to guide thim!

THE WOMAN. Nay, mother, 'twas the shepherds that was guided by the sthar an' to the bed o' the Blessed Babe.

THE OLD WOMAN. Aye, so 'twas. What be I thinkin' of? The little Blessed Babe! [*She smiles and sits staring at the stove again for a little.*] But they could not find Him to-night. 'Tis so dark an' no sthars shinin'. [*After another pause.*] An' what would shepherds do in a ghreat city? 'Twould be lost they'd be, quicker than in any bog. Think ye, Mary, that the boys would be hootin' thin an' the p'lice, maybe, would want to be aristin' thim for loitherin'. They'd niver find the Blessed Babe, an' they'd have to be movin' on. [*Another pause, and then there is the sound of approaching footsteps again.* THE OLD WOMAN *grasps the arms of her chair and leans forward, intently listening.*] That would sure be the girls this time! [*But again the footsteps go by.* THE OLD WOMAN *sighs.*] Ah, but 'tis weary waitin'! [*There is another long pause.*] 'Twas on that day that David an' me was plighted — a brave Christmas Day wid a shinin' sun an' a sky o' blue wid fair, white clouds. An' David an' me met at the early mass in the dark o' the frosty mornin' afore the sun rose — an' there was all day good times an' a duck for dinner and puddin's an' a party at the O'Brady's in the evenin', whin David an' me danced. Ah, but he was a beautiful dancer, an' me, too — I was as light on my feet as a fairy. [*She begins to croon an old dance tune and hobbles to her feet, and, keeping time with her head, tries a grotesque and feeble sort of dancing. Her eyes brighten and she smiles proudly.*] Ay, but I danced like a fairy, an' there was not another couple so sprightly an' handsome in all the country. [*She tires, and, looking pitiful and disappointed, hobbles back to her chair, and drops into it again.*] Ah, but I be old now, and the strength fails me. [*She falls into silence for a few minutes.*] 'Twas the day before the next Christmas that Michael was born — the little man, the little white dove, my little son! [*There is a moment's pause, and then the pallid woman on the bed has a violent fit of coughing.*]

THE WOMAN. Mother, could ye get me a cup o' wather? If the girls was here to get me a bite to ate, maybe it would kape the breath in me the night.

THE OLD WOMAN [*starts and stares at her daughter, as if she hardly comprehended the present reality. She gets up and goes over to the window under which there is a pail full of water. She dips some out in a tin cup and carries it to her bed.*] Ye should thry to get up an' move about some, so ye can enjoy the Christmas threat. 'Tis bad bein' sick on Christmas. Thry, now, Mary, to sit up a bit. The girls'll be wantin' ye to be merry wid the rest av us.

THE WOMAN [*looking at her mother, with a sad wistfulness*]. I wouldn't spoil things for the girls if I could help. Maybe, mother, if ye'd lift me a little I could sit up. [THE OLD WOMAN *tugs at her, and she herself tries hard to get into a sitting posture, but after some effort and panting for breath, she falls back again. After a pause for rest, she speaks gaspingly.*] Maybe I'll feel sthronger lather whin the girls come home — they could help me — [*with the plaint of longing in her voice*] they be so late! [*After another pause.*] Maybe I'll be sthrong again in the mornin' — if I'd had a cup of coffee. Maybe I could get up — an' walk about — an' do the cookin'. [*There is a knock at the door, and again they call, "Come in," in reedy, weak voices. There enters a little messenger boy in a ragged overcoat that reaches almost to his heels. His eyes are large and bright, his face pale and dirty, and he is fearfully tired and worn.*]

THE WOMAN. Why, Tim, boy, come in. Sit ye down an' rest, ye're lookin' weary.

THE OLD WOMAN. Come to the stove, Timmie, man, an' warm yourself. We always kape a warm room an' a bright fire for our visitors.

THE BOY. I was awful cold an' hungry an' I come home to get somethin' to eat before I started out on another trip, but my sisters ain't home from the store yit, an' the fire's gone out in the stove, an' the room's cold as outside. I thought maybe ye'd let me come in here an' git warm.

THE OLD WOMAN. Poor orphan! Poor lamb! To be sure ye shall get warm by our sthove.

THE BOY. The cars are so beastly col' an' so crowded a feller mostly has to stand on the back platform. [THE OLD WOMAN *takes him by the shoulder and pushes him toward the stove, but he resists.*]

THE BOY. No, thank ye — I don't want to go so

near yet; my feet's all numb an' they allays hurt so when they warms up fast.

THE OLD WOMAN. Thin sit ye down off from the sthove. [*Moves the rocking-chair farther away from the stove for him.*]

THE BOY. If ye don't mind I'd rather stand on 'em 'til they gets a little used to it. They been numb off an' on mos' all day.

THE WOMAN. Soon as yer sisters come, Timmie, ye'd betther go to bed — 'tis best place to get warm.

THE BOY. I can't — I got most a three-hour trip yet. I won't get home any 'fore midnight if I don't get lost, and maybe I'll get lost — I did onct out there. I've got to take a box o' 'Merican Beauty roses to a place eight mile out, an' the house ain't on the car track, but nearly a mile off, the boss said. I wisht they could wait till mornin', but the orders was they just got to get the roses to-night. You see, out there they don' have no gas goin' nights when there's a moon, an' there'd ought to be a moon to-night, on'y the clouds is so thick there ain't no light gets through.

THE OLD WOMAN. There's no sthar shinin' to-night, Tim. [*She shakes her head ominously. She goes to the window for the second time, opens it as before, and looks out. Shutting the window, she comes back and speaks slowly and sadly.*] Niver a sthar. An' the shepherds will be havin' a hard time, Tim, like you, findin' their way.

THE BOY. Shepherds? In town? What shepherds?

THE WOMAN. She manes the shepherds on Christmas Eve that wint to find the Blessed Babe, Jesus.

THE OLD WOMAN. 'Tis Christmas Eve, Timmie; ye haven't forgot that, have ye?

THE BOY. You bet I ain't. I know pretty well when Christmas is comin', by the way I got to hustle, an' the size of the boxes I got to carry. Seems as if my legs an' me would like to break up pardnership. I got to work till midnight every night, an' I'm so sleepy I drop off in the cars whenever I get a seat. An' the girls is at the store so early an' late they don't get time to cook me nothin' to eat.

THE WOMAN. Be ye hungry, Timmie?

THE BOY [*diffidently and looking at the floor*]. No, I ain't hungry now.

THE WOMAN. Be ye shure, Timmie?

THE BOY. Oh, I kin go till I git home.

THE WOMAN. Mother, can't you find something for him to ate?

THE OLD WOMAN. To be shure, to be shure. [*Bustling about.*] We always kapes a full cupboard to thrate our neighbors wid whin they comes in. [*She goes to the empty safe and fusses in it to find something. She pretends to be very busy, and then glances around at the boy with a sly look and a smile.*] Ah, Timmie, lad, what would ye like to be havin' now? If you had the wish o' yer heart for yer Christmas dinner an' a good fairy set it all afore ye? Ye'd be wishin' maybe, for a fine roast duck, to begin wid, in its own gravies an' some apple sauce to go wid it; an' ye'd be thinkin' o' a little bit o' pig nicely browned an' a plate o' potatoes; an' the little fairy woman would be bringin' yer puddin's an' nuts an' apples an' a dish o' the swatest tay. [THE BOY *smiles rather ruefully.*]

THE WOMAN. But, mother, you're not gettin' Tim something to ate.

THE BOY. She's makin' me mouth water all right.

[THE OLD WOMAN *goes back to her search, but again turns about with a cunning look, and says to* THE BOY.]

THE OLD WOMAN. Maybe ye'll meet that little fairy woman out there in the counthry road where ye're takin' the roses! [*Nods her head knowingly, turning to the safe again.*] Here's salt an' here's pepper an' here's mustard an' a crock full o' sugar, an', oh! Tim, here's some fine cold bacon — fine, fat, cold bacon — an' here's half a loaf o' white wheat bread! Why, Timmie, lad, that's just the food to make boys fat! Ye'll grow famously on it. 'Tis a supper, whin ye add to it a dhrop o' iligant milk, that's fit for a king. [*She bustles about with great show of being busy and having much to prepare. Puts the plate of cold bacon upon the table where stands the stunted bit of an evergreen-tree, then brings the half-loaf of bread and cuts it into slices, laying pieces of bacon on the slices of bread. Then she pours out a glass of milk from a dilapidated and broken pitcher in the safe and brings it to the table,* THE BOY *all the while watching her hungrily. At last he says rather apologetically to* THE WOMAN.]

THE BOY. I ain't had nothin' since a wienerwurst at eleven o'clock.

THE OLD WOMAN. Now, dhraw up, Timmie, boy, an' ate yer fill; ye're more thin welcome. [THE BOY *does not sit down, but stands by the table and eats a slice of bread and bacon, drinking from the glass of milk occasionally.*]

THE WOMAN. Don't they niver give ye nothin' to ate at the gran' houses when ye'd be takin' the roses?

THE BOY. Not them. They'd as soon think o' feedin' a telephone or an automobile as me.

THE WOMAN. But don't they ask ye in to get warm whin ye've maybe come so far?

THE BOY. No, they don't seem to look at me 'zactly like a caller. They generally steps out long enough to sign the receipt-book an' shut the front door behin' 'em so as not to let the house get col' the length o' time I'm standin' there. Well, I'm awful much obleeged to ye. Now, I got to be movin' on.

THE OLD WOMAN. Sthop an' cilibrate the Christmas wid us. We ain't started to do nothin' yet because the girls haven't come — they know how [*nodding her head*] — an' they're goin' to bring things — all kinds o' good things to ate an' a branch of rowan wid scarlet berries shinin' [*gesticulating and with gleaming eyes*], an' we'll all be merry an' kape it up late into the night.

THE BOY [*in a little fear of her*]. I guess it's pretty late now. I got to make that trip an' I guess when I get home I'll be so sleepy I'll jus' tumble in. Ye've been awful good to me, an' it's the first time I been warm to-day. Good-by. [*He starts towards the door, but* THE OLD WOMAN *follows him and speaks to him coaxingly*.]

THE OLD WOMAN. Ah, don't ye go, Michael, lad! Now, bide wid us a bit. [THE BOY, *surprised at the name, looks queerly at* THE OLD WOMAN, *who then stretches out her arms to him, and says beseechingly*] Ah, boy, ah, Mike, bide wid us, now ye've come! We've been that lonesome widout ye!

THE BOY [*frightened and shaking his head*]. I've got to be movin'.

THE OLD WOMAN. No, Michael, little lamb, no!

THE BOY [*almost terrified, watching her with staring eyes, and backing out*]. I got to go! [THE BOY *goes out, and* THE OLD WOMAN *breaks into weeping, totters over to her old rocking-chair and drops into it, rocks to and fro, wailing to herself.*]

THE OLD WOMAN. Oh, to have him come an' go again, my little Michael, my little lad!

THE WOMAN. Don't ye, dearie; now, then, don't ye! 'Twas not Michael, but just our little neighbor boy, Tim. Ye know, por lamb, now if ye'll thry to remember, that father an' Michael is gone to the betther land an' us is left.

THE OLD WOMAN. Nay, nay, 'tis the fairies that took thim an' have thim now, kapin' thim an' will not ever give thim back.

THE WOMAN. Whisht, mother! Spake not of the little folk on the Holy Night! [*Crosses herself.*] Have ye forgot the time o' all the year it is? Now, dhry yer eyes, dearie, an' thry to be cheerful like for the girls be comin' home. [*A noise is heard, the banging of a door and footsteps.*] Thim be the girls now, shure they be comin' at last. [*But the sound of footsteps dies away.*] But they'll be comin' soon. [*Wearily, but with the inveterate hope.*]

[*The two women relapse into silence again, which is undisturbed for a few minutes. Then there is a knock at the door, and together in quavering, reedy voices, they call, "Come in," as before. There enters a tall, big, broad-shouldered woman with a cold, discontented, hard look upon the face that might have been handsome some years back; still, in her eyes, as she looks at the pallid woman on the bed, there is something that denotes a softness underneath it all.*]

THE OLD WOMAN. Good avnin' to ye! We're that pleased to see our neighbors!

THE NEIGHBOR [*without paying any attention to* THE OLD WOMAN, *but entirely addressing* THE WOMAN *on the bed*.] How's yer cough?

THE WOMAN. Oh, it's just the same — maybe a little bether. If I could on'y get to the counthry! But the girls must be workin' — they haven't time to take me. Sit down, won't ye? [THE NEIGHBOR *goes to the bed and sits down on the foot of it*.]

THE NEIGHBOR. I'm most dead, I'm so tired. I did two washin's to-day — went out and did one this mornin' and then my own after I come home this afternoon. I jus' got through sprinklin' it an' I'll iron to-morrow.

THE WOMAN. Not on Christmas Day!

THE NEIGHBOR [*with a sneer*]. Christmas Day! Did ye hear 'bout the Beckers? Well, they was all put out on the sidewalk this afternoon. Becker's been sick, ye know, an' ain't paid his rent, an' his wife's got a two-weeks-old baby. It sort o' stunned Mis' Becker, an' she sat on one of the mattresses out there an' wouldn't move, an' nobody couldn't do nothin' with her. But they ain't the only ones has bad luck — Smith, the painter, fell off a ladder an' got killed. They took him to the hospital, but it wasn't no use — his head was all mashed in. His wife's got them five boys an' Smith never saved a cent, though he warn't no drinkin' man. It's a good thing Smith's children is boys — they can make their livin' easier!

THE WOMAN [*smiling faintly*]. Ain't ye got no cheerful news to tell? It's Christmas Eve, ye know.

THE NEIGHBOR. Christmas Eve don't seem to prevent people from dyin' an' bein' turned out o' house an' home. Did ye hear how bad the dipthery is? They say as how if it gits much worse they'll have to close the school in our ward. Two o' the Homan children's dead with it. The first one wasn't sick but two days, an' they say his face all turned black 'fore he died. But it's a good thing they're gone, for the Homans ain't got enough to feed the other six. Did ye hear 'bout Jim Kelly drinkin' again? Swore off for two months, an' then took to it harder'n ever — perty near killed the baby one night.

THE WOMAN [*with a wan, beseeching smile*]. Won't you please not tell me any more? It just breaks me heart.

THE NEIGHBOR [*grimly*]. I ain't got no other kind o' news to tell. I s'pose I might's well go home.

THE WOMAN. No, don't ye go. I like to have ye here when ye're kinder.

THE NEIGHBOR [*fingering the bedclothes and smoothing them over the woman.*] Well, it's gettin' late, an' I guess ye ought to go to sleep.

THE WOMAN. Oh, no, I won't go to slape till the girls come. They'll bring me somethin' to give me strength. If they'd on'y come soon!

THE NEIGHBOR. Ye ain't goin' to set up 'til they git home?

THE OLD WOMAN. That we are. We're kapin' the cilebratin' till they come.

THE NEIGHBOR. What celebratin'?

THE OLD WOMAN. Why, the Christmas, to be shure. We're goin' to have high jinks to-night. In the ould counthry 'tis always Christmas Day, but here 'tis begun on Christmas Eve, an' we're on'y waitin' for the girls, because they know how to fix things betther nor Mary an' me.

The Neighbor [*staring*]. But ain't they workin' in the store?

The Old Woman. Yes, but they're comin' home early to-night.

The Neighbor [*laughing ironically*]. Don't ye fool yerselves. Why, they've got to work harder to-night than any in the whole year.

The Woman [*wistfully*]. But they did say they'd thry to come home early.

The Neighbor. The store's all crowded to-night. Folks 'at's got money to spend never remembers it till the last minute. If they didn't have none they'd be thinkin' 'bout it long ahead. Well, I got to be movin'. I wouldn't stay awake, if I was you.

The Old Woman. Sthay and kape the Christmas wid us! We'll be havin' high jinks by an' by. Sthay, now, an' help us wid our jollity!

The Neighbor. Nay, I left my children in bed, an' I got to go back to 'em. An' I got to get some rest myself — I got that ironin' ahead o' me in the mornin'. You folks better get yer own rest. [*She rises and walks to the door.*]

The Old Woman [*beamingly*]. David an' Michael's comin'. [The Neighbor *stands with her back against the door and her hand on the knob, staring at* The Old Woman.]

The Old Woman [*smiling rapturously*]. Yis, we're goin' to have a gran' time. [The Neighbor *looks puzzled and fearful and troubled, first at* The Woman *and then at* The Old Woman. *Finally, without a word, she opens the door and goes out.*]

The Old Woman [*going about in a tottering sort of dance*]. David an' Michael's comin' an' the shepherds, for the fairies will show thim the way.

The Woman. If the girls would on'y come! If chey'd give me somethin' so as I wouldn't be so tired!

The Old Woman. There's niver a sthar an' there's nobody to give thim a kind word an' the counthry roads are dark an' foul, but they've got the little folk to guide thim! An' whin they reach the city — the poor, lonesome shepherds from the hills! — they'll find naught but coldness an' hardness an' hurry. [*Questioningly.*] Will the fairies show thim the way? Fairies' eyes be used to darkness, but can they see where it is black night in one corner an' a blaze o' light in another? [*She goes to the window for the third time, opens it and leans far out for a long time, then turns about and goes on in her monotone, closing the window. She seems by this time quite to have forgotten the presence of the pallid woman on the bed, who has closed her eyes, and lies like one dead.*]

The Old Woman. Nay, there's niver a sthar, an' the clouds are hangin' heavier an' lower an' the flakes o' snow are fallin'. Poor little folk guidin' thim poor lost shepherds, leadin' thim by the hand so gently because there's no others to be kind to thim, an' bringin' thim to the manger o' the Blessed Babe. [*She comes over to her rocking-chair and again sits down in it, rocks slowly to and fro, nodding her head in time to the motion.*] Poor little mite of a babe, so cold an' unwelcome an' forgotten save by the silly ould shepherds from the hills! The silly ould shepherds from the strength o' the hills, who are comin' through the darkness in the lead o' the little folk! [*She speaks slower and lower, and finally drops into a quiet crooning — it stops and* The Old Woman *has fallen asleep.*]

CURTAIN

[*While the curtain is down, the pallid, sick woman upon the bed dies;* THE OLD WOMAN *being asleep does not notice the slight struggle with death. The fire has gone out in the stove, and the light in the lamp, and the stage is in complete darkness when the two girls come stumbling in. They are too tired to speak, too weary to show surprise that the occupants of the room are not awake. They fumble about, trying to find matches in the darkness, and finally discover them and a candle in the safe. They light the candle and place it upon the table by the scraggy little evergreen-tree. They turn about and discern their grandmother asleep in the rocking-chair. Hurriedly they turn to the bed and discover their mother lying there dead. For a full minute they stand gazing at her, the surprise, wonder, awe, misery, increasing in their faces; then with screams they run to the bed, throw themselves on their knees and bury their faces, sobbing, in the bedclothes at* THE WOMAN'S *feet.*]

CURTAIN

Printed in the United States of America.

The MODERN READERS' SERIES

ASHLEY H. THORNDIKE, *General Editor*

THE MODERN READERS' SERIES presents the world's best literature: famous novels, and newer fiction of permanent interest; poetry; noted essays and dramas; eminent works of history, economics, science, philosophy, and education. American literature is prominent. Unusual and hitherto inaccessible books are included as are also translations of foreign books that have become a traditional part of a literary background.

In general, the titles in the series are available in two bindings: the one, a rich, dark green, half leather; the other, a handsome, durable blue cloth.

Volumes Published
IN HALF LEATHER OR IN CLOTH
(All of these titles are unabridged)

ADDISON: *Essays*
*AESOP: *Fables.* Ed. by Jacobs
ALCOTT: *Little Women*
ALDRICH: *The Story of a Bad Boy*
ALLEN: *A Kentucky Cardinal and Aftermath*
*ARISTOTLE: *Poetics; and Longinus on the Sublime*
ARNOLD: *Culture and Anarchy*
AUSTEN: *Emma*
BACON: *Essays*
BARNUM: *Struggles and Triumphs*
BORROW: *Lavengro*
BRONTË: *Jane Eyre*
BRONTË: *Wuthering Heights*
BROWN: *Edgar Huntly*
*BROWNING: *Selected Poems*
BURNS: *Selected Poems*
*BUTLER: *The Way of All Flesh*
BYRON: *Don Juan*
CARLYLE: *Past and Present; Sartor Resartus*
*CELLINI: *The Autobiography of Benvenuto Cellini*

*CHEKHOV: *Short Stories*
COLERIDGE: *Biographia Literaria*
CONGREVE: *Comedies*
COOPER: *The Last of the Mohicans; The Spy*
DANA: *Two Years before the Mast*
DARWIN: *The Origin of Species*
DEFOE: *Robinson Crusoe*
DICKENS: *A Tale of Two Cities; David Copperfield* (2 vols.)
*DOSTOEVSKY: *Crime and Punishment*
*DOUGLAS: *South Wind*
DUMAS: *The Three Musketeers*
EGGLESTON: *The Hoosier Schoolmaster*
*ELIOT: *Middlemarch*
EMERSON: *Essays*
*FRANCE: *Thaïs*
FRANKLIN: *The Autobiography of Benjamin Franklin*
*GILBERT: *The Mikado and Other Operas*

(*Continued*)

71530   * Cannot be sold in British Dominions

(Continued from previous page)

GOLDSMITH: *The Vicar of Wakefield*

*HARDY: *The Return of the Native*

HARTE: *The Luck of Roaring Camp* and *Selected Stories* and *Poems*

HAWTHORNE: *The Scarlet Letter*

HAZLITT: *Essays*

*HÉMON: *Maria Chapdelaine*

HOLMES: *The Autocrat of the Breakfast Table*

*HOMER: *The Iliad; The Odyssey*

HUXLEY: *Essays*

*IBSEN: *Plays*

IRVING: *The Sketch Book*

*JAMES: *Daisy Miller* and *An International Episode*

KEATS: *Complete Poems*

LAMB: *The Essays of Elia*

*LONDON: *The Call of the Wild* and *Other Stories*

MACAULAY: *Historical Essays*

*MARCUS AURELIUS ANTONINUS: *To Himself*

MELVILLE: *Moby Dick* (2 vols.)

*MEREDITH: *The Ordeal of Richard Feverel*

MILL: *On Liberty* and *Other Essays*

MILTON: *Areopagitica* and *Other Prose Writings*

*MULOCK: *John Halifax, Gentleman*

NEIHARDT: *The Song of Three Friends* and *The Song of Hugh Glass*

PARKMAN: *History of the Conspiracy of Pontiac; The Oregon Trail*

*PATER: *Marius the Epicurean*

POE: *Selected Poems; Tales*

POLO: *The Book of Ser Marco Polo* ("*Travels*")

RUSKIN: *Time and Tide* and *Munera Pulveris*

SCOTT: *Kenilworth; Selected Poems*

SHERIDAN: *Plays*

*STEVENSON: *Treasure Island*

STOWE: *Uncle Tom's Cabin*

SWIFT: *Gulliver's Travels*

*TENNYSON: *Idylls of the King*

THACKERAY: *Henry Esmond; Vanity Fair* (2 vols.)

THOREAU: *Walden*

TROLLOPE: *Barchester Towers*

TWAIN: *The Innocents Abroad*

WHITE: *A Certain Rich Man*

WHITMAN: *Leaves of Grass*

WILKINSON: *Contemporary Poetry*

WORDSWORTH: *Poems*

WYSS: *The Swiss Family Robinson*

IN BLUE CLOTH ONLY

(Unabridged titles are indicated by †)

BARKER: *Forty-Minute Plays from Shakespeare*

BLACKMORE: *Lorna Doone*

CERVANTES: *Don Quixote*

COOPER: *The Pathfinder*

DICKENS: *David Copperfield*

DUMAS: *The Three Musketeers*

*GARLAND: *A Son of the Middle Border*†

HOMER: *The Iliad*

KINGSLEY: *Hypatia*

NEIHARDT: *The Song of the Indian Wars*†

*PALGRAVE: *The Golden Treasury*†

PORTER: *The Scottish Chiefs*

RIIS: *The Making of an American*†

SCOTT: *The Heart of Midlothian; Ivanhoe*

SMITH: *Short Plays by Representative Authors*†

THACKERAY: *Vanity Fair*

WATTS: *Nathan Burke*†

WISTER: *Lady Baltimore*†

For further details, and titles in preparation, write for circular.

* Cannot be sold in British Dominions